PENS OF
MANY COLOURS
A CANADIAN READER

PENS OF MANY COLOURS

A CANADIAN READER

SECOND EDITION

Eva C. Karpinski

Seneca College

HARCOURT
BRACE
CANADA

Harcourt Brace & Company, Canada

Toronto Montreal Fort Worth New York Orlando
Philadelphia San Diego London Sydney Tokyo

Copyright © 1997
Harcourt Brace & Company Canada, Ltd.
All rights reserved

Every reasonable effort has been made to acquire permission for copyright material used in this text, and to acknowledge all such indebtedness accurately. Any errors and omissions called to the publisher's attention will be corrected in future printings.

Canadian Cataloguing in Publication Data

Karpinski, Eva C.
 Pens of many colours : a Canadian reader

2nd ed.
ISBN 0–7747–3510–4

1. College readers.   2. Readers - Multiculturalism - Canada.   3. Multiculturalism - Canada - Literary collections.   I. Title.

FC104.P45 1997   808'.0427   C96–930299–1
F1035.A1P4 1997

Director of Product Development: Heather McWhinney
Acquisitions Editor: Kelly V. Cochrane
Projects Manager: Liz Radojkovic
Developmental Editor: Laura Paterson Pratt
Editorial Co-ordinator: Jeannine Maxfield
Director of Publishing Services: Jean Davies
Editorial Manager: Marcel Chiera
Production Editor: Louisa Schulz
Production Manager: Sue-Ann Becker
Production Co-ordinator: Sheila Barry
Copy Editor: Gail Marsden
Cover and Interior Design: The Brookview Group Inc.
Typesetting and Assembly: Matthew Beck & Sharon Moroney
Printing and Binding: Best Book Manufacturers, Inc.

Cover Art: Bob Boyer, *I'm a Happy Hippy Hopi from Oraibi.*
Collection: Galerie Dresdnere, Toronto.
Photography: Helena Wilson, Toronto.
Reproduced by permission of the artist.

This book was printed in Canada.
1 2 3 4 5   01 00 99 98 97

PREFACE

Putting together the first edition of *Pens of Many Colours* in 1993, Ian Lea and I tried to recognize a growing need among the reading audience to explore the areas outside of what used to be called the literary mainstream. The 1980s and 1990s have seriously put into question the centrality of culture that has been mostly white, European-based, and male-dominated. The so-far marginalized or silenced groups of women, minority, Native, or immigrant writers have become visible and active participants in a dialogue for a pluralistic society. Of primary importance in the process of revising cultural assumptions and traditional literary canons is the increasingly multi-ethnic and multicultural make-up of Canadian society. To reflect this changing reality, which is also the reality of our classrooms, we have to be prepared to respect our differences as well as to be able to learn from them. It is hard to imagine a better first step than exposure to a mosaic of texts that embody those diverse voices reverberating throughout Canada.

The major goal of our multicultural reader is to give a realistic account of the presence of women and men of Native and immigrant stock in our society and to celebrate their contributions to Canadian life and letters. In order to avoid stereotyping, they speak for themselves, in their own voices, which for most of them means speaking and writing in English. We have sought, within the widest compass, representative voices of Canadians, new and old, hyphenated or assimilated, that articulate hopes, resentments, fears, and joys of being here. We have tried to show those men and women in a variety of roles and situations, including nonconventional ones, so as to give the reader an insider's view of a distinctly individual lifestyle and history, which might help to awaken a greater empathy and understanding among people sharing the same social and geographical space.

The book has been arranged as a flexible tool. Although its primary thrust is directed towards multicultural themes and their literary expression, its secondary purpose is pedagogical: the selections have been chosen also for their merit as compositional models. Their content rests firmly on the structural foundations of rhetorical form. In fact, the extended apparatus of discussion questions/writing suggestions, attached to the readings, encourages the rhetorical analysis as a way of determining the authorial purpose in writing, the reader's profile, and the sonority and effectiveness of the message. As a result, this text can not only be used as a cross-cultural thematic reader, but it can also hold inherent interest for English composition courses.

For instructors who wish to employ these selections as models of rhetorical forms and devices, we have included an alternative Contents, identifying which of two or three modes each work fits into, predominantly. Of course, many of these pieces could provide good illustrations of almost all of the modes. Some fiction, primarily narrative, has been omitted from this list.

The organization of this anthology corresponds with the goals outlined above. For practical purposes, we have divided the experience of multiculturalism in Canada contained in this volume into somewhat discrete units, though no individual selection can be isolated entirely from the themes of other units. Nonetheless, each unit has its own guiding structure, which is meant to order the rich tapestry of multicultural life into intelligible patterns. Each unit, moreover, contains a variety of genres—oral history, journalism, personal essay, letter, fiction—to identify how the cultural energy finds its outlet in different forms of expression. In addition, each unit begins with a poem that is relevant to its concerns and highlights its theme.

Furthermore, each unit begins with a brief Introduction to give context and whet the appetite of the reader. Each selection has a brief biography of the author at its beginning and Topics for Exploration at its end, designed to open the structure and content to further thought and scrutiny by the reader. After each unit, Suggestions for Further Study have been included to encourage comparative and divergent thinking, and perhaps further research into the subject. Finally, a Selected Bibliography of over thirty titles published in recent years has been included at the end of the book to facilitate reading and research in depth. It includes Canadian anthologies of short stories, essays, autobiography, and other writing related to multicultural, multi-ethnic, or immigrant experience, excluding, however, poetry anthologies and individual authors' collections (which have usually been acknowledged in the short biographies preceding each reading).

For this edition of *Pens of Many Colours,* I have made a few changes related mostly to the content of our collection. Following the reviewers' comments and the feedback from those who as teachers or students have been using the book, several selections have been removed as too academic, difficult, or irrelevant to our readers' concerns. In several cases, copyright restrictions have forced me to abandon valuable readings. However, I hope that new replacements will make up for the absence of some old favourites. The new readings add the experiences that have been missing from the first edition, such as those of French missionaries, Arab-Canadians, or Mennonites. The geographical regions covered by the selections have also been expanded to include Newfoundland, and more attention is given to British Columbia and Western Canada. Finally, a touch of humour has been brought in by some new stories. Thus revamped and refreshed, the book is being offered to the readers as a tool for promoting greater democratization in education by encouraging individual growth and understanding of others.

The overall vision of *Pens of Many Colours,* commitment to a multicultural perspective, fairly balanced representation of diverse racial, ethnic, or cultural groups, and strong support to antiracist and antisexist struggle, have been maintained throughout. Introducing multicultural voices to the college classroom through such texts as *Pens* can be seen as part of a larger effort to create a more inclusive learning environment. Ideally, any such revisions of the curriculum should be accompanied by changes in our teaching practices as well. Along with our willingness to work with these new voices, we might try to open up to less conventional pedagogical procedures and ways of student self-expression. If we agree that it is through "voice" that various experiences can enter the classroom, we must remember that it is not just the voices allowed in as texts, but also the students' voices as well as the teacher's voice that are engaged in this dialogical exchange.

Class-testing the material included in both editions of *Pens,* and also discussing it with students and other teachers, I have found out that readers' responses can be unpredictable and far more complex than expected. As teachers, we cannot forget that the same text read by different people can produce denial and identification, silence and outspokenness, resistance to being treated as victims or "native informants" and empowerment through recognition. We should use such classroom situations to try to get across the point that no single culture controls signification. Instead of training students how to arrive at one "correct" reading of a particular text, teachers and students in multicultural classrooms must constantly practise negotiating meaning. We must remember that our own and students' interpretations are strongly influenced by our different backgrounds and individual circumstances, and even if certain comments appear "unusual" or "illegitimate," such comments may reveal a lot about the situatedness of our knowledges and highlight some important differences that would otherwise go unnoticed.

Research shows that exposure to diverse viewpoints and perspectives is beneficial to both students of mainstream backgrounds and students of diverse backgrounds (even though this distinction is only provisional as the same person can belong to either of these categories, depending on whether race, gender, ethnicity, class, sexuality, or language is taken to be a dominant factor). Multicultural texts like *Pens of Many Colours* provide successful models of people striding both cultures; validate the experience of students of diverse backgrounds and affirm their cultural identity; promote mutual understanding and empathy; increase the awareness of the complexity of Canadian society; and de-emphasize the dominant culture view of history and introduce other perspectives on the historical and economic forces that have given Canada its present shape. However, teachers and students alike should also be aware of the potential dangers of this version of "multiculturalism" inherent in the very form and structure of a multicultural reader. Very often such textbooks are underwritten by the pseudo-egalitarian "we-are-all-the-same" type of philosophy or, alternately, by the orientalist or voyeuristic fascination with difference. Through their false "democratic" pretensions, these textual "mosaics" may create the context where real, material differences can easily be forgotten, and any claims to "uniqueness" can be diffused by a variety that is quantitative rather than qualitative. Therefore, to alleviate this intrinsic problem of the genre of multicultural reader, in *Pens of Many Colours* we have tried to avoid voice appropriation; to place mainstream voices alongside multicultural voices, thus refusing to "ghettoize" the latter or marginalize them as "other than"; and to remind the reader of the specificity of recorded oppression or privilege through introductions and questions attached to the readings.

I have decided to place in this Preface the above theoretical comments because I think that we need a forum for sharing our experiences of working with multicultural readers. We often work in isolation and are left alone with our doubts. It is my personal belief that every effort made to transform models of education so that they reflect a multicultural standpoint is necessary and desired today. Against the rhetoric of economic restraint that reduces teachers and students to less than subjects in the teaching/learning process, we must insist on humanizing the institutions of education. Embracing the idea of multicultural education is an important step towards this change.

As usual, many people have contributed their knowledge, intelligence, and enthusiasm to the preparation of this book. I would like to thank the editors at Harcourt Brace, Heather McWhinney, Kelly Cochrane, Louisa Schulz, and especially Laura Paterson Pratt, who has been a wonderful Developmental Editor; the reviewers, Francis Aspinall at Centennial College, Maureen Coleman at Sheridan College, Graham Forst at Capilano College, David McCarthy at Centennial College, Maureen Shaw at Kwantlen College, and Judi Szeszycki at Keewatin College, and all my colleagues and students who have offered their helpful comments and suggestions.

Eva C. Karpinski
Seneca College

A Note from the Publisher

Thank you for selecting *Pens of Many Colours*, Second Edition, by Eva C. Karpinski. The author and publisher have devoted considerable time to the careful development of this book. We appreciate your recognition of this effort and accomplishment.

We want to hear what you think about *Pens of Many Colours*. Please take a few minutes to fill out the stamped reply card at the back of the book. Your comments and suggestions will be valuable to us as we prepare new editions and other books.

CONTENTS

UNIT THREE
SELF AND OTHER: LANGUAGE

UNIT FOUR
GROWING UP: EDUCATION

UNIT FIVE
DRIFTING APART: GENERATION GAP

UNIT SIX
MAPS OF MEMORY: PLACES REVISITED

UNIT SEVEN
DOUBLE BIND: CANADIAN IDENTITY

RHETORICAL CONTENTS

PROCESS ANALYSIS

DIVISION AND CLASSIFICATION

CAUSE AND EFFECT

DEFINITION

COMPARISON AND CONTRAST

COMING HERE: ORIGINS

INTRODUCTION

"**V**oyages to the new world" have been the stuff of adventure since the beginning of time—even when that beginning has been forgotten. The motives have been as various as the voyagers: imperial ambition, enforced migration by slavery, transportation by charitable patrons, flight from misery and massacre, perhaps simple curiosity. In this unit we have selected from a multitude of origins, periods, and motives; no two of these voyages are alike in any of these respects.

Though their migration to this continent during the Ice Age has been forgotten, for the Cree Indians of Saskatchewan the most recent voyage of discovery has been through time, not space. Pat Deiter-McArthur (Day Woman) presents a brief history of five generations of her people since their first interaction with white explorers and settlers. Their culture shock is not the bewilderment of facing a new environment, but rather the impact of a colonizing force that comes upon their world from the outside. She chronicles the changes forced upon her culture by European invaders, changes whose effects her people are still experiencing.

Of the earliest literature documenting the period of exploration, trade, missionary expansion, and early settlement, we have journals, letters, chronicles, reports, and other records—all of them intended to convey impressions from the "wilderness" to the "civilized world" back at home. Marie de l'Incarnation, a Catholic nun, writes about her experiences in seventeenth-century Quebec. In a prose ripe with religious passion, she describes a series of natural disasters interpreted as God's punishment for the sins committed in this country. Her apocalyptic imagery reminds us of the spiritual character of her mission while at the same time revealing difficulties of daily survival in a strange land.

In the 1800s, Catharine Parr Traill—like her sister, Susanna Moodie, another pioneer of early immigrant literature—crossed the Atlantic to redeem lost status, ill prepared though she was for the hardships ahead. Now, a century later, the population of what was once the British Empire can still find life in one former colony more attractive than in another. Writing of the voluntary migrants who, like Traill, seek a better life in the "new world," Rohinton Mistry describes several motives that have brought these recent voyagers from the East to the West.

Not all immigration to Canada, however, has been voluntary. We have records of Black slaves in Nova Scotia dating back to 1606. Furthermore, there have always been many immigrants who arrive in Canada under duress, in flight. Their search for a future in Canada is less pressing than escape from their past elsewhere. The eighteenth-century autobiographical account written by Boston King presents the ordeals of a Black Loyalist who escapes the bondage of slavery to find refuge in Nova Scotia.

For modern-day refugees from Europe and the so-called Third World, war, hunger, and tyranny are the reasons they flee their homes. Miriam Rosenthal gives eloquent testimony to the motives of those who wanted to escape the genocidal chaos inflicted on Europe by Nazi Germany before and during World War II.

In the last twenty years, the plight of the refugees has become widespread. Violence and misery in the world are never lacking.

Helga (Kutz-Harder) Mills has observed some trouble spots of the globe and assembled a brief anthology of the experiences of its women refugees. Each of them, in flight from a different catastrophe—civil war, starvation, foreign invasion—articulates the problems of culture shock in a new society to which she cannot assimilate very quickly. These women bring with them the burden of painful memories and straitened circumstances that life in Canada cannot alleviate. For them there is no voyage of return.

Multiculturalism

I continue to sing of other loves,
Places...moments when I am furious;
When you are pale and I am strong
As we come one to another.

The ethnics at our door
Malingering with heritage,
My solid breath, like stones breaking;
At a railway station making much ado about much,
This boulder and Rocky Mountain,
CPR heaving with a head tax
As I am Chinese in a crowd,
Japanese at the camps,
It is also World War II.
Panting, I am out of breath.

So I keep on talking
With blood coursing through my veins,
The heart's call for employment equity,
The rhapsody of police shootings in Toronto,
This gathering of the stars one by one, codifying them
And calling them planets, one country, really...

Or galaxies of province after province,
A distinct society too:
Québec or Newfoundland; the Territories...
How far we make a map out of our solitudes
As we are still Europe, Asia,
Africa; and the Aborigine in me
Suggests love above all else—
The bear's configuration in the sky;
Other places, events; a turbanned RCMP,
These miracles—

My heritage and quest, heart throbbing;
Voices telling me how much I love you.
YOU LOVE ME; and we're always springing surprises,
Like vandalism at a Jewish cemetery
Or Nelson Mandela's visit to Ottawa
As I raise a banner high on Parliament Hill
Crying "Welcome!"—we are, you are—
OH CANADA!

—*Cyril Dabydeen*

Cyril Dabydeen, who came to Canada from Guyana in 1970, is a novelist and poet living in Ottawa. From 1984 to 1987 he was Poet Laureate of Ottawa. His published volumes of poetry include Distances, This Planet Earth, *and* Coastland: New and Selected Poems. *He also edited the anthology* A Shapely Fire: Changing the Literary Landscape *(1987).*

Pat Deiter-McArthur (Day Woman)

*Pat Deiter-McArthur (Day Woman) is a Cree Indian deeply committed to
Native history and rights. She has written two books:* Dances of the
Northern Plain *and* Games of the Plains Cree. *She works as a private
consultant in ethno-historical research and training. Herself a member of
the "fifth generation," she examines in the following excerpt the five generations of Native people's history since the initial contact with Europeans.*

Saskatchewan's Indian People— Five Generations

It has been about five generations since Saskatchewan Indian people
have had significant contact with European settlers. The First
Generation strongly influenced by Europeans were the treaty-signers.
The key characteristic of this generation was their ability to have some
input into their future. They retained their tribal cultures but realized
that they had to negotiate with the Europeans for the betterment of
future generations. They did not give up their language or religion or
the political structures of nationhood. They were perceived by
government as an "alien" nation to be dealt with by treaty.

The Second Generation (1867–1910) of Indian people were the
objects of legal oppression by the government. This generation lived
under the absolute rule of an Indian agent, a government employee.
Through the Indian Act, this generation was denied their religion,
political rights, and freedom to travel off their reserves. A pass and
permit system was strictly adhered to on the prairies; every Indian
person required a pass to leave the reserve and a permit to sell any
agricultural produce. All children were required to attend residential
schools run by the churches. The goals of their schools were, first, to
make Christians out of their students and to rid them of their pagan
lifestyles and, second, to provide a vocational education.

Tuberculosis was a major killer of Indian people during this time and contributed to decimating their population in Saskatchewan to a low of five thousand in 1910. This generation was treated as wards and aliens of Canada.

The laws which served to oppress the second generation were in place until the early 1950s. The Third Generation (1910–1945) was greatly affected by these laws and schooling. This generation can be described as the lost generation. These people were psychologically oppressed. They rejected their Indianness but found that because of the laws for treaty Indians they could not enjoy the privileges accorded to whites. This third generation was our grandfather's generation. Many Indians at this time could speak their language but would not because of shame of their Indianness. They were still required by law to send their children to residential schools, to send their sick to Indian hospitals, and to abide by the Indian agent. They rarely had a sense of control over their own lives. This generation was considered wards of the government and denied citizenship.

Our father's time, the Fourth Generation since treaty-signing, can best be described as the generation of an Indian rebirth. This generation (1945–1980) is characterized by a movement of growing awareness—awareness that being Indian was okay and that Indian people from all tribes are united through their aboriginality, historical development, and special status.

This generation saw the rise of Indian and Native organizations across Canada, the return of traditional ceremonies, and an acknowledgement of the need to retain traditional languages and cultural ways.

Indian people of this generation were given the right to vote in 1960. The pass and permit system was abandoned in the late 1930s. In 1956, Indian children could attend either residential schools or the local public schools. However, the effects of this generation being raised within an institution and their parents being raised in the same way had a severe impact on these individuals. The residential school not only taught them to suppress their language but also to suppress their feelings and sense of individualism. The continued attack on Indian languages by residential schools left this generation with an ability to only understand their language, but many were not sufficiently fluent to call their Native language their first language.

During the sixties, there was a rise in Indian urbanization, a trend that continues today. This generation also contributed to an Indian baby boom that is estimated to be eight to ten years behind the non-Indian baby boomers. The federal and provincial vote allowed Indian people to legally consume alcohol. Alcoholism, suicides, and violent deaths were on the rise for this generation.

This was a period of experimentation by both the Indian communities and the government. Unfortunately, neither side was ready for each other. The intended government goal of assimilation was besieged with problems of racism, poverty, maladjustment, and cultural shock.

Today's Indian people are part of the Fifth Generation. The fifth generation is faced with choices: assimilation, integration, or separation. Indian people are now able to intermarry or assimilate with non-Indians without the loss of their Indian status. Indian leaders across Canada are seeking a separate and constitutionally recognized Indian government. Indian government is to provide its own services within Indian reserves. Integration allows Indian people to retain a sense of their cultural background while working and living within the larger society.

The fifth generation people are the first children since treaty-signing to be raised by their parents. Many of this generation are not able to understand a native language. Their first and only language is English. This generation is generally comfortable about their Indianness without strong prejudicial feelings to others. However, this generation is challenged to retain the meaning of Indian identity for their children.

TOPICS FOR EXPLORATION

1. What is the purpose that prompted Pat Deiter-McArthur to write this essay? Who will make up her readership? What does she hope her readers will learn? What role is she playing for her audience? Although she presents the facts objectively, is she also trying to persuade?

2. In what order has the author chosen to present her materials? How has she chosen to divide her analysis? How effective is that pattern?

3. In her essay, she analyzes the impact of interactions with white culture on First Nations people whose first encounter with white settlers is seen as the historical threshold. What are the five steps she identifies in this process analysis? What are the characteristics of each step? How does one step compare with another?

4. What challenges to Native people's identity are chronicled in Pat Deiter-McArthur's essay? What were some of the negative effects of European influence upon the Native population in each period she discusses? Were there any positive effects?

5. What were some methods that white governments in Canada used in order to repress Native culture? Find examples of assimilation, integration, and separation as patterns of the Native–white interactions described in the text.

6. What effect does the author of this Native history hope to have on the future (or sixth) generation of her people in light of the recent struggle for Native self-determination and self-government?

Marie de l'Incarnation

Marie de l'Incarnation (1599–1672) was a Frenchwoman who devoted her life to God's service. She left her marriage and children to enter a French convent. Subsequently, she was sent to New France and founded an Ursuline school there. Her experiences in early Canada were documented in her letters, one of which is reprinted below.

The Earthquake

Quebec, 20 August, 1663

My very dear son:

I have waited to give you an account separately of the earthquake this year in our New France, which was so prodigious, so violent, and so terrifying that I have no words strong enough to describe it and even fear lest what I shall say be deemed incredible and fabulous.

On the third day of February of this year 1663 a woman Indian, but a very good and very excellent Christian, wakening in her cabin while all the others slept, heard a distinct and articulated voice that said to her, "In two days, very astonishing and marvellous things will come to pass." And the next day, while she was in the forest with her sister, cutting her daily provision of wood, she distinctly heard the same voice, which said, "Tomorrow, between five and six o'clock in the evening, the earth will be shaken and will tremble in an astonishing way."

She reported what she had heard to the others in her cabin, who received it with indifference as being a dream or the work of her imagination. The weather was meanwhile quite calm that day, and even more so the day following.

On the fifth day, the feast of St. Agatha, Virgin and Martyr, at about half past five in the evening, a person of proven virtue [Mother Marie-Catherine de Saint-Augustin], who has frequent communication with God, saw that he was extremely provoked against the sins committed in this country and felt at the same time disposed to ask him to deal with these sinners as they deserved. While she was offering her prayers for this to divine Majesty, and also for souls in mortal sin, that his justice be not without mercy, also beseeching the martyrs of Japan, whose feast was being held that day, to consent to make application for this as would be most suitable to God's glory, she had a presentiment—or rather an infallible conviction—that God was ready to punish the country for the sins committed here, especially the contempt for the ordinances of the Church.

She could not refrain from desiring this chastisement, whatever it might be, since it was fixed in God's decree, though she had no indication of what it would be. Forthwith, and a little before the earthquake came to pass, she saw four furious and enraged demons at the four corners of Quebec, shaking the earth with such violence it was evident they wished to turn it right over. And indeed they would have succeeded in this if a personage of wondrous beauty and delightful majesty, whom she saw in the midst of them, giving rein to their fury from time to time, had not restrained them just when they were on the point of destroying everything.

She heard the voices of these demons saying, "Now many people are frightened. There will be many conversions, we know, but that will last but a little time. We will find ways to get the world back for ourselves. Meanwhile let us continue to shake it and do our best to turn everything over."

The weather was very calm and serene and the vision still had not passed when a sound of terrifying rumbling was heard in the distance, as if a great many carriages were speeding wildly over the cobblestones. This noise had scarcely caught the attention than there was heard under the earth and on the earth and from all sides what seemed a horrifying confusion of waves and billows. There was a sound like hail on the roofs, in the granaries, and in the rooms. It seemed as if the marble of which the foundation of this country is almost entirely composed and our houses are built were about to open and break into pieces to gulp us down.

Thick dust flew from all sides. Doors opened of themselves. Others, which were open, closed. The bells of all our churches and the chimes of our clocks pealed quite alone, and steeples and houses shook like trees in the wind—all this in a horrible confusion of overturning furniture, falling stones, parting floors, and splitting walls. Amidst all this the domestic animals were heard howling. Some ran out of their houses; others ran in. In a word, we were all so frightened we believed it was the eve of Judgment, since all the portents were to be seen.

So unexpected a calamity, when the young people were preparing to spend the carnival season in excesses, was a clap of thunder on everyone's head, they expecting nothing less. It was rather a clap of

God's mercy upon the whole country, as was seen by its results, of which I shall speak elsewhere. From the first tremor consternation was universal. And as no one knew what it was, some cried "Fire!", thinking it was a conflagration; others ran for water to extinguish it; others snatched up their arms, believing it was an army of Iroquois. But as it was none of these things, everyone strove to be first out of the houses, which seemed on the point of falling down.

No greater safety was to be found without than within, for we at once realized by the movement of the earth, which trembled under our feet like agitated waves under a shallop, that it was an earthquake. Some hugged the trees, which clashed together, causing them no less horror than the houses they had left; others clung to stumps, the movements of which struck them roughly in the chest.

The Indians, who were extremely frightened, said the trees had beaten them. Several among them said they were demons God was using to chastise them because of the excesses they had committed while drinking the brandy that the wicked French had given them. Some other less-instructed Indians, who had come to hunt in these regions, said it was the souls of their ancestors, who wished to return to their former dwelling. Possessed by this error, they took their guns and shot into the air at what they said was a band of passing spirits. But finally our habitants and our Indians, finding no more refuge on the ground than in the houses, grew weak with fear and, taking better counsel, went into the churches to have the consolation of perishing there after they had made their confession.

When this first tremor, which lasted more than half an hour, had passed, we began to breathe once more; but this was for only a little while, for at about eight o'clock in the evening the shaking began again and in the space of an hour was twice repeated. We said matins in the choir, reciting it partly on our knees in a humbled spirit, surrendering ourselves to the sovereign power of God. There were thirty-two new earthquakes that night, as I was told by a person that counted them. I, however, counted only six because certain of them were weak and almost imperceptible. But at about three o'clock there was one that was very violent and lasted for a long time.

These tremors continued for the space of seven months, though irregularly. Some were frequent but weak; others were rarer but strong and violent. So, since the evil only left us in order to pounce upon us with greater strength, we had scarcely time to reflect upon the misfortune that threatened us when it suddenly surprised us, sometimes during the day but more often during the night.

If the earth gave us reason for alarm, heaven did no less so—both by the howls and shrieking we heard resounding in the air and by distinct and frightening voices. Some said, "Alas!" Others said, "Let us go! Let us go!" and others, "Let us stop up the rivers!" The sounds were heard sometimes of bells, sometimes of cannon, sometimes of thunder. We saw fires, torches, and flaming globes, which sometimes fell to the earth and sometimes dissolved in the air. A man of fire was seen with flames pouring from his mouth. When our domestics went of necessity to bring in wood at night, they saw fires of this sort five or six times a night. Terrible spectres were also seen, and, as the demons sometimes join with the thunder, though it is but an effect of nature, it was easy to believe that on this occasion they had joined with the earthquakes, to increase the fear that agitated nature would cause us.

Amidst all these terrors we did not know where the whole thing would end. When we found ourselves at the close of the day, we made ready to be swallowed up by some abyss during the night. When day came, we were in continual expectation of death, seeing no assured moment of our life. In a word we sickened in the expectation of some universal misfortune....

A month passed thus in fear and uncertainty of what was to come; but finally when the earth's movements began to diminish, being now rarer and less violent (except two or three times when they were very strong), we began to discover the usual results of violent earthquakes—namely, a great many crevices in the earth, new torrents, new springs, and new hills, where they had never been before; the earth levelled where there had formerly been mountains; in some places new chasms whence rose sulphurous vapours, and in others great empty plains that had formerly been laden with woods and brush; rocks overturned, farms moved, forests destroyed, some of the trees being uprooted and others buried in earth to the tips of their branches. Two rivers were seen to disappear and two new springs were found—one white as milk and the other red as blood. But nothing astonished us more than to see the great St. Lawrence River which, because of its prodigious depth, is never changed, either by the melting of the snow that usually changes rivers or by the junction of more than five hundred rivers that flow into it, not to speak of the more than six hundred springs, very heavy for the most part—nothing astonished us more, I say, than to see this river change and assume the colour of sulphur and retain it for a week.

When several Indians that fear had driven from the woods wished to return to their cabin, they found it buried in a lake that had formed there. A granary near us was seen to lie first on one side, then on the other, and finally to settle upright again. At the Beaupré church, which is that of the parish of Château-Richer, the earth shook so roughly on Ash Wednesday that its walls trembled visibly, like cardboard. The Blessed Sacrament, which was exposed, likewise trembled. It did not fall, however, being retained by a little crown of artificial flowers. The lamp, which was extinguished, fell three times but, when the ecclesiastic who has the care of that church lit it and set it back in its place, it did not fall again.

We learned from some gentlemen that came from Tadoussac that the earthquake made a strange disorder there. For the space of six hours it rained ashes in such quantity that they lay an inch thick on the ground and in the barks. It is inferred from this that the fire enclosed in the earth touched off a mine and, through the opening thus made, flung up ashes, which were like burned sugar. These gentlemen say that the first tremors terrified them in the extreme because of the strange effects they caused....

From Word from New France, *translated by Joyce Marshall*

TOPICS FOR EXPLORATION

1. What warnings of the impending disaster were received before the earthquake? Who were the people who had these premonitions? Were they given credence?

2. Marie de l'Incarnation describes the onset of the earthquake using apocalyptic imagery. How does this imagery correspond with her religious interpretation of the disaster?

3. What different reactions to the first tremor did she observe among the Indians? How did the people at the mission pass their time awaiting what they thought was inevitable death?

4. What supernatural phenomena accompanying the earthquake are mentioned in her letter? Were there any miraculous occurrences that could increase the number of conversions?

5. What did the land look like after the earthquakes? Why does Marie de l'Incarnation see the results of the earthquake as "a clap of God's mercy upon the whole country" rather than a calamity?

Boston King

One of the most important waves of Black migration to Canada took place during the American Revolutionary War. The British promised freedom and land to those Black slaves who would support the Crown against American fighters for independence. Boston King (1760–1802) was a Methodist minister and a former slave who joined British forces and was transported to Nova Scotia. However, disappointed with life there, in 1792, King together with a group of other Black Loyalists went to Sierra Leone in Africa, where he became a missionary.

Memoirs of the Life of Boston King, a Black Preacher, Written by Himself During His Residence at Kingswood School

I t is by no means an agreeable talk to write an account of my Life, yet my gratitude to Almighty God, who considered my affliction, and looked upon me in my low estate, who delivered me from the hand of the oppressor, and established my goings, impels me to acknowledge his goodness: And the importunity of many respectable friends, whom I highly esteem, have induced me to set down, as they occurred to my memory, a few of the most striking incidents, I have met with in my pilgrimage. I am well aware of my inability for such an undertaking, having only a slight acquaintance with the language in which I write, and being obliged to snatch a few hours, now and then, from pursuits, which to me, perhaps, are more profitable. However, such as it is, I present it to the Friends of Religion and Humanity, hoping that it will be of some use to mankind.

I was born in the Province of South Carolina, 28 miles from Charles-Town. My father was stolen away from Africa when he was young. I have reason to believe that he lived in the fear and love of

God. He attended to that true Light which lighteth every man that cometh into the world. He lost no opportunity of hearing the Gospel, and never omitted praying with his family every night. He likewise read to them, and to as many as were inclined to hear. On the Lord's-Day he rose very early, and met his family: After which he worked in the field till about three in the afternoon, and then went into the woods and read till sun-set: The slaves being obliged to work on the Lord's-Day to procure such things as were not allowed by their masters. He was beloved by his master, and had the charge of the Plantation as a driver for many years. In his old age he was employed as a mill-cutter. Those who knew him, say, that they never heard him swear an oath, but on the contrary, he reproved all who spoke improper words in his hearing. To the utmost of his power he endeavoured to make his family happy, and his death was a great loss to us all. My mother was employed chiefly in attending upon those that were sick, having some knowledge of the virtue of herbs, which she learned from the Indians. She likewise had the care of making the people's clothes, and on these accounts was indulged with many privileges which the rest of the slaves were not.

When I was six years old I waited in the house upon my master. In my 9th year I was put to mind the cattle. Here I learnt from my comrades the horrible sin of Swearing and Cursing. When 12 years old, it pleased God to alarm me by a remarkable dream. At mid-day, when the cattle went under the shade of the trees, I dreamt that the world was on fire, and that I saw the supreme Judge descend on his great white Throne! I saw millions of millions of souls; some of whom ascended up to heaven; while others were rejected, and fell into the greatest confusion and despair. This dream made such an impression upon my mind that I refrained from swearing and bad company, and from that time acknowledged that there was a God; but how to serve God I knew not. Being obliged to travel in different parts of America with race-horses, I suffered many hardships. Happening one time to lose a boot belonging to the Groom, he would not suffer me to have shoes all that winter, which was a great punishment to me. When 16 years old, I was bound apprentice to a trade. After being in the shop about two years, I had the charge of my master's tools, which being very good, were often used by the men, if I happened to be out of the way: When this was the case, or any of them were lost, or misplaced, my master beat me severely, striking me upon the head, or any other part without mercy. One time in the holy-days, my master and the men being from home, and the care of the house devolving upon me and the younger apprentices, the house was broke open, and robbed of many valuable articles, thro' the negligence of the apprentice who had then the charge of it. When I came home in the evening, and saw what had happened, my consternation was inconceivable, as all that we had in the world could not make good the loss. The week following, when the master came to town, I was beat in a most unmerciful manner, so that I was not able to do any thing for a fortnight. About eight months after, we were employed in building a store-house, and nails were very dear at that time, it being in the American [Revolutionary] war, so that the work-men had their nails weighed out to them; on this account, they made the younger apprentices watch the nails while they were at dinner. It being my lot one day to take care of them, which I did till an apprentice returned to his work, and then I went to dine. In the mean time he took away all the nails belonging to one of the journeymen, and he being of a very violent temper, accused me to the master with stealing of them. For this offence, I was beat and tortured most cruelly, and was laid up three weeks before I was able to do any work. My proprietor, hearing of the bad usage I received, came to town, and severely reprimanded my master for beating me in such a manner, threatening him, that if he ever heard the like again, he would take me away, and put me to another master to finish my time, and make him pay for it. This had a good effect, and he behaved much better to me, the two succeeding years, and I began to acquire a proper knowledge of my trade. My master being apprehensive that Charles-Town was in danger on account of the war, removed into the country, about 38 miles off. Here we built a large house for Mr. Waters, during which time the English took Charles-Town. Having obtained leave one day to see my parents, who lived about 12 miles off, and it being later before I could go, I was obliged to borrow one of Mr. Waters's horses; but a servant of my master's, took the horse from me to go a little journey, and stayed two or three days longer than he ought. This involved me in the greatest perplexity, and I expected the severest punishment, because the gentleman to whom the horse belonged was a very bad man, and knew not how to shew mercy. To escape his cruelty, I determined to go to Charles-Town, and throw myself into the hands of the English. They received me readily, and I began to feel the happiness of liberty, of which I knew nothing before, altho' I was most grieved at first, to be obliged to leave my friends, and reside among strangers. In this situation I was seized with the smallpox, and suffered great hardships; for all the Blacks afflicted with that disease, were ordered to be carried a mile from the camp, lest the soldiers should be infected, and disabled from marching. This was a grievous circumstance to me and many others. We lay sometimes a whole day without anything to eat or drink; but Providence sent a man, who belonged to the York volunteers whom I was acquainted with, to my relief. He brought me such things as I stood in need of; and by the blessing of the Lord I began to recover.

Soon after I went to Charles-Town, and entered on board a man of war. As we were going to Chesepeak-bay, we were at the taking of a rich prize. We stayed in the bay two days, and then sailed for New-York, where I went on shore. Here I endeavoured to follow my trade, but for want of tools was obliged to relinquish it, and enter into service. But the wages were so low that I was not able to keep myself in clothes, so that I was under the necessity of leaving my master and going to another. I stayed with him four months, but he never paid me, and I was obliged to leave him also, and work about the town until I was married. A year after I was taken very ill, but the Lord raised me up again in about five weeks. I then went out in a pilot-boat. We were at sea eight days, and had only provisions for five, so that we were in danger of starving. On the 9th day we were taken by an American whale-boat. I went on board them with a chearful countenance, and asked for bread and water, and made very free with them. They carried me to Brunswick, and fed me well. Notwithstanding which, my mind was sorely distressed at the thought of being again reduced to slavery, and separated from my wife and family; and at the same time it was exceeding difficult to escape from my bondage, because the river at Amboy was above a mile over, and likewise another to cross at Staten-Island. I called to remembrance the many great deliverances the Lord had wrought for me, and besought him to save me this once, and I would serve him all the days of my life. While my mind was thus exercised, I went into the jail to see a lad whom I was acquainted with at New-York. He had been taken prisoner, and attempted to make his escape, but was caught 12 miles off: They tied him to the tail of a horse, and in this manner brought him back to Brunswick. When I saw him, his feet were fastened in the stocks, and at night both his hands. This was a terrifying sight to me, as I expected to meet with the same kind of treatment, if taken in the act of attempting to regain my liberty. I was thankful that I was not confined in a jail, and my master used me as well as I could expect; and indeed the slaves about Baltimore, Philadelphia, and New-York, have as good victuals as many of the English; for they have meat once a day, and milk for breakfast and supper; and what is better than all, many of the masters send their slaves to school at night, that they may learn to read the Scriptures. This is a privilege indeed. But alas, all these enjoyments could not satisfy me without liberty! Sometimes I thought, if it was the will of God that I should be a slave, I was ready to resign myself to his will; but at other times I could not find the least desire to content myself in slavery.

Being permitted to walk about when my work was done, I used to go to the ferry, and observed, that when it was low water the people waded across the river; tho' at the same time I saw there were guards posted at the place to prevent the escape of prisoners and slaves. As I was at prayer one Sunday evening, I thought the Lord heard me, and would mercifully deliver me. Therefore putting my confidence in him, about one o'clock in the morning I went down to the river side, and found the guards were either asleep or in the tavern. I instantly entered into the river, but when I was a little distance from the opposite shore, I heard the sentinels disputing among themselves: One said, "I am sure I saw a man cross the river." Another replied, "There is no such thing." It seems they were afraid to fire at me, or make an alarm, lest they should be punished for their negligence. When I had got a little distance from the shore, I fell down upon my knees and thanked God for this deliverance. I travelled till about five in the morning, and then concealed my self till seven o'clock at night, when I proceeded forward, thro' bushes and marshes, near the road, for fear of being discovered. When I came to the river, opposite Staten-Island, I found a boat; and altho' it was very near a whale-boat, yet I ventured into it, and cutting the ropes, got safe over. The commanding officer, when informed of my case, gave me a passport, and I proceeded to New-York.

When I arrived at New-York, my friends rejoiced to see me once more restored to liberty, and joined me in praising the Lord for his mercy and goodness. But notwithstanding this great deliverance, and the promises I had made to serve God, yet my good resolutions soon vanished away like the morning dew: The love of this world extinguished my good desires, and stole away my heart from God, so that I rested in a mere form of religion for near three years. About which time, [in 1783,] the horrors and devastation of war happily terminated, and peace was restored between America and Great Britain, which diffused universal joy among all parties, except us, who had escaped from slavery, and taken refuge in the English army; for a report, prevailed at New-York, that all the slaves, in number 2000, were to be delivered up to their masters, altho' some of them had been three or four years among the English. This dreadful rumour filled us all with inexpressible anguish and terror, especially when we saw our masters coming from Virginia, North-Carolina, and other parts, and seizing upon their slaves in the streets of New-York, or even dragging them out of their beds. Many of the slaves had very cruel masters, so that the thoughts of returning home with them embittered life to us. For some days we lost our appetite for food, and sleep departed from our eyes. The English had compassion upon us in the day of distress, and issued out a proclamation, importing, that all slaves should be free, who had taken refuge in the British lines, and claimed the sanction and privileges of the Proclamation respecting the security and protection of Negroes. In consequence of this, each of us received a certificate from a commanding officer at New-York, which dispelled all our fears and filled us with joy and gratitude. Soon after, ships were fitted out, and furnished with every necessity for conveying us to Nova Scotia. We arrived at Burch Town [Shelburne] in the month of August, where we all safely landed. Every family had a lot of land, and we exerted all our strength in order to build comfortable huts before the cold weather set in.

That winter, the work of religion began to revive among us, and many were convinced of the sinfulness of sin, and turned from the error of their ways. It pleased the Lord to awaken my wife under the preaching of Mr. Wilkinson; she was struck to the ground, and cried out for mercy: she continued in stress for near two hours, when they sent for me. At first I was much displeased, and refused to go; but presently my mind relented, and I went to the house, and was struck with astonishment at the sight of her agony. In about six days after, the Lord spoke peace to her soul: she was filled with divine consolation, and walked in the light of God's countenance about nine months. But being unacquainted with the corruptions of her own heart, she again gave place to bad tempers, and fell into great darkness and distress. Indeed, I never saw any person, either before or since, so overwhelmed with anguish of spirit on account of backsliding, as she was. The trouble of her soul brought affliction upon her body, which confined her to bed a year and a half.

However, the Lord was pleased to sanctify her afflictions, and to deliver her from all her fears. He brought her out of the horrible pit, and set her soul at perfect liberty. The joy and happiness which she now experienced, were too great to be concealed, and she was enabled to testify of the goodness and loving-kindness of the Lord, with such liveliness and power, that many were convinced by her testimony, and sincerely sought the Lord. As she was the first person at Burch Town that experienced deliverance from evil tempers, and exhorted and urged others to seek and enjoy the same blessing, she was not a little opposed by some of our Black brethren. But these trials she endured with the meekness and patience becoming a christian....

Soon after my wife's conversion, the Lord strove powerfully with me. I felt myself a miserable wretched sinner, so that I could not rest night or day. I went to Mr. Brown, one evening, and told him my case. He received me with great kindness and affection, and intreated me to seek the Lord with all my heart. The more he spoke to me, the more my distress increased.... On my return home, I had to pass thro' a little wood, where I intended to fall down on my knees and pray for mercy; but every time I attempted, I was so terrified, that I thought my hair stood upright, and that the earth moved beneath my feet. I hastened home in great fear and horror, and yet hoped that the Lord would bless me as well as my neighbours.... I thought I was not worthy to be among the people of God, nor even to dwell in my own house; but was fit only to reside among the beasts of the forest. This drove me out into the woods, when the snow lay upon the ground three or four feet deep, with a blanket, and a fire-brand in my hand. I cut the boughs of the spruce tree and kindled a fire. In this lonely situation I frequently intreated the Lord for mercy. Sometimes I thought that I felt a change wrought in my mind, so that I could rejoice in the Lord; but I soon fell again thro' unbelief into distracting doubts and fears, and evil-reasonings....

As my convictions increased, so did my desires after the Lord; and in order to keep them alive, I resolved to make a covenant with him in the most solemn manner I was able. For this purpose I went into the garden at midnight, and kneeled down upon the snow, lifting up my hands, eyes, and heart to Heaven; and intreated the Lord, who had called me by his Holy Spirit out of ignorance and wickedness, that he would increase and strengthen my awakenings and desires, and impress my heart with the importance of eternal things; and that I might never find rest or peace again, till I found peace with him, and received a sense of his pardoning love. The Lord mercifully looked down upon me, and gave me such a sight of my fallen state, that I plainly saw, without an interest in Christ, and an application of his atoning blood to my conscience, I should be lost to all eternity. This led me to a diligent use of all the means of Grace, and to forsake and renounce every thing that I knew to be sinful.

The more convictions increased, and the more I felt the wickedness of my own heart; yet the Lord helped me to strive against evil, so that temptations instead of prevailing against me, drove me nearer to him. The first Sunday in March, as I was going to the preaching, and was engaged in prayer and meditation, I thought I heard a voice saying to me, "Peace be unto thee!" I stopped and looked round about, to see if any one was near me. But finding myself alone, I went forward a little way, when the same words were again powerfully applied to my heart, which removed the burden of misery from it; and while I sat under the sermon, I was more abundantly blessed. Yet in the afternoon, doubts and fears again arose in my mind. Next morning I resolved like Jacob, not to let the Lord go till he blessed me indeed. As soon as my wife went out, I locked the door, and determined not to rise from my knees until the Lord fully revealed his pardoning love. I continued in prayer about half and hour, when the Lord again spoke to my heart, "Peace be unto thee." All my doubts and fears vanished away: I saw by faith, heaven opened to my view; and Christ and his holy angels rejoicing over me. I was now enabled to believe in the name of Jesus, and my soul was dissolved into love. Every thing appeared to me in a different light to what they did before; and I loved every living creature upon the face of the earth. I could truly say, I was now become a new creature....

In the year 1785, I began to exhort both in families and prayer-meetings, and the Lord graciously afforded me his assisting presence.... I laboured in Burchtown and Shelwin [four] years, and the word blessed to the conversion of many, most of who continued stedfast in the good way to the heavenly kingdom....

About this time the country was visited with dreadful famine, which not only prevailed at Burchtown, but likewise at Chebucto, Annapolis, Digby, and other places. Many of the poor people were compelled to sell their best gowns for five pounds of flour, in order to support life. When they had parted with all their clothes, even to their blankets, several of them fell down dead in the streets, thro' hunger. Some killed and eat their dogs and cats; and poverty and distress prevailed on every side; so that to my great grief I was obliged to leave Burchtown, because I could get no employment....

The circumstances of the white inhabitants were likewise very distressing, owing to their great imprudence in building large houses, and striving to excel one another in this piece of vanity. When their money was almost expended, they began to build small fishing vessels; but alas, it was too late to repair their error. Had they been wise enough at first to turn their attention to the fishery, instead of fine houses, the place would soon have been in a flourishing condition; whereas it was reduced in a short time to a heap of ruins, and its inhabitants were compelled to flee to other parts of the continent for sustenance....

TOPICS FOR EXPLORATION

1. How does Boston King justify his decision to write an account of his life? What is the purpose of the memoir which has been dedicated "to the Friends of Religion and Humanity?" Of what use can an individual life story like Boston King's be to its readers?

2. Compare the appeal King's narrative must have had at the time of its publication in 1798, to the response his text evokes in contemporary readers. What did it exemplify in the past? What is its value today? Does it still inspire? educate? merely inform?

3. What does Boston King's memoir reveal about the conditions of slavery in the American southern states in the 18th century? What are some examples of maltreatment and hardships endured by Black slaves recorded in King's narrative?

4. After several setbacks, Boston King's quest for freedom leads him to Nova Scotia. His personal history is often played out against the background of the American Revolutionary War. What do we learn about the role of Black people in the conflict between the British and Americans? How were Black Loyalists rewarded for their service?

5. Inasmuch as it views life as a pilgrimage, King's memoir tells a double story, that of his liberation from slavery and of his spiritual awakening through the discovery of religion. Can these two aspects of his narrative be seen as related? Discuss the importance of religion in Boston King's life.

Catharine Parr Traill

Catharine Parr Traill (1802–1899) emigrated from England in 1832 and settled in the Rice Lake–Peterborough area in Ontario. Traill's experiences in "the bush" were described in The Backwoods of Canada *(1836), based on letters she wrote to her relatives in England. Her sister, Susanna Moodie, gave her version of similar experiences in* Roughing It in the Bush *(1852). Traill and her family were bankrupt members of the English gentry who emigrated to Canada to repair their fortunes; they found, however, that their cultural background had not prepared them well for the rigours of "bush farming" in the new world. Both books were designed to inform and warn prospective English immigrants who might have been misguided by exaggerated claims of Canadian developers. In the excerpt Traill introduces her readers to some of the uncomfortable realities of pioneer life.*

from The Backwoods of Canada
LETTER IX

Lake House

April 18, 1833

But it is time that I should give you some account of our log-house, into which we moved a few days before Christmas. Many unlooked-for delays having hindered its completion before that time, I began to think it would never be habitable.

The first misfortune that happened was the loss of a fine yoke of oxen that were purchased to draw in the house-logs, that is, the logs for raising the walls of the house. Not regarding the bush as pleasant as their former master's cleared pastures, or perhaps foreseeing some hard work to come, early one morning they took into their heads to ford the lake at the head of the rapids, and march off, leaving no trace of their route excepting their footing at the water's edge. After many days spent in vain search for them, the work was at a stand, and for one month they were gone, and we began to give up all expectation of hearing any news of them. At last we learned they were some twenty miles off, in a distant township, having made their way through bush and swamp, creek and lake, back to their former owner, with an instinct that supplied to them the want of roads and compass.

Oxen have been known to traverse a tract of wild country to a distance of thirty or forty miles going in a direct line for their former haunts by unknown paths, where memory could not avail them. In the dog we consider it is scent as well as memory that guides him to his far-off home;—but how is this conduct of the oxen to be accounted for? They returned home through the mazes of interminable forests, where man, with all his reason and knowledge, would have been bewildered and lost.

It was the latter end of October before even the walls of our house were up. To effect this we called 'a bee'.[1] Sixteen of our neighbours cheerfully obeyed our summons; and though the day was far from favourable, so faithfully did our hive perform their tasks, that by night the outer walls were raised.

The work went merrily on with the help of plenty of Canadian nectar (whisky), the honey that our *bees* are solaced with. Some huge joints of salt pork, a peck of potatoes, with a rice-pudding, and a loaf as big as an enormous Cheshire cheese, formed the feast that was to regale them during the raising. This was spread out in the shanty,[2] in a *very rural style*. In short, we laughed, and called it a *picnic in the backwoods*; and rude as was the fare, I can assure you, great was the satisfaction expressed by all the guests of every degree, our 'bee' being considered as very well conducted. In spite of the difference of rank among those that assisted at the bee, the greatest possible harmony prevailed, and the party separated well pleased with the day's work and entertainment.

The following day I went to survey the newly-raised edifice, but was sorely puzzled, as it presented very little appearance of a house. It was merely an oblong square of logs raised one above the other, with open spaces between every row of logs. The spaces for the doors and windows were not then chopped out, and the rafters were not up. In short, it looked a very queer sort of a place, and I returned home a little disappointed, and wondering that my husband should be so well pleased with the progress that had been made. A day or two after this I again visited it. The *sleepers*[3] were laid to support the floors, and the places for the doors and windows cut out of the solid timbers, so that it had not quite so much the look of a bird-cage as before.

After the roof was shingled, we were again at a stand, as no boards could be procured nearer than Peterborough, a long day's journey through horrible roads. At that time no saw-mill was in progress; now there is a fine one building within a little distance of us. Our flooring-boards were all to be sawn by hand, and it was some time before any one could be found to perform this necessary work, and that at high wages—six-and-sixpence per day. Well, the boards were at length down, but of course of unseasoned timber; this was unavoidable; so as they could not be planed we were obliged to put up with their rough unsightly appearance, for no better were to be had. I began to recall to mind the observation of the old gentleman with whom we travelled from Cobourg to Rice Lake.[4] We console ourselves with the prospect that by next summer the boards will all be seasoned, and then the house is to be turned topsy-turvy, by having the floors all relaid, jointed, and smoothed.

The next misfortune that happened, was, that the mixture of clay and lime that was to plaster the inside and outside of the house between the chinks of the logs was one night frozen to stone. Just as the work was about half completed, the frost suddenly setting in, put a stop to our proceeding for some time, as the frozen plaster yielded neither to fire nor to hot water, the latter freezing before it had any effect on the mass, and rather making bad worse. Then the workman that was hewing the inside walls to make them smooth, wounded himself with the broad axe, and was unable to resume his work for some time.

I state these things merely to show the difficulties that attend us in the fulfillment of our plans, and this accounts in a great measure for the humble dwellings that settlers of the most respectable description are obliged to content themselves with at first coming to this country,—not, you may be assured, from inclination, but necessity: I could give you such narratives of this kind as would astonish you. After all, it serves to make us more satisfied than we should be on casting our eyes around to see few better off than we are, and many not half so comfortable, yet of equal, and, in some instances, superior pretensions as to station and fortune.

Every man in this country is his own glazier; this you will laugh at: but if he does not wish to see and feel the discomfort of broken panes, he must learn to put them in his windows with his own hands. Workmen are not easily to be had in the backwoods when you want them, and it would be preposterous to hire a man at high wages to make two days' journey to and from the nearest town to mend your windows. Boxes of glass of several different sizes are to be bought at a very cheap rate in the stores. My husband amused himself by glazing the windows of the house preparatory to their being fixed in.[5]

To understand the use of carpenter's tools, I assure you, is no despicable or useless kind of knowledge here. I would strongly recommend all young men coming to Canada to acquire a little acquaintance with this valuable art, as they will often be put to great inconvenience for the want of it.

I was once much amused with hearing the remarks made by a very fine lady, the reluctant sharer of her husband's emigration, on seeing the son of a naval officer of some rank in the service busily employed in making an axe-handle out of a piece of rock-elm.

'I wonder that you allow George to degrade himself so,' she said, addressing his father.

The captain looked up with surprise. 'Degrade himself! In what manner, madam? My boy neither swears, drinks whiskey, steals, nor tells lies.'

'But you allow him to perform tasks of the most menial kind. What is he now better than a hedge carpenter[6] and I suppose you allow him to chop, too?'

'Most assuredly I do. That pile of logs in the cart there was all cut by him after he had left study yesterday,' was the reply.

'I should see my boys dead before they should use an axe like common labourers.'

'Idleness is the root of all evil,' said the captain. 'How much worse might my son be employed if he were running wild about the streets with bad companions.'

'You will allow this is not a country for gentlemen or ladies to live in,' said the lady.

'It is the country for gentlemen that will not work and cannot live without, to starve in,' replied the captain bluntly; 'and for that reason I make my boys early accustom themselves to be usefully and actively employed.'

'My boys shall never work like common mechanics,'[7] said the lady, indignantly.

'Then, madam, they will be good for nothing as settlers; and it is a pity you dragged them across the Atlantic.'

'We were forced to come. We could not live as we had been used to do at home, or I never would have come to this horrid country.'

'Having come hither you would be wise to conform to circumstances. Canada is not the place for idle folks to retrench a lost fortune in. In some parts of the country you will find most articles of provision as dear as in London, clothing much dearer, and not so good, and a bad market to choose in.'

'I should like to know, then, who Canada is good for?' said she, angrily.

'It is a good country for the honest, industrious artisan. It is a fine country for the poor labourer, who, after a few years of hard toil, can sit down in his own log-house, and look abroad on his own land, and see his children well settled in life as independent freeholders.[8] It is a grand country for the rich speculator, who can afford to lay out a large sum in purchasing land in eligible situations; for if he have any judgment, he will make a hundred per cent as interest for his money after waiting a few years. But it is a hard country for the poor gentleman, whose habits have rendered him unfit for manual labour. He brings with him a mind unfitted to his situation; and even if necessity compels him to exertion, his labour is of little value. He has a hard struggle to live. The certain expenses of wages and living are great, and he is obliged to endure many privations if he would keep within compass, and be free of debt. If he have a large family, and brings them up wisely, so as to adapt themselves early to a settler's life, why he does well for them, and soon feels the benefit on his own land; but if he is idle himself, his wife extravagant and discontented, and the children taught to despise labour, why madam, they will soon be brought down to ruin. In short, the country is a good country for those to whom it is adapted; but if people will not conform to the doctrine of necessity and expediency, they have no business in it. It is plain Canada is not adapted to every class of people.'

'It was never adapted for me or my family,' said the lady, disdainfully.

'Very true,' was the laconic reply; and so ended the dialogue.

But while I have been recounting these remarks, I have wandered far from my original subject, and left my poor log-house quite in an unfinished state. At last I was told it was in a habitable condition, and I was soon engaged in all the bustle and fatigue attendant on removing our household goods. We received all the assistance we required from ____, who is ever ready and willing to help us. He laughed and called it a '*moving* bee'; I said it was a 'fixing bee'; and my husband said it was a 'settling bee'; I know we were unsettled enough till it was over. What a din of desolation is a small house, or any house under such circumstances. The idea of chaos must have been taken from a removal or a setting to rights, for I suppose the ancients had their *flitting*,[9] as the Scotch call it, as well as the moderns.

Various were the valuable articles of crockery-ware that perished in their short but rough journey through the woods. Peace to their manes.[10] I had a good helper in my Irish maid, who soon roused up famous fires, and set the house in order.

We have now got quite comfortably settled, and I shall give you a description of our little dwelling. What is finished is only a part of the original plan; the rest must be added next spring, or fall, as circumstances may suit.

A nice small sitting-room with a store closet, a kitchen, pantry, and bed-chamber form the ground floor; there is a good upper floor that will make three sleeping-rooms.

'What a nut-shell!' I think I hear you exclaim. So it is at present; but we purpose adding a handsome frame front as soon as we can get boards from the mill, which will give us another parlour, long hall, and good spare bed-room. The windows and glass door of our present sitting-room command pleasant lake-views to the west and south. When the house is completed, we shall have a verandah in front; and at the south side, which forms an agreeable addition in the summer, being used as a sort of outer room, in which we can dine, and have the advantage of cool air, protected from the glare of the sunbeams. The Canadians call these verandahs 'stoups'. Few houses, either log or frame, are without them. The pillars look extremely pretty, wreathed with the luxuriant hop-vine, mixed with the scarlet creeper and 'morning glory', the American name for the most splendid of major convolvuluses. These stoups are really a considerable ornament, as they conceal in a great measure the rough logs, and break the barnlike form of the building.

Our parlour is warmed by a handsome Franklin stove with brass galley, and fender. Our furniture consists of a brass-railed sofa, which serves upon occasion for a bed, Canadian painted chairs, a stained pine table, green and white curtains, and a handsome Indian mat that covers the floor. One side of the room is filled up with our books. Some large maps and a few good prints nearly conceal the rough walls, and form the decoration of our little dwelling. Our bed-chamber is furnished with equal simplicity. We do not, however, lack comfort in our humble home; and though it is not exactly such as we could wish, it is as good as, under existing circumstances, we could have.

NOTES

1. Any gathering for communal work.
2. Used here in its French-Canadian sense: "workshop."
3. Supporting beams.
4. "If you go into the backwoods your house must necessarily be a log-house," said an elderly gentleman, who had been a settler many years in the country, "for you will most probably be out of the way of a

saw-mill, and you will find so much to do, and so many obstacles to encounter, for the first two or three years, that you will hardly have the opportunity for carrying these improvements into effect.

"There is an old saying," he added... " 'first creep and then go.' Matters are not carried on quite so easily here as at home... At the end of ten or fifteen years you may begin to talk of these pretty improvements and elegancies and you will then be able to see a little what you are about." (Letter V).

5. That is, he placed the glass in the window-frames before putting the frames in place.

6. Fence repairer.

7. Manual labourers.

8. Those who own land without restrictions on its sale or use.

9. Moving from place to place.

10. Spirits (Latin: the deified souls of departed ancestors).

TOPICS FOR EXPLORATION

1. What is Traill's purpose in writing *The Backwoods of Canada*? Who is her audience? What effect is she hoping to have on her readers? What will her readers gain from her account?

2. What are some of the difficulties that Traill and her family encounter, according to this excerpt? How are these difficulties overcome? Find examples of loyalty and community spirit among the early settlers, as shown in her account.

3. What were some of the steps necessary to build a habitable dwelling in Traill's time? What skills must the immigrant have? How do building methods compare with those of today?

4. In the conversation between "the very fine lady" and "the naval officer," the issue of "rank" arises. What do they mean by rank? How do their attitudes toward work differ?

5. For what reasons, according to Traill, do so many immigrants come to Canada? According to the "naval officer" (and Traill), which immigrants will do well in Canada? Who will do poorly? Why?

6. In the opening paragraphs of her letter, Traill dwells for a while on the image of oxen that become a fit symbol of survival through hard work and perseverance. Are there any correspondences between this image and her description of the ideal immigrants? How is she herself equipped with the qualities she lauds in the settlers?

Miriam Rosenthal

Miriam Rosenthal, a Hungarian-Jewish survivor of the Holocaust tragedy, is an eyewitness narrator of the Nazi atrocities in the concentration camps during World War II. Despite the horrors she suffered along with millions of others, she has, as her account amply shows, retained her integrity and humanity. At the end of her narrative, she and her family decide to leave behind Europe's anti-Semitism and settle in Canada; they carry with them painful memories that will inform their choices in Canadian life. This episode has been excerpted from an article about the Holocaust called "We the Living" by Alan M. Gould.

A Holocaust Survivor's Story

We were taken to the Miskolc ghetto, where we stayed for three weeks. They separated the men from the women. I told my husband, "I have a feeling that whatever happens, it will be very bad. So wherever they take us, you go back to Miskolc and I'll go back to the city." I had a feeling that I'd never see him again.

We were smashed into trains like animals, without food or water. After three days, we arrived at Auschwitz. In the same train was my father-in-law, mother-in-law, my sister-in-law, my husband's sister-in-law with her two babies, six weeks and two years old. We were starving. It was hot, stinking, no food. You couldn't go to the washroom. Outside, all we saw was trees and forest.

When we arrived in Auschwitz, we were so happy! Anything was better than the train! Suddenly, we see fences all over. We see SS men and soldiers and Jews in striped uniforms. The Jews ran to the trains and cried "Give the kinder to der mama!" But why? Why should we give the children to the grandparents? They had come to tell us that if we gave the children to our mothers-in-law, like my sister-in-law did, we would be saved. And the old women went to the gas with the children. If the mothers held on to their children they would die with them.

There was Dr. Mengele, in his white gloves—a beautiful soldier. Left-right, left-right, his hand waved. We had to run—no time to look or talk. Thousands of people!

We came to Birkenau and were deloused. They shaved my hair and gave me a striped outfit, no underwear. I did not know then that right was life. I heard after the war that a train with my mother and sister arrived on the same day as my train from Miskolc. She was only twenty-five, and was begged to give up her year-old baby, but she would not do it. So she went to the left with my mother.

We were sent to barracks of five hundred women in Auschwitz. Older inmates told us, "You just come from Hungary? Look how fresh and healthy you are! You see that smoke there? That's your parents and sisters and brothers and children! They are dead!" "What? Are you crazy?" we asked.

It had been so hysterical when they shaved us. They put brown hair in one pile, black hair in another. I don't know what they did with it. There we were, naked. And we looked into each other's eyes—that was the mirror. We looked and started to laugh! We looked like idiots! Like monkeys! It was so terrible, and it was still funny.

I found out I was pregnant, in my fourth month. I didn't know, since no woman had a period at Auschwitz. And after four months, I felt something moving inside me, and I said to myself, "My God— I'm pregnant!" This was the worst possible thing, because every day I saw what happened to pregnant women. I already knew it meant death.

I didn't show until the fifth month, but I knew that every day I was waiting to die. Because one of these days they are going to catch me. And the hunger. There was no food. I begged for more food, and someone who knew I was pregnant would have mercy, and sometimes I'd get a peel of a potato. Each day's food was a tiny bit of margarine and a bit of bread. In the morning, black coffee. At night, soup.

I had been told, if they ask for a number of women to go on a transport out of the camp, to volunteer. And so, after about a month, they asked for five hundred to go to Plasow, another camp. It had been built in a Jewish cemetery.

It was a horrible place. People worked on mountains, like slaves in ancient Egypt, carrying stones. When we arrived a Polish Jewish Kapo named Henry Reisfeld said to me. "I can use twenty women. I will save them in my barrack for work." He had been in the camp for three years already. He was unbelievable. I'd ask him, "Why are you helping me like this?" And he said. "You look like my daughter so much—she was killed here. I'll show you the grave." He survived the war—he wrote me right after. He knew I was pregnant and he got me food—bread, more bread, anything he could. But we didn't stay there too long, maybe a few weeks. It was terrible there, but still better than Auschwitz.

One day he told me. "We got an order; you must go back to Auschwitz. Don't go back. We'll be liberated soon by the Russians." I told him that I wasn't staying. I would go back with the rest of the girls. I wasn't going to leave my friends and my cousin. And so we were shipped back to Auschwitz. He ran after our train with a pail of water throwing it onto the train. Again, selections. Again, Mengele. Left. Right. And already he was selecting weak ones and strong ones. Or those who looked pregnant. I was pretty far—my fifth or sixth month, already showing. And in front of me was my first cousin, who wasn't even married! Mengele called to her in German "You are a pig." She replied "No, I am not a pig." "Yes you are, and don't you dare talk back to me. You go to the left." And he sent her to the gas. Me, he let go. "I can't believe it," I told the girls. I was expecting to die.

Two weeks later, I was put on a transport to Augsburg, in Germany—a Messerschmitt airplane factory. Everyone was so happy! A factory! Better than Auschwitz! And this was the first time we saw other people—Germans. Political prisoners from Holland, Belgium.

We got better food than in Auschwitz. We were still hungry, but it was better. The political prisoners were allowed to go and live in the city at night. The Jews were kept in the barracks. I worked next to a Christian communist. All day on the machine, to help build airplanes.

One day, as I worked, two SS men came in to look closely at every worker. One said to me in German "You pig woman! What are you doing here! You are pregnant? Let's go! Where? Back to Auschwitz." I said good-bye to my friends, who were crying. But it was a relief. I couldn't care anymore. Thank God the suffering would be over. And the fear of what would happen to the baby. But my husband didn't even know that I was pregnant! There was no one there to help.

So they put me on a passenger train. This was December, 1944. I had on big wooden shoes and no stockings, and it was snowing. The two soldiers were very decent. They knew the war was coming to an end. They bought my ticket. I had a classy trip! There were civilized people sitting all around me, and I still didn't have any hair, and I was pregnant, and I looked crazy.

People kept looking at me, and the two soldiers went out to smoke. And a German lady said. "What is happening here?"

"Don't you know?" I said to her. "I'm Jewish. They're taking me to the gas, in Auschwitz. Don't you know what is happening to the Jewish people?" She said she didn't, and was so concerned that she opened her purse and took out a piece of bread and handed it to me. The other people were all staring. They really didn't know. They were polite to me.

The train stopped after a few hours, and the men said, "Let's go. Get off the train." "What happened?" "They bombed Auschwitz. You won't be going to the gas now." "Where are you taking me?" "To Landsberg."

It was a special *lager*, a horrible camp where they worked people to death. They handed me over like a parcel, giving my number, and they left. The work camp was called Kaufring. The same setup. Barbed wire. Electrified fences. No Mengele. I saw men and women in different parts of the camp, with only barbed wire between them. Skeletons. They could hardly work anymore. An SS woman took me to a cabin. My God, what I see in this cabin! Six other pregnant women like me! I went hysterical crying, "Why are you here?"

They called us the Pregnancy Commando. Every day we worked. But we had food. The Germans knew they had lost the war. They wanted to use us as alibis—that they didn't kill infants. So we worked every day. I was in my eighth month. It was bitter cold. We worked in a laundry, to wash lice out of prisoners' clothes and hang them out to dry. Some days we had to carry dead bodies in a wagon, dump them in a big pit, and the SS would dump lime on them.

The women started to give birth—first one, then another. I was the last, the seventh. I helped the first six into the world. The midwife. There was a doctor, a Jewish prisoner. But he was skin and bones. He had been a gynecologist in Hungary. One day the SS brought him to us "He will be your doctor!" We started to laugh. He couldn't even stand up. He should help us? After the SS left the doctor said, "Children how can I help you? I have no strength left. I'm dying!" He was about fifty-five and looked terrible.

David, who was the Jewish Kapo in the kitchen, he saved our lives. He used to hide meat under the coal in a pail. He told us "Look, you have a doctor now. I'm going to fatten him up so that he should have strength to help you have the babies!" So he snuck extra food to Dr. Vadasz. He survived the war; I sent him clothes then, and wrote to him. He soon after passed away. But then the doctor said, "I have no needle, no medicine, no nothing! No diapers! No soap!" But David once stole a sheet, which he tore up for diapers.

One day, he came in with an SS man. He had been a teacher. And he wept and said, "Look, I'm an SS officer. There is no excuse. I know I am going to die. The Americans are very close. But please believe me—I have children at home, too." And under his coat, he had pieces of rags, soap. Two or three times he did this.

The doctor delivered each of the babies. I was very sick. Leslie was ten pounds—and with all that lack of food! I had forty-eight hours of labour. He was a beautiful baby with blonde, curly hair, and blue, blue eyes, and the SS men went crazy over him—he was a little Aryan! I had a very difficult delivery. The doctor told me, "Miriam I'm trying everything. I can do nothing more. Only God can help you."

Finally, my son was born. I didn't even know, on the other side of the electrical fence, where the men were, they were praying all night—psalms—for me. The whole night. Because they heard the screaming from me. I was so overwhelmed by pain, when the men yelled out, "Do you know what day is today—the day you had the baby? It's Purim! It's Purim!"

But then I was very sick. The placenta stayed in. I got fever and was unconscious. My friend who delivered six weeks before me—she now lives in Brazil, and came in for my son's wedding—she nursed Leslie. She saved my son's life. She told me later that she didn't think I would survive, so she had decided to adopt him.

And then the order came that the Americans were coming, and we had to evacuate the camp. We had to go to Dachau—to the gas—with our babies. So they started to empty the camp, but they couldn't take me, because I was so sick. Four soldiers lifted the bed and began to take me to the infirmary. But as they were walking, I started to hemorrhage, and the whole placenta came out. They ran to Dr. Vadasz, who made a cleaning.

I felt better. Leslie was being nursed by my friend. I had one more camp to go to—Dachau. We walked and walked. I had little milk and Leslie began to lose weight. We were put in an open cattle-car in April, 1945.

We saw airplanes and bombs falling. They thought we were Germans! They bombed our trains—they blew up the engine and the first two cars filled with Jews. We kept waving frantically; we are not Nazis! We are Jews! But how could they see?

The train stopped, so we thought the war was over. I tied Leslie to my neck with a piece of cloth and I jumped from a high trestle. It was near a forest, near Dachau. I ran toward a village, and a peasant woman threw bread to me.

All of a sudden, the Germans shot at us, and began to force us back to the train. I had put Leslie by a tree trunk and covered him with leaves and my body. There were bombs falling and the Germans were shooting ... we were led back to the train. They brought a new engine and we continued toward Dachau.

Dachau is a city, and we went through it, in our open car. The train stopped in the middle of the city, across from apartments. We were held up because they could not gas the Jews fast enough—so many were being shipped in from across Europe. So we had to sit and wait. This was already early May. And the baby was hungry and I was hungry and I had very little milk.

Ever since Leslie was born, I had such a will to live again! I had a child, I must take him home, I must save him. He was beautiful! And he never cried. It's as if he knew that he was not supposed to cry. Somehow he knew.

So I got off the train. People cried out "They are going to shoot you! The war is almost over!" But I said, "I don't care! I have no milk and my baby is hungry." And I left the train with Leslie. It was daytime. I crossed the street, went upstairs into an apartment building, knocked on the door. A German woman opened the door. "What do you want?" "I'm hungry. I need milk for my baby. We are Jewish and we are going to be gassed."

She almost went crazy. And I'll never forget that in her hallway there was a long mirror. It was the first time I'd seen myself since before the deportation from the ghetto. I had a little bit of hair. She quickly got a piece of bread and a glass of milk. She knew what was happening, since she must have seen all the trains filled with Jews every day going to Dachau. Where could they have been taking them?

I came back to the train with Leslie. The women were like animals, grabbing the bread from me. A man—a dentist—from our town—a skeleton, came to me and begged for a piece of bread. I gave him my last piece. He survived the war.

Then the train started to go. We got into Dachau at night. There was shouting and yelling and screaming: "Free! Free! You are Free!" It was American soldiers who had broken in. At four in the morning, dead bodies everywhere, chaos and American soldiers. We were screaming. One American gave me a little prayer book—I never part with it—it's in my purse even now.

The Americans wanted to take away the babies with their mothers to a home, to keep us strong. I didn't want to go. I said, "No, I want to go home as soon as I can."

One day I walked through the barracks and my husband's cousin recognized me. "Miriam! My goodness! What happened! Who is this baby?" I told him. "Are you hungry?" he asked. "I'm going to bring you a chicken!" He wrung the neck and plucked it and cooked it and brought it to me. He laughed, "Nice and kosher—you can eat it!" Whenever I see him nowadays, he says, "Remember the chicken?" Who cared if it was kosher or not kosher, as long as you had food?

They drove me in a jeep with a doctor and a nurse from Dachau to Prague. Then I went again in a train—on the top of a coal wagon. Can you imagine? I was nursing and not nursing. I once went to the engineer and got hot water for the baby.

I finally arrived in Komarno. My brother had survived a forced labour camp. He didn't recognize me, and didn't know I had a baby. He took me back to what was left of our family home. Russians lived there—Russian soldiers.

The cousin who I met in Dachau went home before me and he met my husband. He told him, "I met your wife. She's coming home with the baby." And he said, "Yah? What baby?"

"Your Baby! He looks like your father—exactly! It's a beautiful baby!" My husband told him, "You're crazy!" Then he realized that I had probably become pregnant. He said, "Maybe a German soldier. Maybe she was made pregnant by a Nazi." It did happen in the war, of course.

And he started to walk. I don't know how many days, but he walked all the way to my city, Komarno. There was no train. His shoes were completely gone from walking. He had been in a slave labour camp during the war. Until the moment he came to my door, I didn't know he had survived. He knocked and there I stood. He just cried and cried: "He looks like my father." I told him, "You know he has your ears." One of Leslie's ears is bent, just like my husband's. Our reunion was unbelievable.

We wanted to start living like normal human beings. We had thought that after what had happened the world stopped, and everyone would be crying for us. But the Hungarians would say, "Oh look! We thought you wouldn't come back." Or, "Look—more came back than went!" Things like that. We came home broken in body and broken in soul, and that was the welcome. One day I saw a woman wearing my mother's coat walking down the street.

I wrote to my sister in Canada. They wrote back. We had to go to Cuba first. Canadian immigration wasn't open yet, and the United States wouldn't give us a permit to stay temporarily. We had stayed ten months in Paris waiting for papers, and then ten months in Havana. Then we were congratulated by the Canadian consulate: "Good luck!"

First we were in Timmins for a year, where my husband served as rabbi. From there, we went to Sudbury. We stayed sixteen years. We came to Toronto sixteen years ago, and we opened Miriam's Bookstore.

Leslie has a Ph.D. in organic chemistry, and works at Honeywell. He is married with two girls and a boy. Lilian is thirty-two, has a teaching diploma, and has taught kindergarten. Murray is doing his Master's in medieval Jewish history at McGill. He is single.

I tell you, Canadians don't appreciate where they are. To be here in this blessed country—nothing else but freedom! They don't know! To be free; to walk in the streets; you can go to synagogue, do whatever you want, speak your mind. You don't have to worry. What it means to be a person—to live like a human being! People have to learn to appreciate Canada. We have to be thankful every day we are here.

I have nightmares. Not often, but I have them. I feel that I can't find my baby Leslie, and we have to run. Again we are in the trains.

My daughter asks me, "How can you divide yourself and live still like a human being?" And I answer her, "I have to cope. You live, you work, you don't think about it." I very seldom tell my story. And this is but a nutshell of what happened.

I used to feel guilt. Not any more. Why me, I would ask, why did I come home, and not my mother, who was such a pious, honest Jew? Why me?

And the whole question comes up, about religion: why am I still religious? I am asked. And I tell them, "I brought a son back from Hell—how can I not believe in God?"

TOPICS FOR EXPLORATION

1. Whom does Rosenthal have in mind as her audience while she narrates her personal story? What is her purpose: to inform? to persuade? Does she have any other?

2. Rosenthal's narrative does not employ much commentary. Does this make her story more effective? Is commentary even necessary?

3. Rosenthal's text includes examples of the extreme bestiality institutionalized by concentration camps. How did the Nazis "dehumanize" the Jews upon their arrival at the camps? What steps were taken to destroy the prisoners' identities?

4. What were the causes and conditions that brought about these horrors in Europe during World War II? Does Rosenthal consider the causes of the suffering? Why or why not?

5. How was Rosenthal spared so often? What were the circumstances of the chance events that saved her life? Apart from the role of pure chance in the small gestures of help extended to her, what attitude characterized those who managed to survive? How did her "will to live" endure among so many painful experiences?

6. Most of Rosenthal's story relates her imprisonment by the Nazis. Compare that with the brief description of experiences in Canada after the war. Why did she decide to immigrate to Canada?

Rohinton Mistry

Rohinton Mistry was born in Bombay, India, in 1952 and emigrated to Canada in 1975. Educated in economics at Bombay, in Toronto he worked in a bank while studying philosophy and literature at night. In 1985, he was awarded the Canadian Fiction *Contributor's Prize. In 1988, the collection of short stories from which our selection has been taken,* Tales from Firozsha Baag *(1987), was short-listed for the Governor General's Award. His novel* Such a Long Journey *won the Governor General's Award and became a national bestseller in 1991. These fictions have a strong autobiographical element and meticulous, authentic detail. Mistry's stories often reflect the tensions of Bombay life and contrast it with the exotic temptations of life elsewhere, especially in the West.*

Lend Me Your Light

... your lights are all lit—then where do you go with your
lamp? My house is all dark and lonesome,—lend me your light.
Rabindranath Tagore
Gitanjali

We both left Bombay the same year. Jamshed first, for New York, then I, for Toronto. As immigrants in North America, sharing this common experience should have salvaged something from our acquaintanceship. It went back such a long way, to our school days at St Xavier's.

To sustain an acquaintance does not take very much. A friendship, that's another thing. Strange, then, that it has ended so completely, that he has erased himself out of our lives, mine and Percy's; now I cannot imagine him even as a mere bit player who fills out the action or swells a procession.

Jamshed was my brother's friend. The three of us went to the same school. Jamshed and my brother, Percy, both four years older than I, were in the same class, and spent their time together. They had to part company during lunch, though, because Jamshed did not eat where Percy and I did, in the school's drillhall-cum-lunchroom.

The tiffin carriers would stagger into the school compound with their long, narrow rickety crates on their heads, each with fifty tiffin boxes, delivering lunches from homes in all corners of the city. When the boxes were unpacked, the drillhall would be filled with a smell that is hard to forget, thick as swill, while the aromas of four hundred steaming lunches started to mingle. The smell must have soaked into the very walls and ceiling, there to age and rancify. No matter what the hour of the day, that hot and dank grotto of a drill-hall smelled stale and sickly, the way a vomit-splashed room does even after it is cleaned up.

Jamshed did not eat in this crammed and cavernous interior. Not for him the air redolent of nauseous odours. His food arrived precisely at one o'clock in the chauffeur-driven, air-conditioned family car, and was eaten in the leather-upholstered luxury of the back seat, amidst his collection of hyphenated lavishness.

In the snug dining-room where chauffeur doubled as waiter, Jamshed lunched through his school-days, safe from the vicissitudes of climate. The monsoon might drench the tiffin carriers to the bone and turn cold the boxes of four hundred waiting schoolboys, but it could not touch Jamshed or his lunch. The tiffin carriers might arrive glistening and stinking of sweat in the hot season, with scorching hot tiffin boxes, hotter than they'd left the kitchens of Bombay, but Jamshed's lunch remained unaffected.

During the years of high school, my brother, Percy, began spending many weekend afternoons at his friend's house at Malabar Hill. Formerly, these were the afternoons when we used to join Pesi *paadmaroo* and the others for our most riotous times in the compound, the afternoons that the adults of Firozsha Baag would await with dread, not knowing what new terrors Pesi had devised to unleash upon the innocent and the unsuspecting.

But Percy dropped all this for Jamshed's company. And when he returned from his visits, Mummy would commence the questioning: What did he eat? Was Jamshed's mother home? What did the two do all afternoon? Did they go out anywhere? And so on.

Percy did not confide in me very much in those days. Our lives intersected during the lunch routine only, which counted for very little. For a short while we had played cricket together with the boys of Firozsha Baag. Then he lost interest in that too. He refused to come when Daddy would take the whole gang to the Marine Dri *maidaan* on Sunday morning. And soon, like all younger brothers, I was seen mainly as a nuisance.

But my curiosity about Percy and Jamshed was satisfied by Mummy's interrogations. I knew that the afternoons were usually spent making model airplanes and listening to music. The airplanes were simple gliders in the early years; the records, mostly Mantovani and from Broadway shows. Later came more complex models with gasoline engines and remote control, and classical music from Bach and Poulenc.

The model-airplane kits were gifts from Jamshed's itinerant aunties and uncles, purchased during business trips to England or the U.S. Everyone except my brother and I seemed to have uncles and aunties smitten by wanderlust, and Jamshed's supply line from the western world guaranteed for him a steady diet of foreign clothes, shoes, and records.

One Saturday, Percy reported during question period that Jamshed had received the original soundtrack of *My Fair Lady*. This was sensational news. The LP was not available in Bombay, and a few privately imported or "smuggled" copies, brought in by people like Jamshed's relatives, were selling in the black market for two hundred rupees. I had seen the records displayed side by side with foreign perfumes, chocolates, and cheeses at the pavement stalls of smugglers along Flora Fountain.

Sometimes, these stalls were smashed up during police raids. I liked to imagine that one day a raid would occur as I was passing, and in the mêlée and chaos of the clash, *My Fair Lady* would fly through the air and land at my feet, unnoticed by anyone. Of course, there wasn't much I could have done with it following the miracle, because our old gramophone played only 78 rpms.

After strenuous negotiations in which Mummy, Percy, and I exhausted ourselves, Percy agreed to ask his friend if I could listen to the album. Arrangements were made. And the following Saturday we set off for Jamshed's house. From Firozsha Baag, the direction of Malabar Hill was opposite to the one we took to go to school every morning, and I was not familiar with the roads the bus travelled. The building had a marble lobby, and the lift zoomed us up smoothly to the tenth floor before I had time to draw breath. I was about to tell Percy that we needed one like this in Firozsha Baag, but the door opened. Jamshed welcomed us graciously, then wasted no time in putting the record on the turntable. After all, that was what I had come for.

The afternoon dragged by after the sound-track was finished. Bored, I watched them work on an airplane. The box said it was a Sopwith Camel. The name was familiar from the Biggles books Percy used to bring home. I picked up the lid and read dully that the aircraft had been designed by the British industrialist and aeronautical engineer, Thomas Octave Murdoch Sopwith, born 1888, and had been used during the First World War. Then followed a list of parts.

Later, we had lunch, and they talked. I was merely the kid brother, and nobody expected me to do much else but listen. They talked of school and the school library, of all the books that the library badly needed; and of the *ghatis* who were flooding the school of late.

In the particular version of reality we inherited, *ghatis* were always flooding places, they never just went there. *Ghatis* were flooding the banks, desecrating the sanctity of institutions, and taking up all the coveted jobs. *Ghatis* were even flooding the colleges and universities, a thing unheard of. Wherever you turned, the bloody *ghatis* were flooding the place.

With much shame I remember this word *ghati*. A suppurating sore of a word, oozing the stench of bigotry. It consigned a whole race to the mute roles of coolies and menials, forever unredeemable.

During one of our rare vacations to Matheran, as a child, I watched with detachment while a straining coolie loaded the family's baggage on his person. The big metal trunk was placed flat on his head, with the leather suitcase over it. The enormous hold-all was slung on his left arm, which he raised to steady the load on his head, and the remaining suitcase went in the right hand. It was all accomplished with much the same approach and consideration used in loading a cart or barrow—the main thing was balance, to avoid tipping over. This skeletal man then tottered off towards the train that would transport us to the little hill station. There, similar skeletal beings would be waiting with rickshaws. Automobiles were prohibited in Matheran, to preserve the pastoral purity of the place and the livelihood of the rickshawallas.

Many years later I found myself at the same hill station, a member of my college hikers' club, labouring up its slopes with a knapsack. Automobiles were still not permitted in Matheran, and every time a rickshaw sped by in a flurry of legs and wheels, we'd yell at the occupant ensconced within: "Capitalist pig! You bastard! Stop riding on your brother's back!" The bewildered passenger would lean forward for a moment, not quite understanding, then fall back into the cushioned comfort of the rickshaw.

But this type of smug socialism did not come till much later. First we had to reckon with school, school uniforms, brown paper covers for textbooks and exercise books, and the mad morning rush for the school bus. I remember how Percy used to rage and shout at our scrawny *ghaton* if the pathetic creature ever got in his way as she swept and mopped the floors. Mummy would proudly observe, "He has a temper just like Grandpa's." She would also discreetly admonish Percy, since this was in the days when it was becoming quite difficult to find a new *ghaton*, especially if the first one quit due to abuse from the scion of the family and established her reasons for quitting among her colleagues.

I was never sure why some people called them *ghatons* and others, *gungas*. I suppose the latter was intended to placate— the collective conferment of the name of India's sacred river balanced the occasions of harshness and ill-treatment. But the good old days, when you could scream at a *ghaton* and could kick her and hurl her down the steps, and expect her to show up for work next morning, had definitely passed.

After high school, Percy and Jamshed went to different colleges. If they met at all, it would be at concerts of the Bombay Chamber Orchestra. Along with a college friend, Navjeet, and some others, my brother organized a charitable agency that collected and distributed funds to destitute farmers in a small Maharashtrian village. The idea was to get as many of these wretched souls as possible out of the clutches of the village money-lenders.

Jamshed showed a very superficial interest in what little he knew about Percy's activities. Each time they met, he would start with how he was trying his best to get out of the country. "Absolutely no future in this stupid place," he said. "Bloody corruption everywhere. And you can't buy any of the things you want, don't even get to see a decent English movie. First chance I get, I'm going abroad. Preferably the U.S."

After a while, Percy stopped talking about his small village, and they only discussed the concert program or the soloist's performance that evening. Then their meetings at concerts ceased altogether because Percy now spent very little time in Bombay.

Jamshed did manage to leave. One day, he came to say goodbye. But Percy was away working in the small village: his charitable agency had taken on the task full time. Jamshed spoke to those of us who were home, and we all agreed that he was doing the right thing. There just weren't any prospects in this country; nothing could stop its downhill race towards despair and ruin.

My parents announced that I, too, was trying to emigrate, but to Canada, not the U.S. "We will miss him if he gets to go," they told Jamshed, "but for the sake of his own future, he must. There is a lot of opportunity in Toronto. We've seen advertisements in newspapers from England, where Canadian Immigration is encouraging people to go to Canada. Of course, they won't advertise in a country like India—who would want these bloody *ghatis* to come charging into their fine land?—but the office in New Delhi is holding interviews and selecting highly qualified applicants." In the clichés of our speech was reflected the cliché which the idea of emigration had turned into for so many. According to my parents, I would have no difficulty being approved, what with my education, and my westernized background, and my fluency in the English language.

And they were right. A few months later things were ready for my departure to Toronto.

TOPICS FOR EXPLORATION

1. Mistry's story is autobiographical. How does this affect the style? What methods does the author use to give weight and authenticity to his story?

2. The lunches attended by the narrator, his brother, and Jamshed at school and at Jamshed's house are symbolic of the contrast between the respective social levels of their families. How do they differ?

3. Who are *ghatis*? How do they represent the institutional injustice of Bombay? Contrast the lifestyles of the *ghatis* with those who live in the Malabar Hills.

4. How does the narrator as a young boy perceive the West? What are the symbols of its exotic luxury? Is the title Mistry's ironic comment about the West? In the context of his critique of Bombay's social stratification, does the title reflect the idealized longing for Western democracies in post-colonial countries?

5. What is the meaning of the contrast among the three main characters, Jamshed, Percy, and the narrator? How do their motives differ? In the light of their desires, what different goals do they accomplish?

6. What is the process that an Indian immigrant must follow in order to come to Canada?

7. How do you understand the narrator's comment at the end that the idea of emigration has turned into a cliché for so many people in his country? In what way does the story's flashback into the past explain the growth of emigration from post-independence India?

Helga (Kutz-Harder) Mills

The real-life stories collected in Helga (Kutz-Harder) Mills' reportage often have their source in unspeakable suffering and misery that caused their subjects to flee their homelands and become refugees in Canada.

The socio-political backgrounds of these personal experiences are varied. The Iranian Revolution of 1978, led by Ayatollah Khomeini, replaced the Shah's regime with an Islamic government that established a strict Moslem rule. It governed in a way that many people found more repressive than the Shah's reign. In 1978 in Afghanistan, a Soviet-backed military junta seized power, initiating the cycle of civil violence and guerrilla fighting that went on for ten years, until the Soviet troops were finally withdrawn, and continued even afterwards. The civil war left the country devastated and depopulated. From 1979, El Salvador, in Central America, has been the site of relentless battle between the U.S.-supported military government and the leftist popular movement. Thousands of people have been killed or "disappeared"; thousands have sought escape in refugee camps. Burundi, a small African country, has been troubled by long-term political instability that has its roots in ethnic conflicts. For years, it has been unable to escape the bloody civil war between the Hutu majority and the Tutsi ruling class. Somalia, an African republic uniting former British and Italian colonies, is subject to both drought and flood, which places this country in the so-called hunger belt. It has received international economic and technical assistance. Sri Lanka, formerly the British colony of Ceylon, has been wracked since its independence in 1948 by the violent religious, linguistic, and ethnic conflict between the majority Sinhalese Buddhists and the minority Tamils who favour an independent Tamil homeland. The politics of violence and terrorism is the island's everyday reality.

Breaking the Barriers:
Refugee Women in Canada

The stories of the refugee women I have met in Canada fill me with woe and wonder. The realities of their past sometimes defy my imagination. The courage with which they find their place in a settled society like Canada is awe-inspiring. Many of them have an aura of calm and beauty which masks the turmoil inside when they try to hold in tension the unbearable memories of the past, the spirit-defying obstacles of everyday life in a cold new country, and the tentative flame of hope which dares to believe that this is the place where their spirits can flourish.

Many of the refugee women are reluctant to talk of their past, sometimes because they are afraid of unleashing emotional despair which they may not be able to control, and sometimes because they need to bury some of the details in order to be accepted by their people here. Breaking the barriers within themselves requires as much courage as breaking the barriers between them and their new society. The stories which I have gathered here are tributes to this courage. They look inward and outward. They give us truth about ourselves, about us, and about the world in which we live together. The women and their stories are a gift to us.

YOUNG WOMAN FROM IRAN

A young Iranian man started the conversation: "Women in Iran suffer two times more than men." The young widow accompanying him continued the story. Because her husband wrote down his criticism of the government he was imprisoned. Because she was pregnant with his child, she, too, was imprisoned. When he died, the authorities freed her from prison, but she found herself imprisoned by a society which shunned her because of him. She had no right to study, no right to work, no way to survive and feed a child.

She was bitter about her past: "Women are half of a man, except when they have to go to prison the same as a man." She told me that many women with children fill the prisons, and many women are executed. Many children lose both parents and become the lost children of Iran, because "nobody is allowed to help them."

She arrived at a Canadian airport, carrying a small daughter and "horrible memories" of family members' executions, and religious repression, especially of women. Immigration officials treated her well and gave her a hearing only two days later. She came to the meeting tired and worried. She did not know what to do when the official thundered: "Why, why, why don't you go home where you belong? Why are you coming and stealing jobs from Canadians?" In her heart she cried: "I can't go home, I would rather be executed than treated like this. I can't stop crying." She needed to believe that she would be helped, not criticized for why she was where she was.

As a single mother she knew that first of all, she must find work. But before that, she must study French because she was in Montreal. She worried about a lot of things. What could she do with her little girl? How could she manage? How could she live if her baby became sick? She could find work in a factory, but how nice it would be to work at her own profession, even at a minimum wage.

She ended her conversation: "Women aren't refugees because of what they have done, but because of what their husbands have done." She bowed her head and, as her lustrous black hair fell over her shoulders, we wept, men and women alike. Will we ever know what keeps her going day after day?

YOUNG WOMAN FROM AFGHANISTAN

She was one of the privileged few who had ventured out of a tradition in which females are sequestered, to attend the university in Kabul. The times away from campus were still spent with women in whose company love and tradition and nurture were felt and passed on. Men were for marrying and for stability.

Then came the terror of war and the flight from danger. Her mother died in her homeland. One sister found her way to Germany. Other sisters found their way to Australia. She married a countryman along the way, and they came to Canada along with his five unmarried brothers. She and her baby daughter were the only females in the household, and she longed for women to turn to for guidance and cultural continuity.

At twenty-three she saw the advertisement for a youth training program available to anyone unemployed under the age of twenty-four. Toronto apartments are expensive, and a child needs toys and a bed and clothes and books and love. "If I don't take the program now I'll be too old for the age restriction, and when I leave my child with the sitter she cries and will not eat," she explained. At home, a mother or an aunt or sister could have helped. Here, a strange woman with strange customs cares for her child. She sobs over the telephone. I cannot solve her dilemma, but I can listen to her story.

She called again recently. She has moved to the suburbs, far away from public transportation, to be able to offer her child a garden to play in. Her loneliness and alienation are intensified. I wonder how long it will be before she walks with a sense of fulfilled promise.

YOUNG WOMAN FROM EL SALVADOR

A church heard about her fear of returning to El Salvador, and quickly agreed to sponsor her into Canada. She waited eleven months in Buffalo while the Canadian authorities read through the stacks of paper and signed the right ones before she could finally end her journey. The room they provided was so warm and welcoming, and she sank into some pillows, exhausted. Eventually the young man she had met along the way found her, and became her husband.

Like most new immigrants, their monthly income was minimal, unequal to the expectations she placed on herself as a good wife. In her understanding, that included serving expensive cuts of meat and spending the day at home to protect the timing of the evening meal. Meanwhile, her sponsors ate bean sprouts and granola, and watched her weekly allowance used up in apparently inappropriate grocery bills. They advised when they could, and in time the grocery bills got lower; so did her self-esteem as a wife. She learned how to fit into the Canadian economy, but felt she was betraying her cultural values.

How do any of us know which culture should be imposed on which? Will she eventually be a Canadian Salvadorean woman, or a Salvadorean Canadian woman? Either way, she may feel as if she has failed at being a good woman.

YOUNG WOMAN FROM BURUNDI

She had been a refugee in Africa for seven years, and was relieved when Canada selected her as a government sponsored refugee, along with her four small children. She came to Montreal, fluent in French and full of hope. Two children went to school, and two children went to daycare. She was one of the lucky ones; she got a job in a factory. Factory work itself was an unfamiliar experience. She began to sense that no one wanted to talk past her black face. She tried to realize what was happening around her: "I cried in the washroom, and nobody noticed my tears when I came out. I wondered why nobody cared about me until I realized that nobody cared about anybody. Nobody even said 'excuse me' when they stepped on a toe."

Machines frightened her, and she was transferred to a simpler one. It wasn't simple, though, to be working with men for the first time in her life. She finally decided to leave her job, and was amazed that the boss was sad. She realized with surprise that he thought she had been doing a good job. He never told her!

She stayed home for a while and worried about the other women. She had never been involved in collectives of any kind, but she knew they needed each other. She went to an International Centre and told them about her worries and how they could help each other. She filled out complicated forms to create a job to help other women, and got a grant for a new job. Now she works with women and helps them from her own experience in Canada. "All those women are slaves to their culture," she said. "They forget their own possibilities."

Can we ever fully understand why they are here? Can we learn from their experience? Can we understand them as individual women? Will we ever look at them without prejudice?

YOUNG WOMAN FROM SOMALIA

She was highly skilled in Somalia: a typist and telex computer operator. But after her husband disappeared (just one of thousands) her life changed, because in Somalia a working woman needs a male sponsor. At first her uncle sponsored her, but he disappeared, too. And so she was fired, with no place to go. "The war in Somalia is an anarchist war. It is a war on women," she said. Any woman between the ages of eighteen and forty is not safe from being forcibly removed to the army camps to be raped and violated. And that's only the beginning. If her husband finds out, he kills her for the shame of it all; if they know that he has found out, they kill him, too; if he goes into hiding instead, and she won't tell where he is, they kill her.

And so she escaped to Canada, aching because she left a young baby with her sister, who couldn't come to Canada, as protection for her sister: only a girl with a baby is safe from violation. And so she sacrificed her baby daughter to save her sister. Most of all she feels so alone because there are not enough Somalis in Canada to form the kind of community to which she needs to belong, in order to stand upright in the midst of the pain and the memory of the flesh and blood she left behind.

YOUNG TAMIL WOMAN FROM SRI LANKA

As a child she had heard stories of bombings from her mother. Then, one of the bombs killed her young husband, and she felt them in her soul when she realized that her unborn twins would never know their father. She was a high school teacher, and one extra-violent day her principal warned her to stay at home. Frozen with fear, three women watched while thugs ran to the back of the house with torches to burn it down—just because she was a Tamil. Only wit and the need to survive kept them moving to a temporary safe haven, a room 6'x10' for fifty people. "I still feel the scars of that burning," she said.

The nurse who helped her wash the twins asked: "When are you going home?" She remembers bursting into tears because she had no home to go to. They kept moving, sleeping with their clothes on and a bit of food nearby, ready to move when necessary. For three months they stayed in India, then they found their way to England, where a Canadian church heard about them and sponsored their move to Canada. They waited eleven more months before arriving at the welcoming church. One of the first comments from an unthinking person confused her: "You a refugee? Surely immigrant is more like it."

The sponsoring church is kind, but the trauma and depression remain. Holding her teaching skills in her memory, she wonders why only the men are easily given studying opportunities here in Canada. She shared some of her disappointments with us: "The cultural transition lies heavily on the women. The guilt for having left home is heavy." Beneath the warm smile and the classic beauty lies a lot of pain.

These refugee women will never forget the land of their birth. Without doubt, the scars of past traumas will also never be forgotten. Perhaps they did not know much about Canada before they arrived here. But now they know that Canada is their homeland. They know that the peace and safety they have found in Canada will give them a chance to start a new life. Now they have an opportunity to develop their potential and contribute their talents to the land which gave them refuge.

TOPICS FOR EXPLORATION

1. What is the author's role in "Breaking the Barriers"? How objective is Mills' approach to her subject? Whom is she trying to reach in her audience? What is the purpose of this essay?

2. What barriers have these refugee women raised against communication about their own past? Why?

3. Why has the author chosen to concentrate on women in her essay? Why do these women symbolize the problems of their countries so well?

4. What are some of the sacrifices the women have suffered in order to emigrate from their countries? What difficulties do these refugees have in common? What problems are unique to each?

5. What are the major dilemmas that the refugee women face while adjusting to a new environment in Canada? How have their cultural origins affected the choices they have made in Canada?

6. Gender and ethnicity conspire against these refugee women, putting them always at a disadvantage. Find evidence in their stories that they have been victims of inequality in their male-dominated cultures at home. Then try to analyze their present situation in Canada so as to determine how far the double-jeopardy, associated with being both a woman and a member of a visible minority, affects their chances for a better future.

SUGGESTIONS FOR FURTHER STUDY

1. Compare the history of the "five generations" written by Pat Deiter-McArthur and the facts about Black slavery revealed in Boston King's narrative. What experiences have these two distinct groups of people had in common? How do they differ? What causes of oppression do they reveal?

2. Using Marie de l'Incarnation's and Catharine Parr Traill's letters as reference, discuss harsh realities of everyday life faced by early missionaries and settlers. What idea of Canadian wilderness emerges from their writing?

3. Compare the experiences of Catharine Parr Traill coming to Canada from the heart of the British Empire more than a century ago and those of Rohinton Mistry's immigrants arriving today from the former British colonies. How have conditions changed? What has remained unchanged?

4. In this unit there are numerous examples of political refugees. Discuss the similarities binding Miriam Rosenthal's narrative of war-torn Europe to the experiences of refugee women in Helga (Kutz-Harder) Mills' account. How do their stories differ?

5. Boston King criticizes some white settlers in Nova Scotia for their vanity and "imprudence in building large houses." Half a century later, Catharine Parr Traill gives a description of her "humble home" which doesn't quite meet her middle-class aspirations. Is there any ironic clash of perspectives here?

BEING HERE: UNCERTAINTY

INTRODUCTION

Coming here is always a challenge. Sacrificing the familiar, habitual, and comprehensible—whether the sacrifice has been voluntary or necessary—leaves a void to be filled by the new, disconcerting, and confusing messages sent by the unknown environment. Arrival in the new land demands patience, flexibility, and strength to assimilate a new geography and the languages and customs of those who have come before. Even for those born here, the Natives and Inuit, the experience of "being here" is troubled by the arrival of a domineering, consumption-based white culture which they have struggled to understand and, often, resist. Thus, "being here," for new and old

Canadians alike, is marked by an uncertainty that springs from common sources: the disruption of self-definition in an alien milieu; the anxiety of livelihood and economic loss; and the blight of prejudice and racial discrimination.

Jenine Dumont in her essay describes her long struggle with her identity as a Métis. Unaware of her "part-Indian" heritage as a child, she was startled into awareness by discrimination at age eight, but tried to "be white" until thirty. Caught between two cultures, Dumont, who is a descendant of Gabriel Dumont of the Northwest Rebellion, could not freely acknowledge her ancestry—to herself and others—until she was a grown woman and could turn a hidden feeling of insecurity into an outward pride in her heritage.

The outrage of racism comes under open scrutiny in Rosemary Brown's, Joy Kogawa's, and Archie Crail's writing. The effects of racism upon community and individual alike—systemic injustice, personal prejudice, economic and emotional anguish—are all explored candidly. Rosemary Brown's autobiography describes the discrimination she encountered during her first days in Montreal in the 1950s. Discrimination in accommodation, education, and the workplace angered Brown and without doubt contributed to her political activism. Joy Kogawa, widely known for her novel *Obasan*, illustrates a similar difficulty of "being here" experienced by the Japanese-Canadians who were imprisoned or confined in internment camps during World War II. Along with many others who were wrongfully treated, Kogawa has struggled politically to redress the injury and redeem the memory of the victims. The last chapter of *Itsuka*, her sequel to *Obasan*, shows the Canadian government accepting responsibility for its error and making its apology to its wronged citizens.

Archie Crail explores the intersection of corporate power, bureaucracy, and racism through the eyes of a new immigrant. Marius's expectations to be free from racist oppression in Canada are shattered when he discovers how well entrenched racism is in the minds of people and in the institutional structures he encounters in his first Canadian job as an accounting clerk. The story reveals the ironic discrepancy between the official commitment to progressive policies (such as affirmative action) and the lack of individual willingness to unlearn racism in everyday life.

Many immigrants suffer economic problems in the new land. They strive to regain what they have lost "at home" or gain what they have never had before. Canada, from the time of Catharine Parr Traill on, has been portrayed as a land of opportunity for the industrious and ingenious. The reality of "being here," of course, is usually different at the beginning: privation, frustration, and the struggle for livelihood where the old rules of economic success might not apply. Yeshim Ternar's story about an ambitious and intelligent young Turkish woman who pays her way through college by doing house-cleaning addresses the problem of immigrants who often have to work below their qualifications, especially at the start of their life in Canada. Saliha, who was a teacher in Turkey, feels displaced in Montreal in her job as a cleaning woman. She understands that the language barrier between new immigrants and their employers is thus compounded by class barriers. She turns her bitterness against Canadians who too often misjudge the newcomers and remain unaware of the real value of people arriving in this country.

The plight of overqualified immigrants who cannot find adequate jobs in Canada is even more pronounced in Salwa M. Said's story. Nadia and her husband leave behind their privileged social status in Egypt and choose an uncertain future in Canada. Their dreams are initially threatened when they start looking for work. Through perseverance and tenacity they finally succeed in building a good life here. However, for Nadia success is not without its problems. As she ponders the differences between her own and her sister's life, Nadia realizes that she has had to pay dearly for her choices.

The texts in this unit, which attempts to classify some cultural frictions and anxieties, are necessarily a limited sampling. The variety of expression can never be exhausted as long as the manifold ways of "being here" continue to articulate themselves.

Chinese Wall Writings

Notice

Fellow countrymen, read the following notice quickly:
Having amassed several hundred dollars,
I left my native home for a foreign land.
To my surprise, I was kept inside a prison cell!
Alas, there is nowhere for me to go from here,
I can see neither the world outside nor my dear parents.
When I think of them, tears begin to stream down.
To whom can I confide my mournful sorrow,
But to etch in a few lines on this wall.

— Anonymous, from Beiyang, Xinhui County,
Guangdong Province

A Mr. Lee from Taishan County, Guangdong Province, carved a poem on a
wall on 4 September 1911:

Sitting alone in the Customs office,
My heart aches.
Had I not been poor,
I would not have travelled far away from my home.
I went abroad upon my brother's advice.
The black devil here is ruthless,
He forces the Chinese to sweep and clean the floor.
Two meals a day are provided
But I wonder when I will be homeward bound.

An anonymous person wrote the following:

Deserting my parents, wife and children, I come to the Gold Mountain because I am poor. I remember their words that they have tried by various means to raise a thousand and some odd dollars for my passage. I have now safely arrived but unexpectedly the people here wanted to examine my eyes, forced me to strip to the waist and to take off my pants to lay bare my body. I have much been abused and insulted because China is weak and I am poor. I always think of my parents. My dear fellow countrymen, we should return home and help build our mother country strong and rich.

The sorrow and anger of the imprisoned immigrants were vividly expressed in their poems. The following one was written in 1919:

I have always yearned to reach for the Gold Mountain.
But instead, it is hell, full of hardship.
I was detained in a prison and tears rolled down my cheeks.
My wife at home is longing for my letter
Who can foretell when I will be able to return home?

Another poem reads as follows:

I am in prison because I covet riches.
Driven by poverty I sailed over here on the choppy sea.
If only I did not need to labour for money,
I would already have returned home to China.

The above inscriptions, hidden beneath layers of paint and whitewash, were discovered in November 1977, during the demolition of the Immigration Building in Victoria, B.C. Some messages were carved on the cell walls with a sharp point; other messages were written with pen and ink. Dr. David Chuenyan Lai, at that time a geographer at the University of Victoria, managed to read the inscriptions and translate them into English. They were written in traditional verse forms or in running prose. Here they appear in free forms taken from Lai's article "A 'Prison' for Chinese Immigrants," The Asianadian, *vol. 2, no. 4.*

The Immigration Building was built in 1908, and over the years it served a number of purposes. At one time it included cells in which Chinese immigrants were confined until their transit papers could be processed. The "wall writing" attests to the loneliness, humiliation, pride, ambition, and confusion of the immigrants. Each Chinese dreamed that Canada would be, for him, the Gim Shan *(Gold Mountain) where he could seek—and find—his fortune. In these cells each man could only dream.*

Rosemary Brown

Rosemary Brown was born in Jamaica in 1930; she came to Canada in 1950. A social activist and feminist scholar, she was involved in volunteer work and professional counselling for women and children; she also taught Women's Studies at Simon Fraser University. She was the first black woman to be elected to the British Columbia Legislature (1972). She has participated in national and international conferences on peace and human rights. She has often appeared on television; in 1987 she hosted a TVOntario series, Women and Politics. *The following excerpt comes from her autobiography,* Being Brown: A Very Public Life *(1989), where she shares the story of her political career and private life as a struggle for dignity and human rights.*

from Being Brown

Living in Montreal, even in the relative seclusion of Royal Victoria College, the women's residence at McGill University, brought me my first contact with racism, Canadian-style. I had been raised on a diet of poems and stories about the oppression of being Black in the United States, but always there was the rider that Canada was different. Indeed, my family thought that by sending me to university in Canada they were guaranteeing that I would not have to deal with what they referred to as the 'ugliness' of prejudice while receiving a reasonably good education (not as good as I would have received in England, but certainly superior to anything offered in the United States).

I must confess that the graduates of McGill, Dalhousie and the University of Toronto I met before leaving Jamaica fed the myth of a discrimination-free Canada by never mentioning prejudice. They spoke glowingly of their Canadian friends, indulgently of their Canadian professors and lovingly of their Canadian social experience. There were many jokes about the weather, some feeble attempts to include French phrases in their conversation and great bragging about the superiority of the academic standards. The only complaint that I remember hearing concerned the shortage of Jamaican girls enrolled at the universities. The boys felt that they had to justify dating white Canadian girls while extolling the beauty and virtue of the childhood girlfriends left in Jamaica, from whom they had extracted promises of fidelity during their absence and to whom they had pledged eternal love.

I read the brochures sent to me by Royal Victoria College and McGill University avidly. I was hungry to add to my limited knowledge of Canada, which did not go much beyond the country's expanse of snow and ice, the dependence of the world on its prairies for wheat, its brave and loyal support of England during the war (unlike the Americans) and the idiosyncrasies of Prime Minister Mackenzie King (and his mother), who seemed to retain power forever.

I conjured up in my mind's eye a community of plain, simple, gentle folk who lived uneventful lives in a cold uneventful country inhabited by very few Black people and a handful of Native Indians who resided on reserves.

I was happy with the prospect of my studying in Canada; so was Roy. We both assumed that I would not have any interest whatsoever in Canadian men, that I would not be distracted by a glittering social life; I would study, complete my four years, and return to Jamaica, probably to attend the law school that was in its infancy at the University of the West Indies. In any event it was obvious to both of us that we were destined to marry and grow old together, and the four years apart would only serve to strengthen our attachment to each other.

Canada was not what I expected. Three weeks after I had settled into a double room in Royal Victoria College, the assistant warden of women called me into her office and explained that I was being given a single room, because the College had been unable to find a roommate to share the double with me. She tried to break the news to me gently, pointing out how lucky I was to secure a single room and how much more private and quiet that would be for studying. I was moved into a single room at the same rate as the double—and two white women students were immediately moved into the double room.

I was stunned! I could not believe that not one of the other students in residence had been willing to share a room with me. Other West Indian women who had been at Royal Victoria College before me shrugged the matter off as not being surprising; having had similar experiences themselves they had known all along that no roommate would be found to share my room. Every year, West Indian women, given the option, requested the cheaper double room, moved in and were later moved into the more expensive single rooms at the lower double room rate. The bureaucracy was embarrassed by the whole procedure, but had not found a satisfactory way around it. It lived in the vain hope that one year things would change and a student would be found willing to share a double room with a Black student, and so it persisted. Despite the fact that that particular form of racism worked in my favour economically, it made me angry and my anger was compounded by frustration. It eventually became clear that the experience would be typical of the prejudice I ran into during my years in residence—polite, denied and accepted.

The dining room behaviour was another example of the peculiar brand of racism practised in Royal Victoria College at that time. Whenever I entered the dining room at mealtime I would anxiously scan the tables, hoping to find a seat at a table with another Black student. If there was none available, I would look for a seat with one of the two or three white friends I had managed to make (I had made some, including Sue Curtis, whose father was the Attorney General of Newfoundland at the time). If that failed, I just sat anywhere, knowing that I would probably complete my entire meal without anyone speaking to me or including me in their conversation.

At first, because I am outgoing, a bit of an extrovert, I assumed that my tablemates were shy, so I used to initiate conversation with the person sitting beside me or across from me—the cold and unfriendly responses to these overtures soon convinced me to stop.

I was truly grateful for the people who acted as a buffer against the hurts; although they did not transform Royal Victoria College into a home away from home, they managed to give me a glimpse of that other Canada that existed beyond prejudice and discrimination. Dr. Muriel Roscoe, Dean of Women, and her assistant Marie Madeline Mottola monitored our activities to ensure that we did not withdraw into a lonely shell of self-pity, but participated in social events on and around the campus. Mike DeFreitas, the senior custodian and an early West Indian immigrant who had retired from the railroad, took on the responsibility of surrogate father. He never hesitated to chastise us for staying out late during weeknights and made it his business to meet and to know the young men who dated us. The other Caribbean women were a special source of support, and although Dr. Roscoe encouraged us not to confine our social contact to our immediate and exclusive circle, she recognized the value and necessity of the love and nurturing that we gave and received from each other.

I was neither lonely nor unhappy during my stay at McGill. The West Indian community was large, vibrant and close-knit. My closest women friends were two other Jamaicans, Patsy Chen and Merle Darby, who had attended Wolmer's, the same private school that I had, and whom I knew well. In addition, because the ratio of male to female West Indian students was then almost three to one there was never a shortage of dates. Many of the older male students were dating white Canadians but in the early 1950s interracial dating was not as accepted as it is today and many more of the male students either refrained from doing it or did it clandestinely.

Interracial dating was absolutely taboo for West Indian women. We were all very conscious of the sexual stereotypes that we were told inhabited the fantasy world of white males, and at that time it was still very important to West Indian men that the women they married be perceived to be pure and virginal. The tragedy, of course, was that the West Indian male students internalized and accepted the white criteria of beauty, and since the "only life" Black women had to live could not "be lived as a blonde," as a popular TV commercial of the time exhorted, the Black men assumed that white men saw no beauty in us, and therefore their only interest would be in our sexual availability.

Even more tragic was the fact that we Black women students (unlike our counterparts of today) shared this perception of our unattractiveness and consequently closed ourselves off from the world of white males. Tragic because the decision to do so was not based on our assessment of our worth, but on our acceptance of our male colleagues' assessment of our lack of worth.

The real excitement of my academic life at McGill was discovering Hugh MacLennan and Canadian literature. During my voracious reading years as an adolescent and teenager, I had discovered and come to love Mazo de la Roche and Lucy Maude Montgomery, and for me that was all there was to Canadian literature. I had inherited from my English high school teachers the belief that very little of value was being produced by writers in the colonies, so I had no curiosity about Canadian literature. Quite frankly I did not think that there was any.

It was with a sort of bemused inquisitiveness that in my second year I registered for the course in Canadian Literature taught jointly by Hugh MacLennan, the author, and Louis Dudek, the poet. As the works of Gabrielle Roy, Morley Callaghan, Earle Birney and Hugh MacLennan entered my life, they opened up such a rich and exciting world to me that I came to see Canada through new eyes and to develop an addiction to Canadian authors that I have never lost.

In addition, I fell in love with Hugh MacLennan. I found him a kind and inspiring teacher who found the time to talk, discuss and listen as I struggled towards a better understanding of Canadian mores, attitudes and customs. One teacher stands out in memory from my high school: Lucille Waldron (Mair), my history teacher. One teacher stands out in memory from my university years: Hugh MacLennan, my Canadian Literature professor.

The less polite face of racism remained hidden until later. Although the women who shared the residence at Royal Victoria College were content just to treat us as though we did not exist, never acknowledging our presence except when necessary and then only with the minimum of courtesy, the landladies and landlords who lived in the neighbourhoods near McGill had no such inhibitions. There was nothing subtle about the racism of the landlords and ladies of Montreal. During the summer the women's residence was closed and we were all expected to return to our respective homes or seek accommodation elsewhere. Of course, my first summer in Canada, I hastened home to Jamaica and remained there until it was time to return to school. I needed desperately to be free of prejudice and discrimination, to see my family, and to reassure myself that I was still a whole and valued human being; and to assess my feelings for Roy. But by the following year, I was in love with one of the male students and wanted to spend the vacation in Montreal to be near him.

Job hunting in Montreal that summer proved to be a nightmare. My Chinese-Jamaican friend Patsy Chen secured a job immediately as a waitress at a golf and country club. Although I applied to the same club that she did and to others as well, I was never accepted. The employment counsellor kept recommending that I accept childcare jobs or light housework jobs, despite the fact that I explained I was not interested in doing housework or caring for children. She finally explained that although she had personally recommended me for a number of different jobs, only the people seeking domestic servants were interested in hiring me.

The older, wiser, senior West Indian women students, experienced in these matters, had never bothered to seek employment in Montreal. As soon as the academic semester ended, they headed for New York, where they were able to secure any type of work they wanted.

Discouraged by my job hunt, I reported to Gretchen Weston, the assistant warden in residence who was also the designated counsellor for foreign students, that I would be returning to Jamaica for the summer since I had been unable to find employment. Gretchen, who happened to be the daughter of one of the Westons of Weston's financial empire and was herself a student at McGill, was clearly upset by my report; she asked me to allow her to make some enquiries and report back to me in a couple of days. The following day she called to tell me to report to the Weston's plant in Longueil for work the following Monday.

Every summer after that I worked at Weston's Bakeries in Longueil as an office 'gopher.' I started at $35 weekly and worked my way up to $45 weekly by the time I graduated. I enjoyed those summer jobs and made some good friends, although on at least one occasion I'm sure that management regretted its generosity in creating a spot for me. One week, when I was the holiday relief for the person in payroll who computed the work hours of the employees in the plant, I was almost voted most popular person in Quebec when all the workers in the plant discovered that they had received a tremendous raise in pay—it seemed that I had multiplied when I should have added and the results brought loud rounds of applause from all the workers on the plant floor. Management quickly promoted me at the end of that week to filing letters and reports with no responsibility for payroll, although I had earlier been told that I would be working in the payroll department for three weeks.

Marie Mastrojosephs, my friend from those days, tells me that I am still spoken of kindly by many of the workers who were beneficiaries of my brief stint in payroll. And I sometimes wonder as I read about him and see him on TV news if Garfield knows how close I came to wrecking the Weston empire.

Once I had secured a job, thanks to the influence of Gretchen Weston, I had to find an apartment, and that's when I ran into the open, hostile and impolite racism of the landlords and landladies I spoke of earlier. These men and women made no secret of their dislike and distaste for Black people. They were rude, obscene and straightforward about refusing to rent us accommodation, often slamming the doors in our faces to emphasize their rejection of our request. Because I could afford it, I decided that I did not need to live in a shabby apartment near the university, so I sought better accommodations in Notre Dame de Grace and lower Westmount. It soon became absolutely clear that a line had been drawn around the university, in the nature of the U.S. 'red-lining' of a neighbourhood, encompassing approximately six blocks in each direction around McGill, that is, effectively making it a segregated neighbourhood. Blacks were not welcome as residents outside that line, except in the St. Antoine district where most of the Canadian Black families of the day lived.

The mild anger and frustration I had felt for the students in Royal Victoria College turned to hatred for the landladies and landlords of Montreal. I fell into a common, irrational habit of including all members of that group in my rage and outrage, rather than just the specific ones who had hurt me. I knew just enough French to understand the obscenities they spat at me, and various forms of the word Black were present in all of them.

Ten years after graduation, when we returned to Montreal so that Bill could complete his residency at the Allan Memorial Hospital, I found that little had changed. His white colleagues had no problems securing reasonable housing in Westmount and Outremont, while we had to settle for inferior accommodation in the poorest part of Notre Dame de Grace. By then, although the hatred had evaporated, the anger and hurt remained; we were the parents of two small children and the prospect that they would have to face similar treatment because of our decision to make Canada our home added guilt to my feelings of rage.

After that experience, I escalated my efforts to get Bill to decide to leave Canada for some other country, any other country in which our children would be free from racism. He agonized over this situation as much as I did, but he always returned to the conclusion that this was a country whose benefits outweighed the liabilities of racism, and that raising our children with self-esteem despite the experience of prejudice was a challenge we just had to face. I disagreed strongly; I wanted my children to experience my safe, loving and positive childhood, but I was not prepared to take them and return to Jamaica without Bill. So, to my rage about racism was added my anger at being powerless to control my family's choice of country of residence.

But my feelings about landlords and ladies paled in comparison to those I had about another group of people. My nightmares were filled with immigration officers. I hated and feared them because, unlike landladies and landlords, they really had my fate and my future in their hands. They had power. I thought they were stupid and cruel—petty despots who made no attempt to conceal their loathing for Black immigrants and whose sadism was uncontrolled when dealing with us.

Every year at the end of the spring semester West Indian students had to go to the immigration office to ask for an extension of our student visas over the summer. We had to lie through our teeth about not working during this time, saying that we would just be lazing about enjoying the Montreal humidity until time to resume classes in September; as students we had been issued special visas that very clearly forbade us working. Before being accepted as students we had to prove that we were financially able to attend university without needing to work or receive any financial assistance from Canada, and at the beginning of the academic year we had to show a balance of $1,000 in our bank accounts to cover the year's tuition and living expenses. The immigration officers suspected that we were lying about not working but they had no proof, and the frustration drove them into a frenzy. We had to show up at the immigration office with a passport, bank book and letter of acceptance for the fall semester at McGill. We also had to have an address and a phone number, as well as a letter of reference from a respectable member of the community, the Dean of Women for the women, one of the lay preachers from the Student Christian Movement for the men. The officers desperately wanted to find reasons to deport us, and as we sat across from them, watching the rage struggling to erupt as they cross-examined us, we would begin to sweat. For emotional support we would go down to the immigration office in groups.

The day that I was accused of trying to secure two extensions instead of one, because I had the misfortune to show up the day after my brother, who had been down for his renewal, I thought that my world was about to explode. The agent was furious that I thought I could pull the wool over his eyes simply by changing my name from Augustus to Rosemary—after all, the surnames were the same, the colour of skin was the same, we were both students, both at McGill, both from Jamaica and as far as he was concerned, Augustus was a girl's name. I was unable to convince him that I was Rosemary and that Augustus was my brother, thus making the similarity in name, colour, etc., quite understandable—he refused to renew my visa. Two days later, accompanied by two respectable members of the community, one of them a church minister whom I had met at the Student Christian Movement, my brother and I, carrying passports, bank books, university transcripts, birth certificates and letters of acceptance to the fall semester, returned to the immigration office. This time we had a different officer, who looked at our documents, looked at us, looked at our documents, stamped the extension in my passport, yelled "next" and dismissed us without addressing a word to us. As I left, something in me snapped and I wept hysterically, right there on the steps of the building.

I used to think that nothing in my childhood had prepared me to deal with this nightmare phenomenon. I was angry at my family for raising me as though racism were a foreign unpleasantness, which I would be spared; I felt that they should have either protected me or prepared me better for this degradation.

I envied Black Americans their access to violent struggle—they could fight back. As Black students in Canada, we seemed to have no options but to rail against our treatment in private and keep our heads down in public, trying to get through the four years to graduation without incident, determined to leave this country without a backward glance or kind thought. Racism seemed to pit me against everyone, including myself—my powerlessness sent *me* into a frenzy.

I was wrong, of course; my childhood had prepared me better than I realized to deal with prejudice. Unlike Black Americans and Black Canadians, I did not become a member of a racial minority group until I was an adult with a formed sense of myself. By then, it was too late to imprint on me the term 'inferior.' I knew that all the things that we were told Blacks could not do, all the jobs that were closed to us in this country, were in fact being done ably, competently and sometimes in a superior way by Blacks at home and in other parts of the world. And I came to understand that my frustration and rage stemmed not from the attempts to make me feel inferior but from a realization of my powerlessness and vulnerability, as a foreigner, to do anything about it. My upbringing had not taught me to deal with powerlessness. I was swamped by the feeling that there was nothing I could do about employers or landlords or students or complete strangers who built fences around me and placed obstacles in my path; and I thought of what it must be like to be born Black in this country and to live all of one's life with law, media, education and every other social institution carrying and reinforcing the message of your inferiority every day of your life. I thanked God that had not been my fate and at that time I swore that no child of mine would ever be forced to endure such a fate. I was determined to leave Canada the day after writing my last exam—not even staying around long enough for my convocation.

Even as I write this, I also recall how each incident would send me racing to the West Indian community in search of succor and to drown the violence exploding in my mind in the laughter and the humour, the music, the dance and the camaraderie that I found there. Anything to forget the glares of hate, the obscene epithets, or the look that just went through me as though I wasn't there—and my own unbearable powerlessness.

When I sit around with friends and reminisce about McGill, it seems that on the surface my life was no different from that of other students. Study and party, party and study—deadlines, panic, fun, anxiety, relief, graduation. Yet in those years I changed in profound and basic ways—for I was never the same after my encounter with racial discrimination, Canadian-style. With the passage of time, the hatred faded and disappeared. But I never lost the rage at the injustice, stupidity and blind cruelty of prejudice.

TOPICS FOR EXPLORATION

1. Who is Rosemary Brown's audience? What preconceptions about her subject does she hope to dispel? What is her purpose: to inform or educate, both, or any other?

2. What does Brown know about Canada before she comes? Why does Canada initially fail to meet her expectations? What is her reaction to Canadian reality?

3. Explain the meaning of "polite racism" or what Brown calls racism "Canadian-style." How was racism demonstrated during her search for jobs and accommodation? Give other examples of prejudice she had to face as a student in the early 1950s. Have these forms of racism disappeared, or is racism still a serious social problem?

4. How were Black women students at that time personally affected by racial and gender stereotyping? For Rosemary Brown, what were the sources of strength and support against racism and sexism?

5. Brown compares the Black situation in the United States with that in Canada. How are they different? How are they the same? How does her evaluation of the situation in these two countries compare with her childhood experience of Black self-image in Jamaica?

6. How has her own past equipped her for coping with racism? According to Brown, is it advisable to raise children so as to make them aware of racism and prepare them for dealing with it?

Jenine Dumont

Jenine Dumont lives in Edmonton, Alberta. She has a Bachelor of Science degree and works full time as a nurse. Her essay reprinted here was first included in the anthology of writing by Native women of Western Canada, Writing the Circle *(1990).*

I Didn't Know I Was Different

I was born in 1944 to Gabriel Dumont and Victoria Lafromboise at Duck Lake, Saskatchewan. My father was a grandnephew of the famous or infamous Gabriel Dumont of the Northwest Rebellion. To the Métis, Gabriel Dumont was always considered famous, but as a child I interpreted from history that the accepted adjective was infamous.

I was born in Duck Lake but did not live there. My mother returned to her home town to have two children after moving to the Birch River area in Manitoba. My first home was a ranch in the Old Fort district on the Woody River. My father managed the ranch that was owned by a wealthy Duck Lake resident. We probably lived there until I was two years old. I was the first girl after three boys, so I was given a lot of attention by family and friends alike. I was six years younger than the youngest boy and exactly twelve years younger than the oldest whose birthday was two days before mine in December. My oldest brother and I had a special relationship.

We moved to the town of Birch River after leaving the ranch and rented an old house which first looked like an old store-front finished in grey stucco, sprinkled with coloured glass. I remember enjoying the two years we lived there. My brother and I played with neighbouring children without incident. My father worked at various jobs, one I remember was bull cook for the provincial government road gang who were building roads eight miles north of Birch River in the Pasadena district. This led to a job as manager of the community pasture in the area, owned by the Department of Lands

Branch and Wildlife. In the summer of 1949, the family moved out to the pasture and lived in two railroad shacks. The larger building was used for a kitchen, living-room, and sleeping area for my parents and my sister and me. The boys slept out in the smaller shack. In the fall, we moved back into town and rented a small but comfortable house behind the Royal Cafe. My oldest brother had to quit school to help out financially; this was a sore point with him all of his life. I remember that he bought a brown snowsuit for my sister, who was somewhat of a tomboy; it really made her look like a tough little boy. On 9 April 1950, Easter Sunday, my youngest sister was born. When mom brought her home, I said, "She looks like an Indian." I didn't know I was part Indian, and it was two years before I knew.

The next summer, we went back to the pasture and lived in the two railroad shacks again. We spent the winter there, too. The next year, the government built a two-bedroom house with a big yard landscaped by elm and spruce trees and a caragana hedge in the front. We thought it was heaven. The government officials thought they could use the smaller bedroom for an office; I don't know where they thought we would all sleep. They ended up using the larger railroad shack for an office down by the corrals, where it was more appropriately situated.

I began grade one when I was six and a half years old because of my December birthday. I loved school and knew a lot before I started. My youngest brother, who was in grade six, and I were the only family members attending the school. The school was a one-room school with grades one to nine. The two or three pupils in grade nine took correspondence courses and were supervised by the teacher. My first year passed without incident.

For my second year of school, we had the same teacher, and everyone was pleased because she was superb. My brother was in grade seven, and they happened to be studying social studies one day when Duck Lake and the Rebellion was discussed. The teacher, who knew our family, asked my brother if that was where our father was from. His reply was, "Yes, they're all a bunch of Indians there."

Nothing more was said, but a few days later or perhaps the next day the kids started teasing us, calling us Indians and half-breeds! This went on for some time. I couldn't understand why the teacher did not stop them, although the teasing occurred at lunch time and recess. One lunch hour, all the kids stayed inside the school while my brother and I were outside alone. Then one day, because we were Catholic, my brother and I were let out of school half an hour early when the Anglican missionaries came to the school to give a service. We walked and ran the two miles home as fast as we could to get home before the other kids. Our parents were surprised to see us home in thirty minutes. I had a sore throat that night, was in bed with a chest cold the next day, and missed school for two weeks. We must have told our parents about the teasing then. When I went back to school, the teasing had stopped. I assume my parents had intervened. My brother skipped school a lot that year and eventually dropped out. He was fourteen years old.

That was when I realized I was part Indian. I believe that was also the first time my father talked to me about being proud of my heritage. Over the years, he would often say, "Hold your head up high and be proud; it doesn't matter what they say."

I was particularly close to my father and believed him, so I did as I was told.

I walked that way so much that in high school people thought I was a snob; I really was shy and afraid of being hurt. I had some difficulty being proud of my Indian ancestry, as there were constant reminders that Indians were inferior. My own mother referred to Indians as "les sauvages" (the savages), as if they were inferior. I remember thinking, "Why are you saying that, we're part Indian too?"

I got a lot of mixed messages. We had a group of Métis friends with whom we spent holidays. All the women were the same, trying to be white and rather intolerant of Indians or the mixed bloods who had more Indian ancestry than we did. I remember my father as being very tolerant and being friendly to Indians. I never heard any of the other men make any racial statements.

Other memories stay with me. Once, when we lived in Birch River, I went to the butcher shop for my mother. The owner was always very nice to us. He used to give us wieners when we came into the store. This particular day I went in while a salesman was there, and the butcher gave me a wiener as usual. As I took it and turned to leave, the salesman, addressing the butcher, said with a laugh, "One of your little Native friends?"

I remember seeing that the butcher was somewhat embarrassed. Little things like that would keep reminding me that I was not white.

I spent a lot of years trying to be white. We used to always say that we were French. Shortly after I met my husband, I asked him if he was prejudiced. I think he must have replied negatively. It never seemed important to tell him I was part Indian. I think he figured it out himself. He's of Icelandic ancestry, and they seem to be a rather non-judgemental people.

After we were married, we lived in northern Manitoba for a year in a town that had a large Native population. I remember denying my ancestry once while I was there. That bothered me for a long time. It took me until I was thirty years old to really come to terms with being part Indian. I had two children of my own by then, and you can be sure I told them they were part Indian. When my daughter was in grade two she told a friend about her Indian ancestry and this girl started to tease her and call her Indian. I went to the child's mother who stopped the teasing. I certainly didn't want history repeating itself.

When I was thirty-five and my last child was a precocious two year old, we stopped in a small northern Alberta town to buy something at a drugstore. My son was touching things, etc. When I went to the counter to pay for my purchase, the clerk looked through me with disdain and I got this terribly chilled feeling. It's a feeling that I cannot describe. It comes when you know that someone dislikes you because of your race. I thought I had come to terms with my Native blood. Maybe I have, but other people have not.

I think the prejudice I was exposed to as a child affects the way I interact with people as I am not an open person and do not make friends easily. When I compare myself to my sisters, who did not suffer the same prejudices I did, I find them to be much more open and congenial. I would like to think there is less prejudice in the world, but is there? I have a ten-year-old son writing a story about an Indian Chief who killed a white man's wife and then this white man relentlessly hunts down the Indian. The story is supposed to take place one hundred years ago. I guess the stereotypes are still there. Where else would this ten year old get his ideas?

TOPICS FOR EXPLORATION

1. Jenine Dumont didn't know she was Métis until she was eight. What were her parents' motives for hiding the family history from her? How did this ignorance of her roots deny her self-image and proud heritage?

2. Dumont grew up surrounded by "mixed messages," such as the truth about the "famous or infamous" Gabriel Dumont, a founder of Manitoba and hero of the Northwest Rebellion. Why did she have difficulty being proud of her Indian ancestry?

3. How did the sudden discrimination of the schoolroom affect Dumont? How did it contribute to her siblings' lack of success in school?

4. What reasons does Dumont give for trying to pass for white? Why did she deny her ancestry until she was thirty? How is she caught in the double bind of having Native and white ancestry?

5. How has Dumont been affected by racial stereotypes and prejudice in her own life? How are they still affecting the life of her children? Does she offer any strategy for coping with racism?

Archie Crail

*Archie Crail was born in South Africa; he emigrated to Canada in 1980.
In 1992, his collection of short stories,* The Bonus Deal, *was nominated for
the Governor General's Award. In addition to short stories, he has also written numerous plays which have been produced by theatres in Saskatchewan
and South Africa, as well as radio dramas for the CBC. He lives in Regina.*

Affirmative Action

One of the first things the woman at personnel had told him was
that the corporation was now following a policy of affirmative
action.

"Now what does that mean?" Marius had asked, his face beneath
the bushy Afro, expressionless.

"Why, haven't you heard?" the woman answered. "It means that
the search is now on for handicapped persons and visible minorities
to fill positions they're qualified for."

"So, I'm just lucky to have applied when I did, hey!" he had
exclaimed. However, she seemed in no mood for familiarity and had
quickly showed him out of the office.

Finally after months of despair he had found himself a half-
decent job. Even if it were just a job as accounting clerk, he'd work
his way up and show them what he could do. That evening he celebrated by himself in front of the television set with a case of Molson
Canadian.

The job of accounting clerk was relatively easy. Most of his work
dealt with reports of absence. On these forms appeared the
employee's name and the amount of time taken off for sick leave or
vacation. On a card filing system he noted the time taken off from
work and subtracted the hours from the outstanding holidays and
sick-leave days. Sometimes he had come across employees who had
used up all their allowed days of absence. His job was then to deduct

the time taken off from the employee's fortnightly earnings. All this was not really accounting work. It belonged to the personnel department. However, Marius kept his opinions to himself.

The remainder of his day was spent increasing those employees' salaries who had attained a new level of seniority. This of course brought resultant increased deductions in income tax, unemployment insurance and company pension. He fed these into the computerized payroll system. Then he had to send out the paycheques every pay period.

He got quite a shock at the end of the first pay period when two paycheques went missing in the company mail system. After a week of frantic searching and phoning branch offices all over the province, they still couldn't be traced. Unable to provide an answer as to how the cheques got lost, he could only agree lamely with the supervisor that they were indeed lost. Although handwritten cheques were issued in the meantime, he still felt a cloud of responsibility hanging over him. This later grew into a suspicion that perhaps, just maybe, there was a conspiracy to get rid of him.

Like all new brooms, Marius believed that he should do his work well and be seen to be diligent. Every morning he came to work half an hour early and started work right away. None of the chit-chat about last night's happenings could draw him into any of the women's conversations. A few times he'd let out a loud guffaw at something funny Christine related to Rhonda. Both girls had then looked at him strangely, but embarrassed with this sudden attention, he'd just continued working.

Unlike Christine, who was loud and physically aware of herself, Rhonda was the quiet mousy type. She rarely spoke unless spoken to, and on the whole was the sort of person who quietly and unobtrusively got things done her way. Perhaps she knew that her voice was not as melodious as Christine's and it always seemed as if she croaked with a cold.

Marius had gone for the twice-daily coffee breaks in the cafeteria. Usually all the people from the various accounting sections would push a few tables together where they would talk about the most recent game the Rough Riders had just lost or the difficulties in farming in this day and age. He knew very little about prairie farming and didn't particularly like football. Once he tried introducing a book he had recently read and another time a movie showing at the local Odeon. Some of those present stared at him as if this was the most unreal thing to discuss, while others just pointedly ignored him. He finally decided that it was best to avoid the coffee breaks since he couldn't contribute anything to the conversations, and instead of feeling difficult and uneasy, he just remained at his desk.

This latest batch of reports of absence didn't look any different from any previous ones. At the very top of the six-inch pile of paperwork, the first one read: "One and a half hours to see a chiropractor." He quickly found the employee's name in the card file and reduced her remaining sick leave by one and a half hours. He now turned to the next sheet. "A day to get married."

He turned to Christine: "What happens when somebody takes a day off to get married?"

"Don'tcha know?" she screeched. "Has it been signed by the head of the department?"

"Yes," he said.

"Well, fuck," she giggled, "then treat it accordingly."

"You mean I should deduct it from his holidays?" he asked in an almost begging tone. "The guy has got none left."

With a sneer Christine whispered (loud enough for him to hear) to Rhonda, "The guy's an absolute asshole. I don't know why they got these dumb niggers here. All this affirmative action is just a bunch of shit." In a louder voice, she continued, "This is supposed to be compassionate leave. Three weeks on the job and you still can't make out head or tail, hey!"

"Give him time," Rhonda croaked condescendingly. "Just give him time."

He was quiet for a minute. Jumping up from his chair he roared, "Hey! I don't want any of your bloody racist remarks! Why don't you guys bloody well give me a job description list? Every time something new comes up I have to ask you guys! I'm sick and tired of asking what the hell to do every time something new comes up!" He threw the pile of papers on the floor.

The girls were quietly ignoring him. He felt he could punch the life out of both of them. Stooping down, he tried gathering his wits while picking up the papers from the floor. But it was no use.

Suddenly he just got up and marched out of the office. He didn't expect such blatant racism in Canada. Least of all not here, where management had made such a hoo-ha about affirmative action.

Passing the supervisor's office, he wondered whether he should take this matter up with her. When he had got this job, she had told him there was no written job description for the accounting clerks—the reason being that accounting functions and company policy in the area had changed so much over the past year that anything formalized and adopted became invalid within six months. However, she had stressed that Christine and Rhonda as senior clerks would be most willing to be helpful whenever he needed information.

During the first week it was okay and the women seemed to fall over each other trying to be helpful. However, after the second week he could clearly see that they were getting tired of being bothered.

He decided not to talk to the supervisor. She always seemed so busy and angry. Instead he continued to the washroom.

Looking into the mirror, he saw his own agony staring back at him. Opening the cold-water tap wide, he bathed his face repeatedly. Consciously he reminded himself that he was a man and that this was life. Okay, so he did come to Canada with expectations. "Safety from legal racism" was what the immigration officer had told him. Suddenly a new thought struck him. Maybe he should try to be more friendly towards people here. Accept them for what they are. Show them that he also has some fine human qualities. That he's able to crack a joke and share a laugh. Surely life isn't all seriousness and hard work. He might even get fired for that earlier outburst. This sudden fear made him wonder if there wasn't something about "incompatibility with fellow workers" in the union contract.

A sudden swish as the washroom door opened jarred him back to reality.

He was in no mood to talk to anybody now and opened the tap wider in order to make conversation impossible. He saw Bill, one of the junior clerks, staring over his shoulder. He didn't particularly like Bill and saw no reason to start his friendliness campaign with him.

"Hi, and how's things today?" Bill shouted above the rush of water.

"Okay, okay," Marius grunted, again bathing his face in cold water. Before Bill could join him at the washbasin, he shut off the tap, almost running to the paper towel dispenser. Drying his face hurriedly, he left. He didn't find that peace he was looking for in the washroom.

Back in the office he found everybody hard at work. What a relief. He didn't have to talk to them. He wasn't even going to apologize for his earlier outburst. They could all go to hell as far as he was concerned. He started working on the pile of reports of absence again. "Arnold Armbruster," the first one read, "two days vacation." Then there was Emma Emmanuel, who took a day off because she was feeling under the weather.

In Saskatoon there was a man named David Petrovski who took seven days off in order to take his six-year-old boy to Toronto for open-heart surgery. He checked the card file and found that the man had used up all his holidays and sick leave to take his child to various doctors in the province. Surely this should be treated as compassionate leave? He looked at the slip of paper again and saw the manager had added that the "seven days are to be deducted from the employee's wages as all holidays have been exhausted." This of course would mean that Petrovski was only going to get half his fortnightly earnings.

He wondered what had happened to the co-operative interdependence people from this province had spoken so much of. Was there no sense of compassion left in this society? Perhaps their compassion was only for the Third World.

After a moment of further musing he decided that this was not his battle. He was not employed as a human rights activist. His job was that of accounting clerk. Still, he felt a little guilty that he hadn't done anything on David's behalf (whomever he might be) and a slight sense of having betrayed somebody irked at his insides. He started working on the rest of the pile of papers.

After another month on the job, he felt confident and strong. Payroll sheets were submitted for computerization on time. No cheques had subsequently gone missing. Reports of absence were a piece of cake. A feeling of utter well-being took hold of him.

"So, missy," he said to Christine one day when the two of them were alone in the office, "how are things working out in your section?" She looked at him enquiringly. "I thought you might need a hand in getting something done," he continued carefully. "I've met my deadlines and see my desk is all clear."

"Why sure, Marius," she said, brushing a stray blonde curl out of the way. "If you feel so kindly, please post these figures in the ledger for me."

"Anytime, ma'am. Anytime. But what's in it for me, hey!" he asked, swinging the swivel chair sideways so he faced her directly. "Surely one good turn deserves another?"

"Come on, Marius. I thought we were supposed to help each other out," she said, unsure where the conversation was leading.

Getting up from the chair, he stretched his thin frame to its full height of six feet and walked towards her desk. "Well, how about coffee after work," he said, taking the sheet of figures before she changed her mind. He walked the two steps back to his own desk without once letting her out of his gaze.

Christine met his stare. "Can't you offer a lady anything better than that?" she parried.

"Let's say, a drink at your favourite place?"

"Well, I don't know. Maybe. When?"

"Tonight after work." There was a finality to his tone.

"Sure," she said, busying herself with papers.

Christine never turned up for the date. After spending half an hour waiting for her at the main entrance, he assumed she must have gotten cold feet and taken another exit out of the building. On second thought he felt that perhaps he shouldn't have sprung this date on her. Maybe he should have cultivated her friendship first before asking for a date. Perhaps that was the way things were done in this country. Since she didn't give him either an explanation or an apology the next day, he was left wondering for the rest of the week as to why she never turned up.

Going through the alphabetical listing of employees one day, he discovered two employees who shared exact same names and dates of birth. After he had checked their social insurance numbers, he found that except for the last two numerals, the numbers were the same. He quickly decided that this was merely coincidence. Besides, the two female employees worked in different departments.

What disturbed him, however, was that the incident was repeated twice subsequently. On a separate sheet of paper he noted down all the particulars and the following pattern emerged: there were three pairs of employees. Each pair shared the same first and last names as well as dates of birth. As for the social insurance numbers of each employee, only the last two numerals in each pair were different. Checking further, he found that out of each pair, there was one person working the claims department. The other three employees worked in the systems, microfilm and auto departments respectively.

Assuming that three of the six were legitimate employees, what does that make the others, he wondered. He glanced up from his notes and lit a cigarette. Exhaling the smoke slowly through his nostrils, he was at a loss as to what to do with this information. Should he show it to the supervisor? If he did and was proved wrong, he'd end up the laughingstock of the whole accounting department. On the other hand, who knows, perhaps the supervisor was in on the deal. But then, was this right keeping such information to himself when the company was probably losing hundreds of thousands of dollars through this scheme?

He finally decided to keep quiet about what he had detected. It was not his job to play company cop. Auditors were paid to keep a lookout for such fraudulent practices. Besides, he was not going to risk his position with such revelations.

Later in the morning everybody was called to the supervisor's office. In her foreboding manner the supervisor told the payroll clerks that, as from the following week, all reports of absence were going to be handled by the human resources department. Marius was acutely aware that this new arrangement was going to reduce his workload tremendously. He wondered which new duties he was going to be given. Nevertheless, he kept quiet as nothing was directly asked of him. But then in his naiveté he expected that management in their corporate wisdom would arrive at a decision which would meet everybody's needs and tasks. So he said nothing and left the supervisor's office quietly ahead of everybody else.

Back at his desk he found a fresh pile of reports of absence waiting for him. Halfway through the batch, he came upon David Petrovski again. He read that a week ago the man, who earlier had lost a week's pay taking his child to Toronto for open-heart surgery, had requested three days' unpaid vacation to bury his son. Marius felt himself getting very hot and suddenly very cold. Mixed emotions of anger at the bureaucracy of the company and empathy with the unknown man's suffering clouded his thoughts. He reached for his packet of cigarettes and suddenly stopped midway. The idea just struck him that there would be something banal in smoking at a time like this. There was a certain holiness in the suffering of this man. Reaching into his desk, he got hold of a standard memorandum sheet. Writing in his best copperplate he informed David that he had seen his suffering and expressed his deepest sympathy. As an afterthought, he wrote a cheque and added that the man should please accept this gift of one hundred dollars from one human being to another. He sealed both cheque and note in an envelope and marked it for the Saskatoon office.

Looking up from his writing, he saw the supervisor standing in the doorway. "Marius, can I see you in my office for a minute, please?" Averting her eyes to the traffic outside the window, the supervisor led the way to her office.

"Marius," she began, standing behind her desk, "we don't want you to take this personally"—holding a large white envelope in her left hand—"but in view of the new arrangement, we have decided that instead of a month's notice, we'll give you a month's pay."

TOPICS FOR EXPLORATION

1. How well is Marius qualified for his new job? How does he present himself as an employee?

2. What definition of "affirmative action" is given in the story? What attitudes do Marius's co-workers demonstrate towards affirmative action? How is Marius treated by his supervisor? by Christine and Rhonda?

3. What is the effect of David Petrovski's case on Marius? What does the treatment of Petrovski tell Marius about the company he is working for?

4. Marius says that he "didn't expect such blatant racism in Canada." What different forms of racism does he encounter in his office?

5. Is Marius's suspicion that perhaps there is a conspiracy to get rid of him justified by the end of the story?

Yeshim Ternar

Yeshim Ternar, a Montreal writer, was born in Istanbul, Turkey, in 1956. From 1975 to 1979, she lived in the United States; in 1980, she came to Canada. She has published fiction in Canadian, American, and European magazines; her stories have appeared in several anthologies: Telling Differences *(1989),* Other Solitudes *(1990), and* Fire Beneath the Cauldron *(1991). Her first collection of short stories,* Orphaned by Halley's Comet *was translated into Dutch in 1994. In her second book,* The Book and the Veil: Escape from an Istanbul Harem *(1994), she blends essay and fiction to conjure up the world of her grandmother's generation in the harems of the Ottoman Empire. Her third book,* True Romance with a Sailor *(1996) is a collection of short stories.*

Ajax Là-Bas

Saliha Samson sits on one of the empty washing machines in the basement and lights a cigarette. There are three loads of wash in the machines. The wash cycle takes 35 minutes; the drying cycle another 25. The French couple who employ her are very nice people. They leave for work early in the morning, as soon as she arrives at 8:30. They trust her with everything. They know she is a conscientious worker, that she doesn't slack off like some of the other cleaning women.

Madame Rivest tells Saliha to eat whatever she wants from the refrigerator. She always leaves some change in the ceramic vase on the telephone table just in case Saliha needs to get extra detergent, cigarettes, or whatever. Madame Rivest knows she likes to snack on strawberry and blueberry yoghurt, so she always makes sure there is some in the refrigerator for her. This morning she has told her she hasn't done her weekly shopping yet, so she is leaving some money for Saliha especially to buy fruit yoghurt.

Now that's a nice gesture! I wish everyone were like that, thinks Saliha as she takes a deep puff from her cigarette. The Rivests live a long ways off from where she lives. She has to take the 80 bus from Park Extension, then the metro at Place des Arts to Berri, and then change metros at Berri to go to Longueuil; afterwards she has to take yet another bus to come here. But the trip is worth it because some of the people she works for close to home treat her so badly that she'd rather lose an hour on the way and work for Madame and Monsieur Rivest. That's a lot easier than working for the two old spinsters on upper Querbes.

Saliha notices the unbalanced load signal flash on one of the washers, and gets off the machine she is sitting on to straighten things out. As she untangles the heavy blue cotton velour bedspread from the black rotor blades of the washing machine, she thinks it was lucky she decided to take this cigarette break in the basement because if she had gone straight upstairs to continue her vacuuming, she would have lost an extra 25 minutes by having to wait for this load after all the others were completed. That would have thrown her schedule off perhaps by an hour because she would have had to take the elevator up and down twice more and delay other tasks in the meantime. That's how cleaning jobs are. You have to plan what you're going to do and how, and in what order. Otherwise.... Well, the machine starts churning again and she jumps back on the machine she was sitting on before to finish her cigarette.

She has her period again. It's crazy, she thinks. Madame Rivest calls her every two weeks. And every other time she has to work for Madame Rivest, she gets her period. It's either the first day or the second day of her period when she has to make that long trip to come here. I've never had any luck with periods, thinks Saliha as she massages her back with her left hand. Saliha's dream is to be able to lie in bed the whole day when she gets her period. But it never works that way.

The first time she had her period when she was eleven, she was in Istanbul then, she ran up to her mom to announce it. Her mother slapped her. 'Why did you do that?' Saliha asked. 'So that you won't lose your wits.' Saliha went to her room and cried less for the mess of blood than for the fact that she was getting too old to play hopscotch. That was fifteen years ago. Saliha cannot remember when she stopped playing hopscotch, but it was at least a year after she got her first period.

Some things in life are like that. First they come to you like big worries, and you spend days and nights worrying about them, but they have the life span and personality of a soap bubble. They grow and grow like a wart in one's heart and just when you're sure they are big and strong and will never go away, they pop out of your life not even leaving a rind, not even a speck of dust, but the dry flake of a single detergent grain.

Canadians are funny, thinks Saliha. They have detergents and lotions and soaps for everything. Everything has its own cleanser here. And every cleanser has its own name. Like Mr Clean. But Mr Clean is also M. Net. Wisk! What a strange way to call your laundry detergent. And Ajax. Particularly Ajax. George, the Greek *dépanneur* at Park Ex, told her Ajax was a Greek hero. Old heroes live on as detergents in Canada. Saliha smiles at her own joke. She thinks she should write this to her mom.

The wash is done in one of the machines. She opens a dryer and transfers the load there. Just as she starts the dryer, the other two machines go off. So she puts these loads in the dryers too, and feeds quarters to the machines. It's time to go up and vacuum the Rivests' bedroom, she decides.

She goes up on the elevator, happy that no one else is on it. She hates to be seen in her work clothes. She is wearing a pink cotton jumper, a navy blue shirt with the sleeves rolled up underneath that, and knee socks and her red moccasins. She had tied a Turkish scarf on her head with a knot in the back to keep her hair away from her face. Madame Rivest says she looks like a school girl like that. But Saliha feels uneasy in her work clothes. After all, it is hard to resign herself to being a cleaning woman on the sly in Canada.

As she is vacuuming the Rivests' bedroom, she remembers her friend Frederiki's warning. Frederiki told her to be careful most when she is vacuuming because when you have the vacuum on full blast, you can't hear if someone is approaching from the back. Frederiki said she knows a couple of cases of rape that happened when the cleaning woman was vacuuming and the old geezer tip-toed and caught the cleaning woman and forced her on the bed... Saliha shivers at the thought. She drops the vacuum cleaner and goes to check if she locked both locks on the door. Not that M. Rivest would do anything like that. He has two married daughters, but you never know who might have keys to the apartment.

On her way back from the door, walking through the living room, Saliha checks the time on the mantel clock that she guesses comes from Spain. The clock is set in a gold and black lacework metal fan that reminds one of the Spanish flamenco dancers. The Rivests appear to be well-travelled people. Scattered about the apartment there are several photographs of Madame and M. Rivest, in silver-rimmed frames, from various countries. The one on the side table next to the loveseat in the living room looks like it was taken in Spain. Madame Rivest, looking several years younger, is smiling in front of a white-washed Mediterranean-type house with red gardenias blooming in clay pots along the window sill. She is slightly tanned. It is a sunny photograph, making Madame Rivest whose face carries many wrinkles from cold Canadian winters look out of place in the country where Saliha assumes the true residents greet the sunshine with less suspicion and distress.

Nevertheless, Madame Rivest smiles in that photograph as all middle-aged tourists do on well-deserved holidays. A straw handbag hangs from her left shoulder, and in her right hand, she holds something like a camera lens cover.

Saliha notes that the dryers must have completed their cycle, so she goes back to the bedroom and quickly finishes off the corners of the room with the special attachment Madame Rivest has taught her to use.

She takes along the yellow plastic laundry basket to carry the wash. She gets unlucky going down. A young housewife and her son step into the elevator on the second floor and ride with her to the main floor. Saliha tries to act oblivious to the woman's presence, but she winks surreptitiously at the little boy. The boy responds with a blank face.

Saliha is relieved when they get out. In the basement she quickly piles all the wash together in the laundry basket and after turning the drums around and feeling around the ridges for a stray sock or handkerchief, she goes up to the Rivests' apartment to sort the clothes. She is folding the towels and the sheets neatly and mechanically when she looks up at the ceiling of the Rivests' bedroom for an instant and starts remembering.

She is back in fourth grade at her elementary school on the Asian side of Istanbul. It was late September, several weeks into the fall term when the school principal had given the all-important Monday morning speech to the whole elementary school population: rows of fidgety kids lined up in twos behind overweight maternal teachers.

They had all finished pledging allegiance to the Turkish nation and Turkish morality. In unison, they had proclaimed the following verses with pride:

'I am Turkish, I am honest, I am industrious. My motto is: to love my inferiors, to respect my superiors, to love my country and my people more than my own life. May my existence be a gift to the existence of the Turkish people.'

It was after the whole schoolyard had fallen silent that the old principal had cleared his throat, adjusted his glasses with a nervous push of the index finger of his right hand, and straightened the arms of his worn navy blue jacket by pulling at the sleeves. He had then solemnly said, more like a poet than the disciplinarian that the Ministry of Education demanded him to be:

'My dear children, today I would like to tell you about your counterparts in America. Little boys and girls your age in America are very different from you in some very important respects. For one, they are often more industrious, and they are better behaved. I felt it was my duty to remind you of this after the very grave accidents your wild running about in the schoolyard during recesses last week has caused. Several of your friends are not at school today because they gashed their heads or sprained their ankles from all the savage games they have been playing. The weather has been very nice. The school year has just begun. Your teachers and I understand that you are all happy to join your friends after the summer holidays, but school is not a place where you come to play unruly games of tag and hide-and-seek. School is a place where you come to learn about the vital skills that you will need for all your lives and where you receive the benefits of civilization. Your counterparts in America understand what school is all about. At recess, they don't run around like you, but make use of their time to practise the knowledge that they learn in the classroom. For example, when they go out into the schoolyard—and let me remind you that not all of them are blessed with a schoolyard such as ours—they examine their surroundings. Look at all the leaves on the ground about you. You have perhaps not noticed them during all your frenzied horseplay. An American child, however, would pick up a leaf, examine it, do research to identify it, and record his observations in his notebook. An American child would do the same for an ant, a worm, or a spider instead of madly crushing it. If you, as young Turks, the adults of the future, learn to do the same, you will help to build a better nation and honour this country that our great Ataturk had offered to you as your most cherished gift.'

With this, the principal ended his speech. Saliha felt she was one of the few who had heard the true message of the principal's words. She looked about and saw, for the first time, the mounds of leaves in the schoolyard and the shady corners teeming with insects. After that day, every dry copper-coloured leaf, every quiet ant bespoke of her new task to pay attention to the world.

Saliha went on to finish her primary school education with distinctions despite some uncomfortable failures in the science class of her fifth year. Then she went to teacher's college to become a primary school teacher. After teaching in remote Anatolian villages where she gained the awe and respect of the peasants, she came to Canada to join her brother who is an auto mechanic in Montreal. She is presently enrolled at Plato College on Park Avenue to learn English and French.

Saliha folds all the towels and linen neatly. She separates Madame Rivest's lingerie from M. Rivest's underwear and pairs up his socks. She puts away all of the clean laundry on the appropriate shelves in the closet and the dresser. She does not neglect to arrange what was already there before she puts away the newly washed clothes.

Everything looks fresh and clean! Only some light dusting remains to be done. Then she will clean the bathroom. First she'll throw away the dirty water in the pail from mopping the floors, then she'll rinse out the cleaning rags and put away all the cleaning materials. Afterwards she'll take her shower and scrub the bathtub clean.

But before she finishes up the remaining tasks, Saliha decides to take a cigarette break on the blue floral patterned armchair in the living room. She makes some fresh coffee in the kitchen, brings her cup over to the living room and lights a cigarette. She unties her scarf and lets her wavy black hair down. As she sips her coffee in between puffs, Saliha goes over her cleaning appointments for the next two weeks. To remember the exact dates, she visualizes the Chrysler calendar in her kitchen with pictures of different kimono-clad Japanese geishas for each month.

She has to clean for the two spinster sisters on Thursday. She certainly doesn't look forward to that one. They are very messy people. They are also very careful with their money.

Contrary to the Rivests, they always follow her around and check how much detergent and soap she uses. They never offer her much at lunchtime. Not that she would eat what they eat. They always eat some strange food that she is unaccustomed to, things like blood sausage and sauerkraut; topping it off with stale Mae West cakes they buy at Steinberg or Provigo. Saliha prefers to keep to herself when she works there.

On Friday afternoon, she will clean for the old Czech at Côte des Neiges. He is a kind and quiet man who doesn't demand much from Saliha. He is glad to have a woman clean up once every few weeks. When she is there, Saliha cooks a couple of light dishes for him. He is always grateful for that and gives her an extra two dollars.

Saliha hopes that Eleni will call her on the weekend to confirm a cleaning job next week. Eleni lives close to where Saliha lives in Park Extension. But the best part of working for Eleni is that at the end of the work day when she is done at her hairdressing salon downstairs, Eleni comes upstairs to have coffee with Saliha and trims her hair and manicures her nails as a gesture of appreciation. Eleni's house is large and demands all of Saliha's energy but the extra reward makes the effort worth it. Eleni expects the cleaning to be done well, but always offers refreshments like Kool-aid and Tang. Last time Saliha worked there, Eleni gave her some of her daughter's old clothes. Saliha hopes she might receive a reasonable sweater next time because she badly needs something a little fashionable for the end of the term party at Plato College.

Sipping the last of her coffee, Saliha rises from the armchair and looks around the living room to plan her dusting strategy. She will do just the outside panels of the display cabinet this time, leaving the silver goblets and British china for the next time. Then she will dust the buffet and the little figurines on top of it, taking care to dust off the folds of the Chinese jade Buddha. She decides not to waste too much time polishing the wood this time as all the wooden surfaces are still sparkling from the last time she did them. The Rivests don't seem to have invited anyone over for dinner in the meantime because the guest sets remain as she last arranged them.

Saliha has just finished drying her hair and changing into her street clothes after her shower when Madame Rivest comes back from work. She greets Saliha in French, glances around the house and shows her approval with many 'Ooh's and 'Wonderful's, stretching her words to make Saliha understand her heart-felt appreciation. Then she says in French that she will call Saliha again next week to confirm their next cleaning date. As she says this, Madame Rivest gestures as if she were dialing and holding on to the receiver of an imaginary telephone.

Of course Saliha can understand everything Madame Rivest is saying without the added gestures, but Madame Rivest is being so kind and helpful that Saliha decides not to use a couple of appropriate French phrases she has recently learned at Plato College.

Madame Rivest goes into her bedroom and comes back out with a sealed white envelope containing Saliha's thirty-five dollars. The Rivests are the only people that put Saliha's earnings in an envelope. They are considerate people.

As Saliha takes the envelope, she says, 'Merci beaucoup, Madame Rivest.' Stepping out the door, she switches the plastic bag containing her work clothes from her right hand to her left hand and extends her right hand to Madame Rivest and says, 'Bonjour, Madame Rivest,' and smiles. These are the first real words she has uttered since she woke up that morning.

In the elevator, going down, Saliha is alone. She checks the contents of the envelope and smiles with satisfaction. Before the elevator reaches the ground floor, Saliha has time to reflect on her day. She has earned enough for the week's food and cigarettes. Last week, she paid the last instalment for her tuition at Plato College. She is tired but life is under control. Her only regret is that she hasn't answered Madame Rivest in longer sentences. But she chases away her regrets with a light shrug and admits the reality.

We come here to speak like them, she thinks; but it will be a long time before they let us practise.

TOPICS FOR EXPLORATION

1. How are we to interpret Saliha's joke that "old heroes live on as detergents in Canada?" Does this statement in any sense illuminate her own and some other immigrants' situations in Canada?

2. How does Saliha feel about working as a cleaning woman? What is her self-image? What are her ambitions?

3. What does a flashback into Saliha's childhood reveal about her background? In what ways was America idealized in the principal's speech? What was the effect of this speech on Saliha?

4. What is Madame Rivest's attitude to Saliha? Why does Saliha decide not to reveal her newly acquired fluency in French to Madame Rivest?

5. Comment on the last sentence of the story: "We come here to speak like them,...but it will be a long time before they let us practise." According to the story, what barriers often separate new immigrants from other Canadians?

Joy Kogawa

Joy Kogawa was born in Vancouver in 1935; she is a nisei, *a second-generation Japanese-Canadian. After the attack on Pearl Harbor and the Japanese capture of Hong Kong in 1941, Japanese-Canadian civilians were rounded up by the Canadian government, their possessions were auctioned off, and they were transported to internment camps away from the British Columbia coast. Kogawa and her family were evacuated to Slocan, B.C., and later to Alberta. The experience of this forced migration of innocent people informs much of Kogawa's work, especially her celebrated novel* Obasan *(1981). The same theme has also recurred in her poetry and in her children's book* Naomi's Road *(1986), most recently made into a play. Kogawa has been active in the legal fight for reparations due to Japanese-Canadians unfairly treated during World War II. This fragment from her novel* Itsuka *(1992), which is a sequel to* Obasan, *describes the apology made to Japanese-Canadians in Parliament. At the end of the excerpt is a government document of "acknowledgement," formally stating Canada's responsibility.* Itsuka *means "someday."*

from Itsuka

Dreams dreams dreams.

It begins in earliest infancy, this journey through the world's many borderlands. It proceeds through the day of the odourless fawn, past summer, into the mustier season of leaves, orchards, the harvest with its memories and dance. To be without history is to be unlived crystal, unused flesh; is to live the life of the unborn.

What I've wakened to in this new autumn day is hunger. My eyes are hungry. The palms of my hands are hungry for this square inch of space we are inhabiting today. Our bite-sized moment of life. I'm as small and as hungry as a newborn sparrow.

September 22, 1988. Ottawa.

Perhaps it's in the scheme of things that when life is most bleak, miracles break through. It's such a mystery. And so completely unexpected. I first heard about it last night. Last night was another lifetime ago.

I was still at *Bridge* when Aunt Emily called around seven. Dan had just called her. She immediately called Anna and me. She couldn't call any others because it's still completely confidential. All she said was "Come over immediately. I can't tell you why." I rushed up to the apartment and found her looking around abstractedly. She packed in silence, mechanically. We tried to sleep. We were up before the alarm. Anna, looking like a blimp, came by with Brian at 5:30 a.m., and we've been driving the four and a half hours along the 401 towards the cut-off at the Tweed highway. We're in a daze.

Our president, Mick Hayashi, Dan and others on the strategy team, unlike most of us, had felt something would have to happen following the American resolution, but over the many months and years they'd grown wary of false optimism. They did not communicate a word of hope to the rank and file. There had been so much debility and loss of morale when repeatedly, after promises of negotiations, there'd be a collapse in talks. Then suddenly, three weeks ago, the team was called to a Montreal hotel, and after a weekend of nonstop negotiating the unbelievable happened. An agreement was reached. There's to be a full acknowledgement of the injustices, individual compensation of $21,000 each to those affected (the Americans are to receive $20,000), a community fund and a race-relations foundation. It's a $350,000,000 package.

"All that? Just like that? But—was there no warning?"

The team was sworn to secrecy. They were told that if the news leaked out in any way, and if the Legion, for instance, objected, the whole thing could be jeopardized. Even now, everything could be stopped. Dan took his oath so seriously that he went north to an isolated cabin.

"It's a miracle. What happened, do you think?"

Brian thinks it's because it's election time. Plus they're copying the Americans, for sure. Maybe it's because of a few key people—like John Fraser, the Speaker of the House.

Young John Fraser, Aunt Emily tells us, was a child in Vancouver when we all disappeared. His father took him to the cenotaph in Stanley Park where Japanese Canadian veterans of the First World War were memorialized. "I fought beside those men," he told his son. John Fraser never forgot.

Whatever the reasons may or may not be, we're so used to pessimism that the fact of a settlement isn't really registering. Aunt Emily says she doesn't want to say another word until she's actually in the House and the papers are actually signed. Dan told her the whole thing is so precarious anything could still stop it.

"How do you think Nikki's going to react?" Anna asks.

"Publicly?" Aunt Emily says. "She'd be a fool to oppose it. And Nikki's no fool."

"Privately, she'll break out in a rash," Brian says.

Privately, I'm wondering if Nikki is still convinced the NJCL are greedy opportunists. Vultures, I think she called us. Could there be any truth in her statement that history will condemn us and vindicate her? That, I suppose, is something none of us can know. What we as a community decide to do from this day on will reveal who we are.

Brian is familiar with the route. We take a rest break at Tweed, get to Ottawa shortly after ten, check in to a friend's house on Gilmour Avenue near the Lord Elgin Hotel, collapse for a second on our beds. And now here we are in this city, the country's capital, the four of us, walking up to Parliament Hill under the blue-white September sky.

I think of the years of labour, the rally half a year ago that Aunt Emily missed—how we walked along in the drizzle and how I wasn't feeling a whisper of hope even though I was carrying the yellow ribbons of hope, and suddenly this unbelievable, this most astonishing day.

If I were a watcher in the skies, I might notice small antlike groupings of people walking up Parliament Hill this morning, up past the Centennial flame; up the wide walk and the steps and into the lobby of the Centre Block with its high vaulted ceiling. Dan flew up last night. Others from the strategy team are here with Mick Hayashi, plus some people from the Ottawa community. Only a few passes have been arranged since it's all such a secret. We hand over our cameras and notebooks at a desk, go down the marble hall, enter the high narrow gallery above the House of Commons and look down directly on the members of Parliament facing each other from their two tiers of benches. So few members present. The speaker is on a dais to our left. To our right is the public gallery, without a single person in it. The huge chamber seems almost empty. Just a handful from our community. So little flesh, but so many ghosts.

Mick Hayashi, Dan and all the main people plus a couple of senior citizens are on the side of the gallery facing the Prime Minister. A few other people from Ottawa, Aunt Emily, Brian, Anna and I sit in the opposite balcony. Anna waves a finger to our team. Below us are the people who lead the country. We can see the top of Prime Minister Mulroney's head from the back and, opposite him, Mr. Broadbent, leader of the New Democratic Party. The leader of the Liberal Party is not present.

11:00 a.m.

The Prime Minister stands. The magic of speech begins—this ritual thing that humans do, the washing of stains through the speaking of words.

"Mr. Speaker," the Prime Minister begins. "Nearly half a century ago, in the crisis of wartime, the Government of Canada wrongfully incarcerated, seized the property, and disenfranchised thousands of citizens of Japanese ancestry...." Even as I strain to hear and remember the many words, they are gone and speech is a trickster, slipping and sliding away. "To put things right," the Prime Minister says in his low voice. And again, "to put things right." And once more. "To put things right."

"Most of us in our own lives," he is saying, "have had occasion to regret certain things we have done. Error is an ingredient of humanity. So too is apology and forgiveness. We all have learned from personal experience that, as inadequate as apologies are, they are the only way we can cleanse the past so that we may, as best we can, in good conscience face the future...."

In the future I know we will look back on this moment as we stand and applaud. We'll remember how Ed Broadbent crossed the floor to shake the Prime Minister's hand and we'll see all this as a distant sun, a star, an asterisk in space to guide us through nights that yet must come. The children, the grandchildren, will know that certain things happened to their ancestors. And that these things were put right.

Sergio Marchi, the Liberal Party representative, is commending our president and community "for their never-ending determination and deep belief in the cause that they carried so well for so long. Today's resolution, no doubt, is a tribute to their sense of purpose, but it is also an appropriate response to those who continue to question the legitimacy and motivation of the leadership...."

I feel us wanting to jump up and cheer but we are contained. And as I look down I can see Mr. Broadbent, who was married to a nisei and knows our story from the inside. I'm glad to be on this side, facing him. He appears agitated, his hands shuffling papers, his eyes glancing up to where we sit. And then he rises and speaks and he's fighting to control his voice. "They, as Canadian citizens, had done no wrong," Mr. Broadbent says. "They had done no wrong...."

This feast of words is too wonderful, too sad, too joyful. I'm numb. Aunt Emily too is listening from some great slow distance of time and space. We are seated at a banquet table that was a hope for people yesterday and will feed us with hope tomorrow. The power of this hour is being stored now in our hearts as a promise fulfilled, a vision realized, and the healing rises up to us, the healing falls about us, over the countryside, here and there, today and tomorrow, touching the upturned faces filled with the waiting and longing of all the wordless years.

The speeches end and it's all going by so fast, so fast, and we're back in the west hallway, in a room where a small throng is gathering. The signing of the agreement is happening here and I catch just a glimpse of the Prime Minister again, no more or less real than any other person as he steps into the room. The TV cameras are directed upon him and our president, smiling, shaking hands, then sitting at a table, the strategy team standing behind. A flashing of lights and cameras clicking. And it's done.

Then, like a gathering swarm of bees, politicians, staff members, the NJCL vanguard in a block, TV crews and reporters all move down the hall, the wide stairs. We walk back down the middle of the Hill to the press conference on the other side of Rideau Street. Aunt Emily is sleep walking.

We can't get into the room where the press conference is and we go with the overflow, up the crowded elevator to a sixth-floor lounge and a television screen, then back down again into the world of microphones and cameras, and catch up with Dan and the others as they walk back up to the Parliament Buildings for a reception.

I want some way to slow down the day, but the waterfall refuses to be contained in a cup and we're swept along in the swift liquid hour, into a room with tables of food, glib words, glazed eyes, cameras flashing, and Aunt Emily is standing with Mr. Broadbent and she looks stunned and not altogether coherent.

"I feel I've just had a tumour removed," one of our friends from Ottawa says to me. "Can you believe it, Naomi?"

We're in a buzz of sounds whirring about.

"Let me congratulate you, Mick. I think you've created a vaccine."

"Yes?"

"Against fatigue. A vaccine against compassion fatigue."

Cedric, Morty, Marion and Ken have just flown up from Toronto and Cedric has the most joyful tearful smile I have ever seen. He comes rushing up to me and in all that crowd he takes me in his arms. "Watch out, world," he whispers. "The mouse has roared."

I laugh. I am whole. I am as complete as when I was a very young child. Marion puts her arms around us both. "God bless us every one," she says.

Aunt Emily and Dan are talking with a man from the Secretary of State who asks Aunt Emily, "How did you feel when you heard the apology?"

Aunt Emily is in a trance and can't reply. My aunt of the so many words. How does she feel as this day speeds by? How does the grass feel in the cool autumn air? How does the sky feel? And the community across the country as it hears the news today?

Ken says, "I finally feel that I'm a Canadian." You can hear the trembling in his voice.

Aunt Emily and I look at each other and smile. We've all said it over the years. "No, no, I'm Canadian. I'm a Canadian. A Canadian." Sometimes it's been a defiant statement, a demand, a proclamation of a right. And today, finally, finally, though we can hardly believe it, to be Canadian means what it hasn't meant before. Reconciliation. Liberation. Belongingness. Home.

Anna and Brian, Cedric, Morty, Aunt Emily and I walk back to Gilmour Avenue. We let ourselves smile. "Well?" Aunt Emily asks, looking up at the sky. That's all she can say.

We make some tea and catch the TV news on every channel we can find. We gasp when we see the official shots. By focusing on the Prime Minister and the MPs behind him, the camera makes the House seem packed, when in fact, it certainly wasn't—not that it mattered. There's a brief report on the radio that Nikki was contacted in Toronto. She said she was very happy about the announcement. We all applaud and toast Nikki with our cups of tea.

The Vancouver contingent phones and we go off to meet for supper. Someone is doing an interview with Mick outside the restaurant. We go in. Wait. Mick arrives. We eat. A few Ottawa people drop by. Then Cedric and I excuse ourselves and leave, ducking past a man taking pictures. We walk hand in hand out into the evening air, up Elgin Street, along Rideau, where strangers are standing at their bus stops, waiting for their many buses, walk past and up to the grounds of Parliament Hill again. We're walking off the stage of the day with its hovering of well-wishers and the great happy crush of the press— away from the speeches, the interviews, the congratulations, the shaking of hands at the restaurant, where some people are still looking at one another, pinching themselves, asking if it's true.

We're taking time, taking time to quieten this day, to bring it back from its already past. We're stretching it out on the canvas of the night air, shaking it out like a blanket to wear.

Oh Aunt Emily, Aunt Emily, is it not the happiest day of your life? I want to remember everything. Savour it all. Our frantic search for a safety pin for the tie on Anna's skirt. The man who honked his horn on Rideau Street and waved. The pattern of sand on the Centre Block steps. Mick, our brave president, with a hand in his hip pocket as he walked briskly ahead of us. I want to etch the day onto the permanent airwaves of memory, replay it over and over until it starts to seem real. Aunt Emily, I want to be able to see you for ever and ever the way you were this morning, walking happily, happily up the hill in your brown trenchcoat and your good walking shoes, my dear warrior aunt. I want to call all the ghosts back again to share this day that none of us can believe is happening.

In my pocket, I have the folded piece of paper that contains the government statement. I read the words again and I take them into my childhood home. I pile them like firelogs, one by one. I warm my limbs.

"As a people, Canadians commit themselves to the creation of a society that ensures equality and justice for all...."

I hand the paper to Cedric and he reads it aloud as we stand looking out over the shadowy trees and bushes on the slope, to the Ottawa River below. In a month's time the leaves of the trees will change colour, and then they will fall as they've been falling for ever, year after year, each leaf with its own tiny story twirling into every other ongoing tale.

This hill is not unlike the slope to the Old Man River near Granton, though it's steeper here and the river is more wide. Sixteen years ago I stood with my uncle on the Granton coulees in the coolness of a night like this, looking down at the ocean of grass, and he said, as he always did, "Umi no yo." It's like the sea.

It's like the sea tonight, Uncle. A busy bubbling trembling sea of the almost sighted and the sometimes blind, the swimmers, the drifters, and those who don't know how to swim. We are here together, and it's enough.

Sixteen years ago this month, my uncle died. And two years later, so did my Obasan. I'm thinking of them and of the rapids, the waterfalls, the eddies in the journey to the sea, and how today we've touched the sounds of the waves on the shore, the applause, the pulse of earth's heart still beating. And I'm thinking of Uncle's words and the words of an old man in Slocan.

"There is a time for crying," they said. "But itsuka, someday, the time for laughter will come."

This is the time, dear Uncle, dear Ojisan. The dramatics, the tears and cheers, have arrived in their own way in their own time. We have come to the hour when the telling leaps over the barricades and the dream enters day.

I can hear the waves from childhood rippling outwards to touch other children who wait for their lives. I can hear the voices, faint as the far-away sound of a distant, almost inaudible wind. It's the sound of the underground stream. It speaks through memory, through dream, through our hands, through our words, our arms, our trusting. I can hear the sound of the voice that frees, a light, steady, endless breath. I can hear the breath of life.

Thank you for this.

ACKNOWLEDGEMENT

As a people, Canadians commit themselves to the creation of a society that ensures equality and justice for all, regardless of race or ethnic origin.

During and after World War II, Canadians of Japanese ancestry, the majority of whom were citizens, suffered unprecedented actions taken by the Government of Canada against their community.

Despite perceived military necessities at the time, the forced removal and internment of Japanese Canadians during World War II and their deportation and expulsion following the war, was unjust. In retrospect, government policies of disenfranchisement, detention, confiscation and sale of private and community property, expulsion, deportation and restriction of movement, which continued after the war, were influenced by discriminatory attitudes. Japanese Canadians who were interned had their property liquidated and the proceeds of sale were used to pay for their own internment.

The acknowledgement of these injustices serves notice to all Canadians that the excesses of the past are condemned and that the principles of justice and equality in Canada are reaffirmed.

Therefore, the Government of Canada, on behalf of all Canadians, does hereby:

1) acknowledge that the treatment of Japanese Canadians during and after World War II was unjust and violated principles of human rights as they are understood today;

2) pledge to ensure, to the full extent that its powers allow, that such events will not happen again; and

3) recognize, with great respect, the fortitude and determination of Japanese Canadians who, despite great stress and hardship, retain their commitment and loyalty to Canada and contribute so richly to the development of the Canadian nation.

TOPICS FOR EXPLORATION

1. "To be without history is to be unlived crystal, unused flesh." Why does the narrator feel she is without history? Find other examples of Joy Kogawa's use of figurative language to convey the "unspeakable."

2. What are the details of the reparations offered to Japanese-Canadians? Are the reparations adequate to compensate them for the losses in property, the years of hardship, and the belated recognition of the injustice done to them?

3. In her narrative, Kogawa presents real people, such as Brian Mulroney and Ed Broadbent. What is the effect of introducing historical personages into the fictional world of the novel? What does it tell us about the margin between fact and fiction?

4. "The washing of stains through the speaking of words" is what humans do, says Kogawa. Why does she believe that the "stain" may be washed clean by the government's public apology? How does the same generalization apply to her own writing and its cleansing, therapeutic function?

5. One of the characters, Ken, says, "I finally feel that I'm a Canadian." How, on this most astonishing day, has the meaning of being Canadian changed for those Japanese-Canadians who were there to hear the announcement and receive the apology?

6. How does Kogawa's text celebrate the sense of purpose in the Japanese-Canadian community? How do its members view their responsibility toward the past and future generations?

7. Why has Kogawa included the government "Acknowledgement" at the end of this fiction? How effective is putting together a fictionalized account and a genuine document, both related to the same historical event? What do they contribute to each other?

Salwa Mohareb Said

Salwa Mohareb Said has an M.A. in English from the American University in Cairo, Egypt. She has written short stories for children, been published in England by Longman's, and been broadcast by the Egyptian Broadcasting Service. At present, she is Director of Pensions for the Canadian Life and Health Association. The story reprinted here first appeared in the collection Arab-Canadian Writing: Stories, Memoirs, and Reminiscences *(1989), edited by Kamal A. Rostom.*

Choices

It was uncommonly cool for a mid-August evening, but Nadia remained in her chair in the backyard because she did not want to interrupt the thoughts flowing through her mind. Any movement would shatter the fragile network of sweet and cruel memories. If she could pull through those tough times ... surely she could survive the current crisis!

So what if they move to St. John's where she does not know a soul? So what if they have to sell the house she has grown to love? She has done all this before. The girls would have to leave their friends and change schools. Hala will be going to university next year ... it's too bad she could not stay in her school until graduation. She wondered how the girls would react to the news ... "Your father has been offered a promotion if he goes to head the company's operations in Newfoundland. I'm going to resign, and we're all moving to St. John's." Fear gripped her heart as she rehearsed what she was going to say to her daughters. She must be getting old. Where is that resilience that carried her through a much bigger move twenty years ago? Surely the risk involved then was far greater than today's. The distance between Toronto and St. John's is but a fraction of the distance between Canada and Egypt, physically, emotionally, and culturally. If she could pull up roots then and come this far, she can do it now. Compared to that major move of twenty years ago, this pales by comparison. Yet the fear and emptiness inside her were overwhelming.

She recalled herself as a young bride in her early twenties, full of drive and ambition. Nothing ever stopped her from going after her dream. She and her husband were two young professionals with a great future ahead of them, by local standards. They had their education, and their families' wealth and social clout to reinforce their claim to success. But they wanted more. They turned their backs on that security to chase a dream all the way across the Ocean. Was it courageous or foolhardy? Her sister, Mona, thought it was foolhardy. But she too was swept by the current of emigration. She did it grudgingly, not by choice, but because she was caught in the tide. Mona had looked around her to find all those she held near and dear leaving ... her best friend was off to Oxford to work on her doctoral dissertation. Her two dearest cousins were in Princeton, and Nadia, her beloved twin sister, was leaving for Canada. So, when Sami came home one day announcing that he had just come from the Canadian Embassy, she knew, in her sinking heart, what her husband was about to announce, and felt powerless to fight the overwhelming tide of departures which was about to engulf her too.

Nadia was all excitement and hope for the future. She looked forward to the challenges of a new life. Mona, on the other hand, looked on the move with dread and fear. The risks were too great! "We're leaving jobs, money, family, and social status to go to an unknown land with different culture, different values ... we'll never belong. We'll always be outsiders with no social position, no status." Nadia had nothing but ridicule for that position. "What great pleasure do you derive from your blessed social status? It's confining and tedious to have your every move watched. I feel like a prisoner of the family name and the social demands. I'd love to go where I can be a drop in the sea ... that would be the ultimate freedom." Little did she know, at the time, how often she would find herself in situations that would make her eat those words.

As she sat in her garden, twenty years later, she recalled those early years of adjusting to being a drop in the sea ... or worse, an outsider, an alien. There were more occasions than she cared to remember, where she had to admit that she really hated being the proverbial drop in the sea. She had the honesty to admit it, but she also had the determination to fight it.

She fought it during those early, miserable cold days, when, as newcomers, she and her husband went looking for work and getting turned down time after time. They were overqualified ... underqualified, or lacked the relevant experience ... and a host of other fictitious reasons to avoid the true reason, they were an unknown, and few are willing to take a chance on an unknown. Having her intelligence and her education discredited was painful. Being distrusted because she looked different and spoke with an accent was painful. Coming back to their tiny apartment to find mail that invariably said "... we regret ..." was painful. But, the most painful of all was a feeling she would never admit to anyone, a feeling that the dream she pursued across the Ocean was unattainable. She refused to admit to those moments of doubt, not even to her husband. She had been a strong force behind their immigration, and felt the full weight of that responsibility and guilt.

Then, after her persistence and tenacity were tested to the limit, small accomplishments started to encourage her to go on. One day she went for an interview for a very junior position with a large organization. She knew that if one of them did not get a job soon, the money they were permitted to emigrate with would run out. She had secretly set a deadline in her own mind that if nothing turned up by the end of that month, they would have to concede defeat and return to Egypt. She went for the interview determined not to let her graduate degrees get in the way of her earning a living. She neglected to mention all her educational accomplishments on the application form. The interview went extremely well and she felt confident that she would be hired. Suddenly, the interviewer asked, "Do you have a university education?" The unexpected question took her by surprise. She hesitated for a moment wondering if she should lie, "y-yes," she stammered in spite of herself, looking down at her cold hands now trembling on her lap. "It's nothing to be ashamed of!" the interviewer said kindly. "Why were you reluctant to tell me?" "Because I really need the job. I can't get work at my real level because I have no Canadian experience. On the other hand, I keep getting turned down for junior jobs because I'm overqualified ..." "Well, the truth is you are. But, I'm prepared to offer you the job anyway. If all works out, you can move up within the company."

Heaven—sheer heaven! She had a job. It didn't matter how low the pay was. Someone finally accepted her. Someone was willing to give her a chance. When her husband had suggested that if things did not open up within another month or two, they should go back, she had resisted. "Yusif! We have to make this work. We always said that we would burn our boats so we wouldn't be tempted to sail right back when the going got tough. We have to think it out." Now that she had a job, she would not have to go back on those words. They can now build a life here. And so they did.

Those were difficult times. A lot of newcomers they knew faced the same problems. Some, like her, were undaunted and tenaciously fought their way up to varying measures of success. Her sister, Mona, was not one of those people. Mona and Sami had their share of problems in adjusting. But Mona cried a lot, and nagged a lot, and never stopped comparing past and present. Her preference was always the past. She had no desire to fight and struggle to create a new life here. It was too hard and required too many sacrifices. She was forever blaming her husband for unsettling her life and forcing her to change.

Sami finally conceded that they would never be happy here. He drove a cab to make a living, while he was studying to qualify for the Canadian equivalent of his engineering degree. Coming home to an unhappy wife and stacks of books to study, day after day, with no relief in sight, was too much to take. So, Sami and Mona made another momentous decision, and returned to Egypt.

Nadia and Mona were fraternal twins. They grew up in the same environment and went to the same schools, had many of the same friends. But their personalities were very different. Their friends used to joke about the disparity in their approaches to life. Mona was gentle, docile, and very conservative, while Nadia relished change and took on every challenge. Their mother used to watch them as they demonstrated their opposing solutions to problems, and shake her head knowingly with only one explanation for the great difference between the two. "The same fire which melts the butter, hardens the egg!"

Mona could not adapt to change, and had no desire to do anything contrary to what her mild nature dictated. Adapting required an effort and a fighting spirit. Mona refused to fight. She preferred to go home. For Nadia home was now here. She belonged here in this Suburban Toronto garden. She also belonged to the beautiful skyline she saw every time she looked up from her desk in the office. She would never entertain the delusion that she was absolutely at home or at peace anywhere, but this was as close as she would ever get.

The front door, which she had left open, was blown shut by a sudden gust of wind, and the sound startled her out of her brief encounter with those forgotten memories.

She forced herself out of her reverie and out of her comfortable chair and walked absentmindedly to the kitchen. She poured herself a cup of coffee and reached out mechanically to push the "play" button on the cassette player perched precariously on the edge of the table. There was an old tape in it. An old Egyptian song she had forgotten about. The singer had long since died. But the beautiful voice was still there. Nadia felt a lump in her throat as she remembered the first time she heard that song twenty-five years ago. A simple song from days gone by could still awaken in her feelings ... feelings whose intrusion she could not allow too often, or she could not function. Feelings of love and longing for a land and a people she abandoned years ago, but never forgot. She did not want to forget, but just to dampen the pain that accompanied the memory, and to lessen the longing she would always feel. Forgetting was not within her power. The Nile that this voice from the dead was singing about ran in Nadia's very veins. She had no power to change that. There were thoughts and feelings and expressions that came alive in her mother tongue. There was a way of thinking, a tolerance, a sense of humor, a twist of phrase, and a whole view of life that were her birthright, and that no distance, physical or temporal, could possibly erase.

The voice from the scratched old tape rose in a familiar refrain, and Nadia felt warm tears running down her face. The same kind of tears she shed when she first came to this new land and homesickness overcame her. Tears no one knew about, then or now. She was the strong one, the fighter, the one who rose to every challenge and moved ahead undaunted. She never could permit herself such moments of weakness, except when she was alone. She did have an image to preserve. Besides, she always managed to fight her moments of weakness. Mona gave in to hers.

Nadia was a little annoyed with herself for allowing a song to invoke such a sentimental and emotional reaction. She had not reacted that way for years. Yearning, perhaps, but not tears! Was she becoming overemotional and sentimental, or was the thought of uprooting herself again too much to take? The first time she did that she was taking an immense risk, but her youthful enthusiasm overshadowed the magnitude of the step she was taking. With that experience to draw upon, she was approaching this new venture both stronger and weaker. Stronger because she was better prepared for the pain to come, but weaker because she now knew that the pain may recede with time, but it never completely disappears. It was here right now! Something reopened the old wound ... a voice from the past, singing in a language she rarely used now, of a river which, though she had not seen it for many years, was a part of her very being. She remembered Shakespeare's "What's gone and what's past help/should be past grief."

She wished it were so. But grief was ever present. She felt like Orestes, destined to be forever pursued by the Furies—never to be at peace. There may be moments of acceptance and even contentment. Moments when logic would convince her that she was as close to being happy as she could ever hope to be. But she knew, even during those brief moments, that her own Furies were lurking in the shadows ready to torment her. They were insidious creatures that manifested their presence in different ways and had a million disguises. Right now, they were in the form of her undying love for the land she chose to leave, for reasons she could no longer remember. It must have been those same Furies that posed as the reasons that made her leave in the first place. She ran then, and continued to be driven all her life. Her own Furies, at times appearing as dissatisfaction, at times as a driving ambition. Whatever their disguise, they always achieved their aim—to keep her running. Running from home and country ... Running in search of a dream ... Running towards success ... always running ... The end result being that she was never allowed to rest or be at peace. She did not believe that some angry creature from the underworld had really set them upon her to punish her. She had made choices in her life that courted them and drew them to her. She had defied the order of things by not accepting anything without questioning it, modifying it, changing it. She had declared herself a challenger to anything and everything that would presume to enter into her life. She had announced that she was in charge, and would change her world to what she wanted it to be, and would not acquiesce and take the easy predetermined route. By choosing to challenge, change and fight, she created the very Furies that would forever haunt her existence.

Nadia shuddered. She was sure it was not from the brisk breeze blowing in from the kitchen door, but from the realization that she had created these monsters, and, given a second chance, she would probably make the same kind of choices that led to their creation.

The girls came in from the movies. "Hi, Mom!" She asked how the movie was. "Boring," said Hala, the youngest. "I thought it was great," was the response from Leila.

Nadia told her daughters about the upcoming move. Hala was full of enthusiasm and wanted to start planning right away. "Great! Absolutely fantastic ... it'll be exciting to live in a new place ..." Leila was quick to interrupt her younger sister, "what do you mean 'Great,' you twit? We'll have to leave all our friends and ..."

Nadia watched the girls arguing and realized that she had really known how her daughters would react to the upcoming change. Their argument reminded her of her arguments with Mona, and of her mother saying, "the same fire that melts the butter, hardens the egg."

Nadia had not melted under the fire. Her youngest daughter was like her. The eldest was definitely the kind that would melt like butter. She would be the kind that always invokes sympathy and protection. She would never be called upon to fight any battles or put out any fires.

Somehow, Nadia felt sorry for the one who appeared to be the stronger and tougher of the two. The youngest would seek out challenges. She would never accept what life hands her down without questioning it. She would never give in to defeat. But, in demonstrating all that apparent strength, she will be inviting perpetual battle. She will appear to be choosing to be in charge of her world. But what she will, in reality, be creating, are her own Furies—who will relentlessly pursue her all her life.

TOPICS FOR EXPLORATION

1. Twenty years earlier Nadia had made a big move from Egypt to Canada; today she is facing another major move in her life. What is the difference this time? What difficulties does prospective relocating from Toronto to St. John's pose for Nadia and her family?

2. What motives did Nadia and her husband have for coming to Canada? How did their reasons for leaving their homeland differ from those of Nadia's sister, Mona?

3. What are Nadia's recollections of their early immigrant years? Why did she feel that "her intelligence and education" were discredited by Canadian employers?

4. Why did Mona and her family decide to return to Egypt? Compare different responses the sisters had to the problem of difficult adjustment to a new life in Canada. How are their differences accounted for?

5. What recipe for success does the story offer to immigrant readers? Is there an implied message that success in a new country always necessarily involves a certain degree of assimilation? How does Nadia's life illustrate the last point? What is the cost of choices she has made?

SUGGESTIONS FOR FURTHER STUDY

1. Compare the two young female characters in Yeshim Ternar's fiction and Rosemary Brown's essay: What do they have in common? In what ways are they different? Is there a difference between the two central figures resulting from education, race, class, or expectations? What are their chances to succeed?

2. Compare "racism Canadian-style" as it affects different groups such as Métis people in Jenine Dumont's narrative, African-Canadians in Rosemary Brown's autobiography and Archie Crail's story, and the Japanese-Canadians of Joy Kogawa's *Itsuka*. What have been the consequences of racism upon each group?

3. Compare the situation of overqualified immigrants struggling to find adequate jobs in a new country, as presented in the short stories written by Yeshim Ternar, Archie Crail, and Salwa Mohareb Said.

4. What prospects and experiences in the new land might be determined by the newcomers' expectations and their social background? Compare on the basis of real and fictional accounts of migration in the writing of Rohinton Mistry (Unit One), Helga (Kutz-Harder) Mills (Unit One), Yeshim Ternar, Rosemary Brown, and Salwa Mohareb Said.

5. The Chinese Canadian National Council has sought reparations for past injustices committed against Chinese immigrants to Canada. On the basis of "Chinese Wall Writings" and Joy Kogawa's *Itsuka*, compare the role that the Canadian government had played in both encouraging immigration and disenfranchising these Asian immigrants.

SELF AND OTHER: LANGUAGE

INTRODUCTION

Learning to speak is like learning to think. It is possible that the way we learn to think is a direct consequence of the way language structures our thinking. Therefore, expression in one's first language is as clear and easy as the breath that generates it.

However, there is no universal spoken language that would enable us to communicate without the structures that custom enforces. Thus, the languages of the world, in their diversity, set up barriers between mental processes and their expression. Those who cross geographical barriers also cross the boundaries of language.

Crossing these barriers means learning to think again in the patterns imposed by a new culture. Of course, the level of language intentionally acquired in adulthood can be either enhanced by curiosity or limited by inhibitions and fears. On the one hand, living in a foreign language can impose constraints or lead the newcomer to cling to the known; on the other hand, it can double the resources of those who dream in two vocabularies. Most of the voices in this unit think in one or several other languages while speaking in English. Most of them find unique advantages in this richness, but there are difficulties, too.

For Eva Hoffman, an author who straddles English and Polish, the difficulty of being transplanted into a new cultural and linguistic context is the severing of "signifier from signified," or the word (and its associations) from experience. She describes the frustrating ironies of learning a second language and the attendant loss of self-definition; she also explores how fluency in a language sets up a class structure. All in all, "linguistic dispossession" is a division of self from culture.

The barriers of language, then, are sometimes difficult to transcend. Genni Gunn deals with the dilemma of conserving one culture while living in another. In "The Middle Ground," Rosalba wants to keep her son Claudio "from being Canadian" because she fears he will lose the Italian heritage so important to her. Nevertheless, as a teacher, she deplores the conservatism of the older generation of Italian immigrants, exemplified by the repressive cultural limits set upon her disabled student, Peppi, by his Italian parents. Garry Engkent communicates a different problem. In "Why My Mother Can't Speak English," the narrator's mother has lived in Canada for decades but has never learned English for a variety of reasons: the rigidity acquired in old age, her preference for her original culture, the limitations set by her patriarchal husband, and so on. The isolation of having one language amidst the culture of another cuts her off from the possibility of understanding Canadian customs and patterns of behaviour and interpreting them in a correct way. Engkent understands that the old woman fears to learn English because it would "change her Chinese soul," even though, in her case, language might act as a barrier to attaining Canadian citizenship.

In a brief essay, Lucy Fazio recounts her introduction to the Canadian school system and the English language. Describing her first day at school as an immigrant child, she stresses the importance of support and assistance needed by such children to integrate successfully into a new cultural and linguistic reality. She pays tribute to her first English teacher, whom she perceived as a "beacon of compassion and understanding."

In a style radically different from that of Fazio, Karim H. Karim interrogates the term "multiculturalism" and the way it functions in public discourse. Along with multiculturalism, he problematizes several other concepts such as "minority," "ethnic," and "immigrant" that are currently used to express the idea of diversity in Canadian society. His analysis reveals that language can be a dangerous political instrument of exclusion and privileging for certain groups.

In this Unit, the contrast between the liberating articulation and hindering muteness that we observe throughout the continuum of language is indeed striking. Despite the frustrations experienced by those who struggle to communicate in a new language, most of them persist in trying to break the language barrier.

The Laundress

She worked as a housemaid, then as a laundress
in small town Winnipeg, full of emigres speaking
every language except her own: she was Icelandic
and as she worked she sang the old Icelandic hymns
and songs: the songs had all her joy, they brought
all her peace. She kept reaching for the language
that got lost in her life. She could never speak it
again, though it always measured her breath.

Late one summer, as she lay dying, she sang again
the Icelandic hymns, sang in her mother tongue,
an other tongue for us; and as we lay her
in a foreign grave, we, who know no Icelandic,
who know then almost nothing of what she loved
and lived by, say our prayers over her in English.

—Einar Pall Jonsson

Einar Pall Jonsson's poem comes from the collection Volvox *(1971), and
has been translated from the Icelandic by Michael Patrick O'Connor and
Thorvaldur Johnson.*

Eva Hoffman

Eva Hoffman was born in Poland in 1945; her family left for Canada when she was fourteen years old. After a few years in Vancouver, she went to study in the United States, where she completed her Ph.D. in English at Harvard University. She now lives in New York and works as an editor for The New York Times. *The following excerpt has been taken from her autobiography,* Lost in Translation *(1989), in which she analyzes her experience of immigration and the difficulties of living between two cultures. Her most recent book is* Exit into History: A Journey through the New Eastern Europe *(1993).*

from Lost in Translation

Every day I learn new words, new expressions. I pick them up from school exercises, from conversations, from the books I take out of Vancouver's well-lit, cheerful public library. There are some turns of phrase to which I develop strange allergies. "You're welcome," for example, strikes me as a gaucherie, and I can hardly bring myself to say it—I suppose because it implies that there's something to be thanked for, which in Polish would be impolite. The very places where the language is at its most conventional, where it should be most taken for granted, are the places where I feel the prick of artifice.

Then there are words to which I take an equally irrational liking, for their sound, or just because I'm pleased to have deduced their meaning. Mainly they're words I learn from books, like "enigmatic" or "insolent"—words that have only a literary value, that exist only as signs on the page.

But mostly, the problem is that the signifier has become severed from the signified. The words I learn now don't stand for things in the same unquestioned way they did in my native tongue. "River" in Polish was a vital sound, energized with the essence of riverhood, of my rivers, of my being immersed in rivers. "River" in English is cold—a word without an aura. It has no accumulated associations for me, and it does not give off the radiating haze of connotation. It does not evoke.

The process, alas, works in reverse as well. When I see a river now, it is not shaped, assimilated by the word that accommodates it to the psyche—a word that makes a body of water a river rather than an uncontained element. The river before me remains a thing, absolutely other, absolutely unbending to the grasp of my mind.

When my friend Penny tells me that she's envious, or happy, or disappointed, I try laboriously to translate not from English to Polish but from the word back to its source, to the feeling from which it springs. Already, in that moment of strain, spontaneity of response is lost. And anyway, the translation doesn't work. I don't know how Penny feels when she talks about envy. The word hangs in a Platonic stratosphere, a vague prototype of all envy, so large, so all-encompassing that it might crush me—as might disappointment or happiness.

I am becoming a living avatar of structuralist wisdom; I cannot help knowing that words are just themselves. But it's a terrible knowledge, without any of the consolations that wisdom usually brings. It does not mean that I'm free to play with words at my wont; anyway, words in their naked state are surely among the least satisfactory play objects. No, this radical disjoining between word and thing is a desiccating alchemy, draining the world not only of significance but of its colors, striations, nuances—its very existence. It is the loss of a living connection.

The worst losses come at night. As I lie down in a strange bed in a strange house—my mother is a sort of housekeeper here, to the aging Jewish man who has taken us in return for her services—I wait for that spontaneous flow of inner language which used to be my nighttime talk with myself, my way of informing the ego where the id had been. Nothing comes. Polish, in a short time, has atrophied, shriveled from sheer uselessness. Its words don't apply to my new experiences; they're not coeval with any of the objects, or faces, or the very air I breathe in the daytime. In English, words have not penetrated to those layers of my psyche from which a private conversation could proceed. This interval before sleep used to be the time when my mind became both receptive and alert, when images and words rose up to consciousness, reiterating what had happened during the day, adding the day's experiences to those already stored there, spinning out the thread of my personal story.

Now, this picture-and-word show is gone; the thread has been snapped. I have no interior language, and without it, interior images—those images through which we assimilate the external world, through which we take it in, love it, make it our own—become blurred too. My mother and I met a Canadian family who live down the block today. They were working in their garden and engaged us in a conversation of the "Nice weather we're having, isn't it?" variety, which culminated in their inviting us into their house. They sat stiffly on their couch, smiled in the long pauses between the conversation, and seemed at a loss for what to ask. Now my mind gropes for some description of them, but nothing fits. They're a different species from anyone I've met in Poland, and Polish words slip off them without sticking. English words don't hook on to anything. I try, deliberately, to come up with a few. Are these people pleasant or dull? Kindly or silly? The words float in an uncertain space. They come up from a part of my brain in which labels may be manufactured but which has no connection to my instincts, quick reactions, knowledge. Even the simplest adjectives sow confusion in my mind; English kindliness has a whole system of morality behind it, a system that makes "kindness" an entirely positive virtue. Polish kindness has the tiniest element of irony. Besides, I'm beginning to feel the tug of prohibition, in English, against uncharitable words. In Polish, you can call someone an idiot without particularly harsh feelings and with the zest of a strong judgment. Yes, in Polish these people might tend toward "silly" and "dull"—but I force myself toward "kindly" and "pleasant." The cultural unconscious is beginning to exercise its subliminal influence.

The verbal blur covers these people's faces, their gestures with a sort of fog. I can't translate them into my mind's eye. The small event, instead of being added to the mosaic of consciousness and memory, falls through some black hole, and I fall with it. What has happened to me in this new world? I don't know. I don't see what I've seen, don't comprehend what's in front of me. I'm not filled with language anymore, and I have only a memory of fullness to anguish me with the knowledge that, in this dark and empty state, I don't really exist.

For my birthday, Penny gives me a diary, complete with a little lock and key to keep what I write from the eyes of all intruders. It is that little lock—the visible symbol of the privacy in which the diary is meant to exist—that creates my dilemma. If I am indeed to write something entirely for myself, in what language do I write? Several times, I open the diary and close it again. I can't decide. Writing in

Polish at this point would be a little like resorting to Latin or ancient Greek—an eccentric thing to do in a diary, in which you're supposed to set down your most immediate experiences and unpremeditated thoughts in the most unmediated language. Polish is becoming a dead language, the language of the untranslatable past. But writing for nobody's eyes in English? That's like doing a school exercise, or performing in front of yourself, a slightly perverse act of self-voyeurism.

Because I have to choose something, I finally choose English. If I'm to write about the present, I have to write in the language of the present, even if it's not the language of the self. As a result, the diary becomes surely one of the more impersonal exercises of that sort produced by an adolescent girl. These are no sentimental effusions of rejected love, eruptions of familial anger, or consoling broodings about death. English is not the language of such emotions. Instead, I set down my reflections on the ugliness of wrestling; on the elegance of Mozart, and on how Dostoyevsky puts me in mind of El Greco. I write down Thoughts. I Write.

There is a certain pathos to this naïve snobbery, for the diary is an earnest attempt to create a part of my persona that I imagine I would have grown into in Polish. In the solitude of this most private act, I write, in my public language, in order to update what might have been my other self. The diary is about me and not about me at all. But on one level, it allows me to make the first jump. I learn English through writing, and, in turn, writing gives me a written self. Refracted through the double distance of English and writing, this self—my English self—becomes oddly objective; more than anything, it perceives. It exists more easily in the abstract sphere of thoughts and observations than in the world. For a while, this impersonal self, this cultural negative capability, becomes the truest thing about me. When I write, I have a real existence that is proper to the activity of writing—an existence that takes place midway between me and the sphere of artifice, art, pure language. This language is beginning to invent another me. However, I discover something odd. It seems that when I write (or, for that matter, think) in English, I am unable to use the word "I." I do not go as far as the schizophrenic "she"—but I am driven, as by a compulsion, to the double, the Siamese-twin "you."

My voice is doing funny things. It does not seem to emerge from the same parts of my body as before. It comes out from somewhere in my throat, tight, thin, and mat—a voice without the modulations, dips, and rises that it had before, when it went from my stomach all the way through my head. There is, of course, the constraint and the self-consciousness of an accent that I hear but cannot control. Some of my high school peers accuse me of putting it on in order to appear more "interesting." In fact, I'd do anything to get rid of it, and when I'm alone, I practice sounds for which my speech organs have no intuitions, such as "th" (I do this by putting my tongue between my teeth) and "a," which is longer and more open in Polish (by shaping my mouth into a sort of arrested grin). It is simple words like "cat" or "tap" that give me the most trouble, because they have no context of other syllables, and so people often misunderstand them. Whenever I can, I do awkward little swerves to avoid them, or pause and try to say them very clearly. Still, when people—like salesladies—hear me speak without being prepared to listen carefully, they often don't understand me the first time around. "Girls' shoes," I say, and the "girls'" comes out as a sort of scramble. "Girls' shoes," I repeat, willing the syllable to form itself properly, and the saleslady usually smiles nicely, and sends my mother and me to the right part of the store. I say "Thank you" with a sweet smile, feeling as if I'm both claiming an unfair special privilege and being unfairly patronized.

It's as important to me to speak well as to play a piece of music without mistakes. Hearing English distorted grates on me like chalk screeching on a blackboard, like all things botched and badly done, like all forms of gracelessness. The odd thing is that I know what is correct, fluent, good, long before I can execute it. The English spoken by our Polish acquaintances strikes me as jagged and thick, and I know that I shouldn't imitate it. I'm turned off by the intonations I hear on the TV sitcoms—by the expectation of laughter, like a dog's tail wagging in supplication, built into the actors' pauses, and by the curtailed, cutoff rhythms. I like the way Penny speaks, with an easy flow and a pleasure in giving words a fleshly fullness; I like what I hear in some movies; and once the Old Vic comes to Vancouver to perform *Macbeth*, and though I can hardly understand the particular words, I am riveted by the tones of sureness and command that mold the actors' speech into such majestic periods.

Sociolinguists might say that I receive these language messages as class signals, that I associate the sounds of correctness with the social status of the speaker. In part, this is undoubtedly true. The class-linked notion that I transfer wholesale from Poland is that belonging to a "better" class of people is absolutely dependent on speaking a "better" language. And in my situation especially, I know that language will be a crucial instrument, that I can overcome the stigma of my marginality, the weight of presumption against me, only if the reassuringly right sounds come out of my mouth.

Yes, speech is a class signifier. But I think that in hearing these varieties of speech around me, I'm sensitized to something else as well—something that is a matter of aesthetics, and even of psychological health. Apparently, skilled chefs can tell whether a dish from some foreign cuisine is well cooked even if they have never tasted it and don't know the genre of cooking it belongs to. There seem to be some deep-structure qualities—consistency, proportions of ingredients, smoothness of blending—that indicate culinary achievement to these educated eaters' taste buds. So each language has its own distinctive music, and even if one doesn't know its separate components, one can pretty quickly recognize the propriety of the patterns in which the components are put together, their harmonies and discords. Perhaps the crucial element that strikes the ear in listening to living speech is the degree of the speaker's self-assurance and control.

As I listen to people speaking that foreign tongue, English, I can hear when they stumble or repeat the same phrases too many times, when their sentences trail off aimlessly—or, on the contrary, when their phrases have vigor and roundness, when they have the space and the breath to give a flourish at the end of a sentence, or make just the right pause before coming to a dramatic point. I can tell, in other words, the degree of their ease or disease, the extent of authority that shapes the rhythms of their speech. That authority—in whatever dialect, in whatever variant of the mainstream language—seems to me to be something we all desire. It's not that we all want to speak the King's English, but whether we speak Appalachian or Harlem English, or Cockney, or Jamaican Creole, we want to be at home in our tongue. We want to be able to give voice accurately and fully to ourselves and our sense of the world. John Fowles, in one of his stories in *The Ebony Tower*, has a young man cruelly violate an elderly writer and his manuscripts because the legacy of language has not been passed on to the youthful vandal properly. This seems to me an entirely credible premise. Linguistic dispossession is a sufficient motive for violence, for it is close to the dispossession of one's self. Blind rage, helpless rage is rage that has no words—rage that overwhelms one with darkness. And if one is perpetually without words, if one exists in the entropy of inarticulateness, that condition itself is bound to be an enraging frustration. In my New York apartment, I listen almost nightly to fights that erupt like brushfire on the street below—and in their escalating fury of repetitive phrases ("Don't do this to me, man, you fucking bastard, I'll fucking kill you"), I hear not the pleasures of macho toughness but an infuriated beating against wordlessness, against the incapacity to make oneself understood, seen. Anger can be borne—it can even be satisfying—if it can gather into words and explode in a storm, or a rapier-sharp attack. But without this means of ventilation, it only turns back inward, building and swirling like a head of steam—building to an impotent, murderous rage. If all therapy is speaking therapy—a talking cure—then perhaps all neurosis is a speech dis-ease.

TOPICS FOR EXPLORATION

1. What role does Eva Hoffman adopt when communicating with her audience? What is her purpose in describing the predicament of a person transplanted from one linguistic universe to another?

2. How does a beginner experience a new language? How do the words in a foreign language behave for a new speaker? Why is it that "the signifier has become severed from the signified"?

3. What frustrations and paradoxes are involved in learning a new language? Why does Hoffman feel that any translation from one language to another is inadequate?

4. How does social context determine the use of language? What connection does Hoffman see between the language and the underlying set of cultural assumptions? How do "class signals" affect her perception of accent? What do "self-assurance and control" in the use of language mean to her?

5. Why does Hoffman have trouble deciding which language to use in her private diary? How is Hoffman's voice a reflection of her confusion and uncertainty? In what way does her diary help her recapture her new self through writing?

6. How does Hoffman relate the initial loss of her native tongue to the loss of identity? Why does she feel she "doesn't exist at all"?

7. What are the dangers of "linguistic dispossession" that she describes? Why can it result in frustration and rage?

Genni Gunn

Genni Gunn's publications include a novel, Thrice Upon a Time *(1990),
a short story collection,* On the Road *(1991), a prose/poetry collection*
Mating in Captivity *(1993), and two collections of poetry in translation
from Italian (both by renowned Italian author, Dacia Maraini):* Devour
Me Too *(1987) and* Traveling in the Gait of a Fox *(1993). She has also
recently completed an original opera libretto,* Alternate Visions, *commis-
sioned by Vancouver Opera. Her story, "The Middle Ground" appeared
in an anthology of Italian-Canadian writing called* Ricordi: Things
Remembered, *edited by C.D. Minni.*

The Middle Ground

They came to live in Vancouver after her husband died: Rosalba
and her small son, Claudio—her son who, in spite of her husband's
persistent teachings, grew more Canadian each year. When he was
born, Giulio had made her promise to speak only Italian to the
boy—a rule she insisted upon even now that he was almost six. But
the boy grew more Canadian each year. He would sit on her lap and
listen attentively to stories (in Italian, always in Italian) about her
parents. "*Il nonno e la nonna,*" Rosalba had taught him to say. But he
had no grandparents here, no olive trees and no watermelons to hug.
Claudio told her the other children laughed when he told them
these stories. The boy had never been to Italy. His imagined homeland was no different to him than Canada had been to Rosalba
before she came. It was not his fault that he could not remember the
taste of prickly-pears, persimmons and fresh fruit.

In Vancouver, Rosalba bought persimmons in a little Chinese
store on Commercial Drive. But they had been picked too soon and
she could not find the right words to describe their real taste.

She'd been in Canada almost ten years, had come at nineteen to
live in Victoria where Giulio taught Italian Studies at the University.
But Rosalba had always loved Vancouver, its mountains and ocean

so close together she could almost smell the Adriatic Sea: Trieste leaning lazy against low-slung mountains, rooftops baked ruddy in the hot summers. From the viewpoint up near the Conservatory in Queen Elizabeth Park, she could almost imagine herself sitting on the stone wall of the old castle that overlooked Trieste. Only the cobblestones were missing and the long steep hills and curved narrow roads leading to the university. In Vancouver, a different beauty: the clumps of evergreens, cedar-shake roofs and coloured houses. Then the downtown high-rises jutting into the sky, dwarfed by the backdrop of mountains.

She came to Vancouver to teach Italian at a school set in Little Italy and filled with a mixture of first and second-generation Italian teenagers. It had been the natural thing for her to do, now that Giulio was gone. Many of the students came from small villages in southern Italy and spoke only dialects. Most had never learned proper Italian grammar. Strange that she should be the one to recreate with patience a language and a culture for strangers' children—she, who could not keep her own son from becoming Canadian.

The changes had been subtle. Like the night he'd asked her to read him a story in English, although she always read to him from *Il Tesoro*. She had been raised on it herself. The thick red volume with gold-embossed printing on the cover, the fairy-tales and jokes and pictures—all part of her childhood. She could almost recite each word by heart. She'd said "no," of course, and read him his favourite story. But the next day, seized with unbearable guilt, she'd gone to a book store and bought *Peter Pan*, in English.

And another evening, when he'd asked if they could order pizza with pineapple on top, she'd said, "absolutely not, that's not real pizza," and had made him one at home, the way her mother had taught her. But later, she'd opened a can of pineapple chunks and let him put them on top of his. She was trying to keep him Italian, but the boy grew more Canadian each year.

In the ten-block radius encircling Commercial Drive, a new Italy had been established long before she came. Here, families lived the traditional roles of their homeland. Some women were still clad in dark dresses that reached to below their knees, their elbows covered with shawls and cardigans. It made Rosalba think of Goya's *Disasters of War*. All that black—black skirts, black hair, black eyes. Only the shop windows on Commercial Drive twinkled with vibrant colours. Mannequins sporting the newest fashions from Rome smiled into the street, eyes vacant, smooth blond bobs and turned-up noses. Rosalba wished they didn't look so *American*. She'd always said *America* when she was in Italy, even though she'd been speaking of Canada. From across the ocean, there had been only one continent, no differentiation between countries. She supposed it was the same for Italy. Canadians thought of Italians as one people—all born of the same fat little dark-haired Italian Mother Earth. But she had only to think of her youth, of the many provinces and dialects, of the animosity between North and South, water and mountains.

She had chosen Vancouver, when her husband died, because of Commercial Drive, because of the mountains and the ocean. When the insurance money came, she went house-hunting with Claudio. At first, they looked in the Italian district. Rosalba tip-toed politely from house to house. "The bathroom counters are all marble. My husband had it sent direct from Italy, you know." Windows shuttered, floors glistening, Madonnas mounted on corner altars in the hall. "And that couch belonged to my grandmother. But we're going back. I'll sell it, if you're interested." Plaster busts of Roman Emperors; outdoors, lions guarding a driveway and at the back, a clothesline to the hydro pole. "These dryers make clothes yellow." And the neighbours peering from doorsteps. "And where are you from, Signora?" All so *Italian*. After the fifth house, Rosalba hurried Claudio into the car seat and drove back to their rented apartment. Inside, she took a deep breath and leaned back on the couch. She had panicked back there, among icons, and idols; she felt she might be absorbed into their darkness, their familiarity. She waited a few days, then contacted a real-estate firm. She asked the school secretary to call for her. "It's my accent," she explained apologetically. "They think I'm stupid."

The real-estate lady showed her houses on the West Side, tall beautiful wooden houses made of bleached grey cedar and nicked with skylights that captured the dawn. She loved these monolithic structures, the white inner walls and the echo of her heels on the hardwood floors. Although she longed to live in one of these houses, she settled finally on a sturdy, squat bungalow with precise rectangular windows with nine panes in each. She bought it because of its cream stucco exterior that reminded her of the white stone of her parents' house. She bought it because it seemed more *Italian*, and this was her concession for not buying one within the Italian district.

She enrolled Claudio in first grade at the elementary school just two blocks away from their new home and made arrangements to have a babysitter take him there in the mornings and pick him up at the end of the day. She had to leave much earlier than he did, to drive across town and be settled into the classroom before her students arrived.

"Now don't you let anyone call you anything but *Claudio*," she said on the first morning, squeezing him to her and wishing she could go with him. "Repeat it slowly if they say it wrong." Rosalba hated the way people here pronounced her name "Rozelba" or "Ruzolba," as if there were no such thing as a soft *r* or *s*. Often, she tried to break it down phonetically: "Ross-al-ba," or "Row-sal-ba, like rosary," she'd say. But they forgot too soon.

At her school, she noticed Peppi Armano immediately. He had a physical disability and always entered her ninth grade class after all the other students were seated. He mumbled an apology although his eyes—black moons in round white saucers—were defiant.

He walked slowly, painfully, his small hands grasping the combination locks on the lockers that lined the hallways. Her classroom was upstairs, and she grew accustomed to the shuffling of feet after the bell had rung. At times, she watched Peppi make his way up or down the stairs, one foot at a time on each step. She wanted to help him, to take his free hand, the one which was not so tightly clasped to the banister, and walk down with him, but she was afraid to show her concern because Peppi kept his head down and stared only at his feet. At the end of the first week, he stayed after class and stood in front of her desk until she prompted him, "Is there something I can do?"

He blushed and for a moment let go of her desk with both hands, trying to stand up straight as he spoke. "About my being late," he said in a muffled, quiet voice, "I have to wait until the others have gone. It's easier when I can hold on to the lockers. My legs ... ," he stopped and leaned against the desk and Rosalba felt tears sting her eyes.

"I understand," she said. But she didn't and later, asked the Principal about it.

"Friedreich's ataxia," the Principal told her. "His parents want to buy him a wheelchair, but he won't hear of it. He's a very stubborn boy. We've talked to him on many occasions."

After that, it seemed her ears were attuned to the sound of Peppi's small feet as they dragged through the halls. She could hear lock after lock swinging on its gate after he'd passed. She imagined she could count the lockers by his steps, by his hands which clung to the round black dials. She asked the Principal if she could have a room on the bottom floor. But he said it was impossible to reroute the school for Peppi. There were too many classes, too many students, too many timetables. "We have to do what's best for the majority," he said. And Rosalba lay in bed at night and tried to think of ways to help one small boy.

She noticed that Peppi remained reserved and always a little apart from the rest of the students. On one occasion, when she organized an after-school trip to the Italian Cultural Centre to see an Italian film, Peppi did not come. She waited for him until one of the students told her that his brother had taken him home at the usual time.

Rosalba went to see Mrs. Crombie, the school counsellor, to ask about Peppi's family.

"As far as we can tell," Mrs. Crombie said, "the parents are overprotective. The boy has no friends—in fact, goes nowhere without either one of his parents or his brother. If only he'd agree to use a wheelchair." She paused. "Has he talked to you about it?"

Rosalba shook her head.

"Poor kid. Last year, we tried talking to the parents ... but you know how it is with these families. They believe they're doing what's best for him." She tapped her pen on her desk for a moment, then looked up at Rosalba. "Why don't you talk to them? They might listen to you, if you spoke in their language."

Their language. Rosalba noticed the choice of words. Mrs. Crombie had not said, *your language. Their language,* as if *they* were somehow different from her. She said, "It's *my* language too."

And Mrs. Crombie smiled. "Yes, but you're different."

Strange the concept of foreigners. And how cultures could be massed under one umbrella. Yet individuals were considered separate. She wanted to shout, "I'm Italian." But she shook her head instead and said nothing. When she was still in Italy and the tourist season began, she had thought of all Americans in the same way. She had never considered each person as separate and distinct, but rather had seen Americans as a collective of brash, loud, forward people, with bermuda shorts and cameras. And when she'd had occasion to meet one, she too had thought that one person was different. The prejudice, then, came out of ignorance, out of the stereotypes they all accepted.

"What is a Wop?" Claudio asked.

Rosalba said, "Schoolchildren often give names to things they don't understand. You are *Italian.*"

"I don't want to be Italian," Claudio said, "because Italians are Wops. And I don't want to be a Wop."

The first few weeks of school passed quickly. She was busy with marking papers, remembering names, preparing a five-minute skit in Italian to be performed for the school. I must do something about Peppi, Rosalba thought, just as soon as I'm more settled. She became aware that Claudio had started to speak English to her at home. At first, he began with a sentence here and there that she asked him to repeat in Italian, as if she couldn't understand.

Two months into the school year, Claudio announced, "I'm not going to speak Italian at home any more."

Rosalba pleaded with him (in Italian), "You'll forget the language," she said. Then, "If your father were alive, he'd be heartbroken."

But Claudio was obstinate. "I don't want to," he said. "What's the use of it, anyway? Nobody in my school speaks Italian."

And Rosalba went to bed feeling guilty and thought about what Giulio would have done in this case. Giulio would have enrolled the boy in a school in the Italian district, where he would be with other Italian children. Each day, he grew more Canadian. And she was afraid to draw him back, to make him live a life he'd never known. She noticed that her students at school were distressed, secretive, trying to cope with the mixture of cultures—their survival dependent on the separation rather than the integration of the two. Was it fair, she thought, to force them to abide by rules that made no sense here, rules which had been implemented for a different culture in a different time?

What startled her the most was that the majority of the Italians she'd met adhered to strict oppressive customs to which she had not been exposed even in Italy. They had brought with them a culture several decades old. Things changed, times changed even in Italy, but these people insisted on remaining the same. "If you stand still, you go backward." She'd read that somewhere, and now the words appeared to make much more sense.

Rosalba asked Peppi to come and see her after school.

"I'll have to phone my brother and tell him what time to pick me up."

"I'll call him," Rosalba said, "and tell him not to come."

He looked at her doubtfully. "Oh, he'll come anyway."

Peppi arrived at 4:00 p.m., after the school halls had thinned out. He stood at her desk and when she told him to sit down, he reluctantly did so. She thought that if he could have managed it, he would have run out of the room, so much did he resemble a trapped animal.

She stared at the papers on her desk and tried to find opening words. "Peppi," she finally began. "I had a talk with Mrs. Crombie."

"It's about the wheelchair, isn't it? Why does everyone talk behind my back?"

"No one is talking behind your back. We're all very concerned about you. Your parents—"

"I'm tired of their concern." His voice rose in pitch. "They always decide everything for me. Nobody asks me what I want."

She stared at him for a moment, then asked softly, "What do *you* want, then?"

"I want to—be myself," he said. "I want to do things myself. They treat me like I can't even think."

"Maybe they're trying to do what's best for you." She paused. "If you can think for yourself, then surely you must realize that a wheelchair would help you tremendously."

"I can manage just fine on my own."

She said nothing, waiting, noting the tremor in his words.

"And besides, if I get the stupid wheelchair, they'll never let me out of their sight. I don't want it!"

"You know," Rosalba said after a moment. "It might not be at all how you think. With a wheelchair, you'd be able to get around on your own a lot easier. For instance, you wouldn't need anyone to take you to or from school."

"Oh sure. As if they'd let me go alone." He sat, quiet, staring at his hands. "I'm not even allowed to go to a movie by myself. Not unless Papa drives me. It's *embarrassing*. Being watched all the time. If it wasn't for the law here, I bet I wouldn't even be allowed to go to school; they'd keep me at home always."

"Do you want me to talk to them?" she asked.

He shrugged. "I don't think it would do any good."

A few days later, Rosalba called Peppi's parents and asked them to come to the school to speak to her. She distinctly said she wanted to see them both.

They came a little past six. She'd asked the babysitter to stay late, even though Claudio had insisted that he was old enough to be left alone for a few hours. Mr. Armano was short and round and Rosalba could see that the boy's beauty came from his mother. She was dressed much older than her years. She could not have been much more than thirty, yet she carried herself like an old woman. Her hair was smoothed back into a bun at the nape of her neck, tight and shiny, making her eyes—Peppi's eyes—appear even larger and rounder than they were. Mrs. Armano kept wringing her hands. "Is something wrong?" Mr. Armano said in English as soon as he walked into the room. "Peppi did something bad? We teach him in the house. We give him the manners—"

"No," Rosalba interrupted, and spoke in Italian. "He's done nothing wrong. He's a very good student."

The Armanos looked at her, puzzled. "Then why did you want us to come if there's nothing wrong?"

Rosalba made them sit in two of the desks of the classroom. She explained to them that Peppi was growing up, that he needed to spend time with people his own age. She asked them why Peppi had not come to see the film with the class.

Mrs. Armano clenched and unclenched her hands on her lap. "He's sick," she said.

"He has a *physical* disability," Rosalba said more sharply than she'd meant to, "but this doesn't mean he can't do a lot of things other boys his age do."

Mrs. Armano looked away. "But he might hurt himself—"

"Mrs. Armano, it's part of growing up. You know that. You've raised another boy."

"Yes, but Peppi is different," she said solemnly.

"Perhaps you're trying to keep him different," Rosalba concluded.

And that night, after she tucked Claudio into bed, she thought about the Armanos, about the fine line between protectiveness and suffocation, about Peppi's symbolic stand against it. She heard Claudio's voice a few days earlier:

"Mamma, don't hold my hand when we're out."

"But why not?"

"I'm too old and Jimmy says only babies hold their mother's hand."

She had told him about her family—her brothers and sisters—and how they still held hands even as adults. But he'd slipped his fingers out of hers as she talked and hooked them into the opening of his pocket. Claudio becoming more Canadian—was she, too, trying to keep him different?

She acted as mediator between Peppi and his parents, spoke to them twice more over the next month, and was finally able to convince them to agree to a compromise: they would allow Peppi to come to school alone if he used the wheelchair. It was only a small concession, but for Peppi, the first triumph of a new independence.

She watched him anxiously that first day, his hands caressing the chrome of the large new wheels. He smiled shyly at her at the end of the day, when he left her classroom with the other teens.

She sat at her desk, long after they'd all gone, and thought about Claudio and herself. She too was trying to do what was best for him. She thought of Giulio, his smile there in Trieste. He'd preserved laughter and bittersweet memories like pressed flowers of intense moments with his family and friends. He had not been rigid. He had embraced the new way of life and enriched it with the old. Rosalba remained in her classroom, thinking, until the janitor asked her to leave so he could lock up the school.

When she arrived home, she saw Claudio sitting at his little table, drawing a picture for her. "I missed you," he said in Italian and buried his face in her skirt. "I missed you too, Claudio," she answered in English. Then she took him onto her lap and told him stories of Italy.

TOPICS FOR EXPLORATION

1. Why does Rosalba's protection of her Italian memories seem meaningless to her son Claudio? Why does she want to keep him from being Canadian? What are the "subtle changes" that Claudio undergoes in becoming more Canadian?

2. Myrna Kostash defines the immigrant nostalgia as "that melancholic yearning for the unrecoverable." In what sense is Rosalba afflicted by nostalgia? What similarities and differences does she find between Vancouver and Trieste?

3. What conflicts over the use of the mother tongue may appear in immigrant families? What difficulties in maintaining the mother tongue are highlighted by the story?

4. Why does Rosalba think her accent makes her sound "stupid"? Why does Mrs. Crombie mass different individuals from one culture "under one umbrella"? Prejudice and stereotyping arise out of ignorance. How do stereotypes originate?

5. Why does Rosalba doubt the validity of imposing rules "implemented for a different culture in a different time"? Why does she panic "among icons and idols"? Why might some immigrants to Canada enforce rules not even valid in their homelands today?

6. How does the part of the plot involving Peppi's oppression by his parents contribute to the unity of the story? Does Rosalba learn from this experience something that helps her settle her own problems with Claudio?

Garry Engkent

Garry Engkent was born in Sun Wui county of the Chinese province Guangdong, and immigrated to Canada in the 1950s. He completed his Ph.D. in English at the University of Toronto, where he now teaches creative writing and English literature. He is also working on a novel to be called A Chinaman's Chance. *"Why My Mother Can't Speak English" was first published in the anthology of Chinese-Canadian writing* Many-Mouthed Birds *in 1991.*

Why My Mother Can't Speak English

My mother is seventy years old. Widowed for five years now, she lives alone in her own house except for the occasions when I come home to tidy her household affairs. She has been in *gum san*, the golden mountain, for the past thirty years. She clings to the old-country ways so much so that today she astonishes me with this announcement:

"I want to get my citizenship," she says as she slaps down the *Dai Pao*, "before they come and take away my house."

"Nobody's going to do that. This is Canada."

"So everyone says," she retorts, "but did you read what the *Dai Pao* said? Ah, you can't read Chinese. The government is cutting back on old-age pensions. Anybody who hasn't got citizenship will lose everything. Or worse."

"The *Dai Pao* can't even typeset accurately," I tell her. Sometimes I worry about the information Mother receives from that biweekly community newspaper. "Don't worry—the Ministry of Immigration won't send you back to China."

"Little you know," she snaps back. "I am old, helpless, and without citizenship. Reasons enough. Now, get me citizenship. Hurry!"

"Mother, getting citizenship papers is not like going to the bank to cash in your pension cheque. First, you have to—"

"Excuses, my son, excuses. When your father was alive—"

"Oh, Mother, not again! You throw that at me every—"

"—made excuses, too." Her jaw tightens. "If you can't do this little thing for your own mother, well, I will just have to go and beg your cousin to ..."

Every time I try to explain about the ways of the *fan gwei*, she thinks I do not want to help her.

"I'll do it, I'll do it, okay? Just give me some time."

"That's easy for you," Mother snorts. "You're not seventy years old. You're not going to lose your pension. You're not going to lose your house. Now, how much *lai-shi* will this take?"

After all these years in *gum san* she cannot understand that you don't give government officials *lai-shi*, the traditional Chinese money gift to persons who do things for you.

"That won't be necessary," I tell her. "And you needn't go to my cousin."

Mother picks up the *Dai Pao* again and says: "Why should I beg at the door of a village cousin when I have a son who is a university graduate?"

I wish my father were alive. Then he would be doing this. But he is not here, and as a dutiful son, I am responsible for the welfare of my widowed mother. So I take her to Citizenship Court.

There are several people from the Chinese community waiting there. Mother knows a few of the Chinese women and she chats with them. My cousin is there, too.

"I thought your mother already got her citizenship," he says to me. "Didn't your father—"

"No, he didn't."

He shakes his head sadly. "Still, better now than never. That's why I'm getting these people through."

"So they've been reading the *Dai Pao*."

He gives me a quizzical look, so I explain to him, and he laughs.

"You are the new generation," he says. "You didn't live long enough in *hon san*, the sweet land, to understand the fears of the old. You can't expect the elderly to renounce all attachments to China for the ways of the *fan gwei*, white devils. How old is she, seventy now? Much harder."

"She woke me up this morning at six, and Citizenship Court doesn't open until ten."

The doors of the court finally open, and Mother motions me to hurry. We wait in line for a while.

The clerk distributes applications and tells me the requirements. Mother wants to know what the clerk is saying, so half the time I translate for her.

The clerk suggests that we see one of the liaison officers.

"Your mother has been living in Canada for the past thirty years and she still can't speak English?"

"It happens," I tell the liaison officer.

"I find it hard to believe that—not one word?"

"Well, she understands some restaurant English," I tell her. "You know, French fries, pork chops, soup, and so on. And she can say a few words."

"But will she be able to understand the judge's questions? The interview with the judge, as you know, is an important part of the citizenship procedure. Can she read the booklet? What does she know about Canada?"

"So you don't think my mother has a chance?"

"The requirements are that the candidate must be able to speak either French or English, the two official languages of Canada. The candidate must be able to pass an oral interview with the citizenship judge, and then he or she must be able to recite the oath of allegiance—"

"My mother needs to speak English," I conclude for her.

"Look, I don't mean to be rude, but why didn't your mother learn English when she first came over?"

I have not been translating this conversation, and Mother, annoyed and agitated, asks me what is going on. I tell her there is a slight problem.

"What problem?" Mother opens her purse, and I see her taking a small red envelope—*lai-shi*—I quickly cover her hand.

"What's going on?" the liaison officer demands.

"Nothing," I say hurriedly. "Just a cultural misunderstanding. I assure you."

My mother rattles off some indignant words, and I snap back in Chinese: "Put that away! The woman won't understand, and we'll be in a lot of trouble."

The officer looks confused, and I realize that an explanation is needed.

"My mother was about to give you a money gift as a token of appreciation for what you are doing for us. I was afraid you might misconstrue it as a bribe. We have no intention of doing that."

"I'm relieved to hear it."

We conclude the interview, and I take Mother home. Still clutching the application, Mother scowls at me.

"I didn't get my citizenship papers. Now I will lose my old-age pension. The government will ship me back to China. My old bones will lie there while your father's will be here. What will happen to me?"

How can I teach her to speak the language when she is too old to learn, too old to want to learn? She resists anything that is *fan gwei*. She does everything the Chinese way. Mother spends much time staring blankly at the four walls of her house. She does not cry. She sighs and shakes her head. Sometimes she goes about the house touching her favourite things.

"This is all your dead father's fault," she says quietly. She turns to the photograph of my father on the mantel. Daily, she burns incense, pours fresh cups of fragrant tea, and spreads dishes of his favourite fruits in front of the framed picture as is the custom. In memory of his passing, she treks two miles to the cemetery to place flowers by his headstone, to burn ceremonial paper money, and to talk to him. Regularly, rain or shine, or even snow, she does these things. Such love, such devotion, now such vehemence. Mother curses my father, her husband, in his grave.

When my mother and I emigrated from China, she was forty years old, and I, five. My father was already a well-established restaurant owner. He put me in school and Mother in the restaurant kitchen, washing dishes and cooking strange foods like hot dogs, hamburgers, and French fries. She worked seven days a week from six in the morning until eleven at night. This lasted for twenty-five years, almost to the day of my father's death.

The years were hard on her. The black-and-white photographs show a robust woman; now I see a withered, frail, white-haired old woman, angry, frustrated with the years, and scared of losing what little material wealth she has to show for the toil in *gum san*.

"I begged him," Mother says. "But he would either ignore my pleas or say: 'What do you need to know English for? You're better off here in the kitchen. Here you can talk to the others in our own tongue. English is far too complicated for you. How old are you now? Too old to learn a new language. Let the young speak *fan gwei*. All you need is to understand the orders from the waitresses. Anyway, if you need to know something, the men will translate for you. I am here; I can do your talking for you.'"

As a conscientious boss of the young male immigrants, my father would force them out of the kitchen and into the dining room. "The kitchen is no place for you to learn English. All you do is speak Chinese in here. To survive in *gum san*, you have to speak English, and the only way you can do that is to wait on tables and force yourselves to speak English with the customers. How can you get your families over here if you can't talk to the immigration officers in English?"

A few of the husbands who had the good fortune to bring their wives over to Canada hired a retired school teacher to teach a bit of English to their wives. Father discouraged Mother from going to those once-a-week sessions.

"That old woman will get rich doing nothing. What have these women learned? *Fan gwei* ways—make-up, lipstick, smelly perfumes, fancy clothes—like whores. Once she gets through with them, they won't be Chinese women any more—and they certainly won't be white either."

Some of the husbands heeded the words of the boss, for he was older than they, and he had been in the white devils' land longer. These wives stayed home and tended the children, or they worked in the restaurant kitchen, washing dishes and cooking *fan gwei* foods, and talking in Chinese about the land and the life they had been forced to leave behind.

"He was afraid that I would leave him. I depended on him for everything. I could not go anywhere by myself. He drove me to work and he drove me home. He only taught me how to print my name so that I could sign anything he wanted me to, bank cheques, legal documents . . ."

Perhaps I am not Chinese enough any more to understand why my mother would want to take in the sorrow, the pain, and the anguish, and then to recount them every so often.

Once, I was presumptuous enough to ask her why she would want to remember in such detail. She said that the memories didn't hurt any more. I did not tell her that her reminiscences cut me to the quick. Her only solace now is to be listened to.

My father wanted more sons, but she was too old to give him more. One son was not enough security he needed for old age. "You smell of stale perfume," she would say to him after he had driven the waitresses home. Or, to me, she would say: "A second mother will not treat you so well, you know," and, "Would you like another mother at home?" Even at that tender age, I knew that in China a husband could take a second wife. I told her that I didn't need another mother, and she would nod her head.

When my father died five years ago, she cried and cried. "Don't leave me in this world. Let me die with you."

Grief-stricken, she would not eat for days. She was so weak from hunger that I feared she wouldn't be able to attend the funeral. At his grave side, she chanted over and over a dirge, commending his spirit to the next world and begging the goddess of mercy to be kind to him. By custom, she set his picture on the mantel and burned incense in front of it daily. And we would go to the cemetery often. There she would arrange fresh flowers and talk to him in the gentlest way.

Often she would warn me: "The world of the golden mountain is so strange, *fan gwei* improprieties, and customs. The white devils will have you abandon your own aged mother to some old-age home to rot away and die unmourned. If you are here long enough, they will turn your head until you don't know who you are—Chinese."

My mother would convert the months and the days into the Chinese lunar calendar. She would tell me about the seasons and the harvests and festivals in China. We did not celebrate any *fan gwei* holidays.

My mother sits here at the table, fingering the booklet from the Citizenship Court. For thirty-some years, my mother did not learn the English language, not because she was not smart enough, not because she was too old to learn, and not because my father forbade her, but because she feared that learning English would change her Chinese soul. She only learned enough English to survive in the restaurant kitchen.

Now, Mother wants *gum san* citizenship.

"Is there no hope that I will be given it?" she asks.

"There's always a chance," I tell her. "I'll hand in the application."

"I should have given that person the *lai-shi*," Mother says obstinately.

"Maybe I should teach you some English," I retort. "You have about six months before the oral interview."

"I am seventy years old," she says. "*Lai-shi* is definitely much easier."

My brief glimpse into Mother's heart is over, and it has taken so long to come about. I do not know whether I understand my aged mother any better now. Despite my mother's constant instruction, there is too much *fan gwei* in me.

The booklet from the Citizenship Court lies, unmoved, on the table, gathering dust for weeks. She has not mentioned citizenship again with the urgency of that particular time. Once in a while, she would say: "They have forgotten me. I told you they don't want old Chinese women as citizens."

Finally, her interview date is set. I try to teach her some ready-made phrases, but she forgets them.

"You should not sigh so much. It is bad for your health," Mother observes.

On the day of her examination, I accompany her into the judge's chamber. I am more nervous than my mother.

Staring at the judge, my mother remarks: "*Noi yren.*" The judge shows interest in what my mother says, and I translate it: "She says you're a woman."

The judge smiles. "Yes. Is that strange?"

"If she is going to examine me," Mother tells me, "I might as well start packing for China. Sell my house. Dig up your father's bones, and I'll take them back with me."

Without knowing what my mother said, the judge reassures her. "This is just a formality. Really. We know that you obviously want to be part of our Canadian society. Why else would you go through all this trouble? We want to welcome you as a new citizen, no matter what race, nationality, religion, or age. And we want you to be proud—as a new Canadian."

Six weeks have passed since the interview with the judge. Mother receives a registered letter telling her to come in three weeks' time to take part in the oath of allegiance ceremony.

With patient help from the same judge, my mother recites the oath and becomes a Canadian citizen after thirty years in *gum san*.

"How does it feel to be a Canadian?" I ask.

"In China, this is the eighth month, the season of harvest." Then she adds: "The *Dai Pao* says that the old-age pension cheques will be increased by nine dollars next month."

As we walk home on this bright autumn morning, my mother clutches her piece of paper. Citizenship. She says she will go up to the cemetery and talk to my father this afternoon. She has something to tell him.

TOPICS FOR EXPLORATION

1. Whom does Garry Engkent have in mind as his readers? What is his purpose in using Chinese words and expressions in a story written in English? Does the English-speaking reader feel left out?

2. The narrator can't read Chinese; his mother can't speak or read English. How does this inhibit their ability to relate to each other? Characterize the narrator's attitude to his mother.

3. In what way does the story illustrate that being cut off from the language of the other in the encounter between Canadians and Chinese immigrants may lead to cultural misunderstandings on both sides? How do the mother's old attitudes continue to colour her experience and expectations in Canada?

4. For what reasons has the narrator's mother not learned English? Why did his father discourage her from doing so? Why does she fear that "learning English would change her Chinese soul"?

5. Comment on the narrator's statement that he is "not Chinese enough any more" to justify both his father's double standards for men and women and his mother's stubborn refusal to learn English.

6. What requirements are necessary in order to become a Canadian citizen? Are they valid? Does language, in the final analysis, act as a hindrance to citizenship for the narrator's mother? Why not?

Lucy Fazio

Lucy Fazio lives in Pointe Claire, Quebec, and she is a doctoral student at McGill University, studying education in second languages. She came to Canada from Europe in 1953 with her family. Her essay printed here first appeared in the Montreal Gazette *in 1994.*

An Immigrant Child Remembers

It is for me, still today, 40 years later, a bittersweet memory but at least one which I no longer flinch from recalling or recounting.

My family represents a contributing statistic to the Canadian post-war expansion and immigration boom that was recorded in Canada between 1946 and 1961. Like the bulk of the newcomers, my parents were Europeans who had been devastated by a long and painful world war.

They wished to start anew, to leave an economically unstable land and to seek solace and security in a friendly, healing place. And so it was that in September 1953 my mother, my sisters and I left Italy, and after a week-long journey on an ocean liner, we disembarked in Halifax.

From there we boarded a train that would take a day and a night to arrive in Toronto. This was the designated meeting place where my father, who had already been in Canada for two years, would meet us and drive us to our final destination: Windsor.

Of that entire 10-day span, I remember two things most vividly: first, severe bouts of nausea both on the boat and the train; and second, my first encounter with "English" bread—every slice was uniform in shape and size and by squeezing one in your hand you could actually form it back into dough. After seeing and eating only irregularly shaped, substantive homemade bread for the first six years of my life, this was incredible!

Little did I know that the culture shock had just begun.

Within a few days of our arrival, my older sister and I were dutifully marched off to school. I remember being excited at the prospect of going to school because the kindergarten I had completed in Italy had been an enjoyable experience. My sister and I were marshalled into a classroom where the teacher pointed to two desks and indicated that we were to sit down. She then took her place at the head of the class and began to teach and speak as she wrote on the blackboard. The other children participated in the lesson as the two of us sat obediently and dumbfoundedly in total silence for that morning and many more mornings to come.

At the end of our first day, the teacher presented us with identical books. I remember my book so clearly. It had the dimensions and appearance of a pocket dictionary—the same small print, wafer-thin pages and black and white presentation of material. The contents of the book consisted of what I know today to be verb conjugations, formulaic language and stick figures for the purpose of illustrations. These were the only tools the teacher had to offer us as support in learning a second language. They meant nothing to me. I had no understanding of those strange pages and stick figures just as I had no understanding of the unfamiliar words that kept tumbling out of the teacher's mouth. The result of this submersion into a new country, culture and language was confusion, feelings of alienation, and worst of all—fear.

I was most fearful of losing my voice. I sat there day in and day out but I could not speak. And at times a panic would overtake me and I would convince myself that now, for sure, I had lost my faculty of speech. I would have to check. So I began to make guttural noises and semi-coughing sounds that would reassure me at least temporarily that I did still have my voice.

The teacher must have understood the motive behind my peculiar actions because she never once scolded me or manifested outward anger at my rather frequent disruptive behavior. She was a marvelous lady who lacked the organizational framework and expertise to actively facilitate my second language learning but who, amid the sea of loneliness and bewilderment of those first days, was a beacon of compassion and understanding.

That I can write this article today is testimony to the fact that eventually I did learn to speak, read, and write the English language. The model under which I learned could best be characterized as "sink or swim." Fortunately for me I swam, even though there was no special provision to facilitate my acquisition of the new language. The supposition in those days was that I and all immigrant children could and would learn by exposure to native speakers and through osmosis. And it is true that in time that is exactly what happened.

But I will always remember the process as one that relegates the language-bound immigrant child to the role of tongue-tied, neglected and fearful nonentity in the classroom.

TOPICS FOR EXPLORATION

1. Why did the author's family leave Italy? What were her first vivid memories of Canada?

2. How were Lucy and her sister treated on their first day at school? What tools did the teacher give them to help them learn English? Were these tools helpful?

3. Why did Lucy begin making noises and sounds in class? How did the teacher react to Lucy's behaviour?

4. How does Lucy Fazio evaluate her teacher's qualifications from her perspective today?

5. Is the "sink or swim" method of learning a language described by Lucy Fazio effective? What are positive and negative aspects of total immersion?

Karim H. Karim

Karim H. Karim is a Canadian correspondent for the Luxembourg-based Compass News Features and a doctoral candidate at McGill University. He has published several articles on the issues related to language and communications. The selection reprinted here originally appeared in Language and Society *in 1989.*

Multiculturalism in Public Discourse

A society's distinctive features are often to be found in the particular nuances of the terms that it uses to describe itself. Canadians have not been slow to give new connotations to already existing terms nor to formulate original ones in articulating the conception of an officially bilingual and multicultural country. "Mosaic", "official languages", "heritage languages", "language minorities", "visible minorities" are part of the terminology that is regularly employed in Canadian discussions about language and culture. However, as with much of public discourse, our glossary of linguistic and cultural differentiation lacks precision and at times clouds fundamental issues of national identity.

Administrative meanings
Meanings of terms formulated for administrative purposes are not always clear when used in broader public discussion. Some formulations that have gained currency through frequent bureaucratic and media usage probably manage to bewilder the uninitiated. For example, whereas "official languages" is self-explanatory, the term "heritage languages" appears to deny that other languages are parts of their respective speakers' heritages. In addition to the official categories of Anglophones and Francophones, Quebec has the semi-official designation of "Allophones", those who—in federal parlance—speak "heritage languages". Such terminology appears to emanate from the debate regarding the place of language in culture—left

unresolved in the national compromise of "multiculturalism within a bilingual framework".

"Mosaic" and "multiculturalism", favoured over the American "melting pot", emphasize the coexistence of the various cultural groups residing in this country. The Multiculturalism Act proclaims that "multiculturalism is a fundamental characteristic of the Canadian heritage and identity". But public discourse generally limits the term to describing only part of the nation's citizenry in adherence to a tripartite image of a Canada consisting of the British-French majority, the aboriginal population and the "multicultural community". The media habitually refer to gatherings including people such as Ukrainians, Greeks, Haitians and Indians as "multicultural events", but similar meetings of their Scottish, Welsh and French counterparts are rarely described in the same way. And in Quebec the designation "cultural communities" is officially reserved for those not of French, British or native ancestry. While such use of "multicultural" and "cultural" may facilitate reference to certain sections of the population, it also fosters the institutionalized separation of the mainstream from "les autres".

Ethnicity

"Ethnic" is another, more widely-used term for non-British, non-French or non-aboriginal persons. Although the anthropological definition of the word has to do with any human being's race and culture, its etymology indicates a long-standing purpose in marginalizing various groups. Professor Raymond Williams traces its origin to *ethnikós,* Greek for nation.

While "ethnic" is often substituted for "minority", "minority" does not always denote "ethnic". Public discourse occasionally includes natives among "minorities"; the official term for isolated Anglophone and Francophone communities is "language minorities"; and since the early 1980s "visible minorities" has denoted non-white, non-aboriginal Canadians. Interestingly, with the emergence of the latter term, "ethnic" is increasingly limited to referring to Europeans of non-British and non-French origins. On the other hand, "immigrants" has become almost synonymous with "visible minorities"—reflecting the increase in newcomers from Asia, the Caribbean and Latin America and their greater difficulty in integrating into the national mainstream.

Hazy definitions

The seeming indifference towards the haze surrounding public definitions of language and culture appears venturesome for a country that debates these issues with periodic intensity. Lacking clarity, the various terms are open to manipulation for temporary gains, leaving fundamental problems unresolved. Current usage ostensibly appears to deny Canadians of British, French and native backgrounds heritage, culture and ethnicity and, conversely, places undue emphasis on the other groups' collective identities in underplaying their respective members' individualities. The inconsistent and ambiguous use of words like "heritage", "culture", "ethnic" and "minority" impedes, conceptually and concretely, the "equitable participation of individuals and communities of all origins" in Canadian society envisioned by the Multiculturalism Act. It tends instead to place multiculturalism within a bicultural framework. While a home-grown vocabulary is critical to the exercise of national self-definition, Canadians should be wary of becoming entangled in the webs of words that we ourselves weave.

TOPICS FOR EXPLORATION

1. According to the author, what are the problems with the terms used in Canadian discussions about language and culture? Which terms lack consistency and precision? Why is the term "heritage languages" confusing?

2. What is a tripartite image of Canada as suggested by the term multiculturalism? On the basis of Karim's article, explain how the concept of multiculturalism can divide rather than unite the nation?

3. What is the origin of the word "ethnic"? How is this word currently used? What are the differences between such terms as "minority," "ethnic," and "immigrant"?

4. Does defining all these language terms increase our understanding of people and their culture? Why does the author think that it is important to untangle "the webs of words that we ourselves weave"?

SUGGESTIONS FOR FURTHER STUDY

1. Genni Gunn, Isabel Vincent (Unit Four), and Maara Haas (Unit Five) all address the problem faced by most immigrants, namely a threat the dominant culture poses to one's ethnic identity. Discuss different examples of separation (the "ghetto" mentality), assimilation, and integration (Gunn's "middle ground") as models of immigrant behaviour found in their narratives.

2. Compare the difficulties of expression in a new language as described by Eva Hoffman and Lucy Fazio. How are the problems they confront different? How do they both approach the challenge of overcoming "linguistic dispossession"?

3. Genni Gunn describes the difficulties of letting the past go and accepting the present. Compare Engkent and Gunn. What features of these two cultures, so different in outlook, do their stories have in common?

4. Engkent's narrator thinks he might not be "Chinese enough any more." Rosalba in Gunn's story fears the same change in her Italian self-image. On the basis of these two stories, identify different attitudes to language and culture held by different generations of immigrants.

5. Language is the focus of the author's reflection in both Karim H. Karim's essay and Eva Hoffman's autobiography. What different forms of linguistic complexity do they discuss respectively?

UNIT FOUR

GROWING UP: EDUCATION

INTRODUCTION

Education imposes the information that a culture believes is necessary for its own growth or survival. Institutions of education represent the authority that a dominant culture exercises and which citizens are taught to respect. Unfortunately, where there is power there are abuses, whether conscious or not. Often in the past, and sometimes still today, Canadian schools, rooted in white, Northern European cultural assumptions, could be seen as places of institutionalized racism. The missionary movement was based on such cultural assumptions.

Perhaps the Native peoples of Canada have suffered most from white domination in education. Too often, the values of Native culture have been denigrated, repressed, and lost. In Pauline Johnson's story, written almost a century ago, we see the double standards imposed by white missionaries upon the Native population and in particular on an impressionable Native girl who is betrayed by the missionary family she has trusted. Here the subjugation of Native spiritual values is further complicated by personal prejudices that provoke a violent retaliation. Johnson's fiction finds a later parallel in Carol Geddes's essay, where she describes the Teslin Tlingit people's way of life as it has been transformed by contact with a European wage-based economy and especially by education in residential schools. Only when Geddes attends university as an adult does she reverse the poor self-image inflicted upon her as a Native child by her Christian missionary teachers.

In the two short stories dealing with immigrant themes included in this Unit, the classroom is central. The characters are teachers and their students, who are immigrants or the children of immigrants. Clark Blaise tells the story of an American nightschool instructor in Montreal teaching English to an assortment of new Canadians whose naïve preconceptions and surprising ambitions frustrate and irritate him—particularly since he himself has come to distrust the values of American assimilation. Contact with these students is an ironic lesson for him, too.

Personal morality and the authority of the teacher often become confused. We see the subtleties of this confusion explored in Robyn Sarah's short story in which two Jewish girls—Esther whose father's job was to investigate anti-Semitic propaganda, and Rhoda, the daughter of Holocaust survivors who have succeeded in the West—consider the implications of a personal remark made in the classroom by their teacher. The remark is interpreted by Rhoda's parents as an anti-Semitic slur. The resultant doubt about intention and responsibility disturbs Esther and her understanding of the meaning of blame.

Isabel Vincent in her essay points to her school experience as one of the factors that have contributed to her gradual estrangement from her own roots. The assimilation of her Portuguese parents into the Canadian mainstream is incomplete, but Vincent has removed herself so far from her ethnic community in Toronto and "Canadianized" herself so thoroughly that she is once turned down for a newspaper job because, ironically, she is perceived as too "Anglo-Saxon."

No matter how the purpose of education is distorted and who might be scarred by its application, it has given to many—if only by provoking them to opposition—fruitful experience and the impulse to articulate it. The process of education is as complicated as the cultures that feed it.

Who Are You?

Wen net ki'l?
Pipanimit nuji-kina'muet ta'n jipalk.
Netakei, aqq i'-naqawey;
Koqoey?

Ktikik nuji-kina'masultite'wk
    kimelmultijik.
Na epa'si, taqawajitutm,
Aqq elui'tmasi
Na na'kwek.

Espi-kjijiteketes,
Ma'jipajita'siw.
Espitutmukewey kina'matnewey-
    iktuk eyk,
Aqq kinua'tuates pa'qalaiwaqann
    ni'n nikmaq.

Who are you?
Question from a teacher feared.
Blushing, I stammered
What?

Other students tittered
I sat down forlorn, dejected,
And made a vow
That day

To be great in all learnings,
No more uncertain.
My pride lives in my education,
And I will relate wonders
    to my people.

—*Rita Joe*

Rita Joe is a Mi'kmaq, born in 1932 in Whycocomagh, Nova Scotia. As a child, she was brought up by foster families. She lives on the Eskasoni Reserve in Cape Breton. She has raised eight children of her own, and adopted two more. She says that she writes always with children in mind, so that others may come to understand the right of her people to education and dignity. Her collections of poetry include Poems of Rita Joe *(1978),* Song of Eskasoni: More Poems of Rita Joe *(1988),* Inu and Indians We're Called *(1991), and* Song of Rita Joe: Autobiography of a Mi'kmaq Poet *(1996).*

Pauline Johnson

Pauline Johnson was born in 1861 on the Six Nations Reserve; she died in 1913. She was the daughter of George Johnson, a Mohawk chief, and an English mother. Her stories, poems, and essays were usually published in the United States, although her reputation in Canada and England was widespread and popular. Often romanticized for the taste of the reading public of her day, her narratives, nonetheless, have a realistic edge and authentically portray some of the conflicts emerging at the meeting point of Native and white societies. The following story was first published in The Moccasin Maker *(1913), a collection of articles and short stories.*

As It Was in the Beginning

They account for it by the fact that I am a Redskin, but I am something else, too—I am a woman.

I remember the first time I saw him. He came up the trail with some Hudson's Bay trappers, and they stopped at the door of my father's tepee. He seemed even then, fourteen years ago, an old man; his hair seemed just as thin and white, his hands just as trembling and fleshless as they were a month since, when I saw him for what I pray his God is the last time.

My father sat in the tepee, polishing buffalo horns and smoking; my mother, wrapped in her blanket, crouched over her quill-work, on the buffalo-skin at his side; I was lounging at the doorway, idling, watching, as I always watched, the thin, distant line of sky and prairie, wondering, as I always wondered, what lay beyond it. Then he came, this gentle old man with his white hair and thin, pale face. He wore a long black coat, which I now know was the sign of his office, and he carried a black leather-covered book, which, in all the years I have known him, I have never seen him without.

The trappers explained to my father who he was, the Great Teacher, the heart's Medicine Man, the "Blackcoat" we had heard of, who brought peace where there was war, and the magic of whose black book brought greater things than all the Happy Hunting Grounds of our ancestors.

He told us many things that day, for he could speak the Cree tongue, and my father listened, and listened, and when at last they left us, my father said for him to come and sit within the tepee again.

He came, all the time he came, and my father welcomed him, but my mother always sat in silence at work with the quills; my mother never liked the Great "Blackcoat."

His stories fascinated me. I used to listen intently to the tale of the strange new place he called "heaven," of the gold crown, of the white dress, of the great music; and then he would tell of that other strange place—hell. My father and I hated it; we feared it, we dreamt of it, we trembled at it. Oh, if the "Blackcoat" would only cease to talk of it! Now I know he saw the effect upon us, and he used it as a whip to lash us into his new religion, but even then my mother must have known, for each time he left the tepee she would watch him going slowly away across the prairie; then when he disappeared into the far horizon she would laugh scornfully, and say:

"If the white man made this Blackcoat's hell, let him go to it. It is for the man who found it first. No hell for Indians, just Happy Hunting Grounds. Blackcoat can't scare me."

And then, after weeks had passed, one day as he stood at the tepee door he laid his white, old hand on my head and said to my father: "Give me this little girl, chief. Let me take her to the mission school; let me keep her, and teach her of the great God and His eternal heaven. She will grow to be a noble woman, and return perhaps to bring her people to the Christ."

My mother's eyes snapped. "No," she said. It was the first word she ever spoke to the "Blackcoat." My father sat and smoked. At the end of a half-hour he said:

"I am an old man, Blackcoat. I shall not leave the God of my fathers. I like not your strange God's ways—all of them. I like not His two new places for me when I am dead. Take the child, Blackcoat, and save her from hell."

The first grief of my life was when we reached the mission. They took my buckskin dress off, saying I was now a little Christian girl and must dress like all the white people at the mission. Oh, how I hated that stiff new calico dress and those leather shoes! But, little as I was, I said nothing, only thought of the time when I should be grown, and do as my mother did, and wear the buckskins and the blanket.

My next serious grief was when I began to speak the English, that they forbade me to use any Cree words whatsoever. The rule of the school was that any child heard using its native tongue must get a slight punishment. I never understood it, I cannot understand it now, why the use of my dear Cree tongue could be a matter for correction or an action deserving punishment.

She was strict, the matron of the school, but only justly so, for she had a heart and a face like her brother's, the "Blackcoat." I had long since ceased to call him that. The trappers at the post called him "St. Paul," because, they told me, of his self-sacrificing life, his kindly deeds, his rarely beautiful old face; so I, too, called him "St. Paul," though oftener "Father Paul," though he never liked the latter title, for he was a Protestant. But as I was his pet, his darling of the whole school, he let me speak of him as I would, knowing it was but my heart speaking in love. His sister was a widow, and mother to a laughing yellow-haired little boy of about my age, who was my constant playmate and who taught me much of English in his own childish way. I used to be fond of this child, just as I was fond of his mother and of his uncle, my "Father Paul," but as my girlhood passed away, as womanhood came upon me, I got strangely wearied of them all; I longed, oh, God, how I longed for the old wild life! It came with my womanhood, with my years.

What mattered it to me now that they had taught me all their ways?—their tricks of dress, their reading, their writing, their books. What mattered it that "Father Paul" loved me, that the traders at the post called me pretty, that I was a pet of all, from the factor to the poorest trapper in the service? I wanted my own people, my own old life, my blood called out for it, but they always said I must not return to my father's tepee. I heard them talk amongst themselves of keeping me away from pagan influences; they told each other that if I returned to the prairies, the tepees, I would degenerate, slip back to paganism, as other girls had done; marry, perhaps, with a pagan—and all their years of labor and teaching would be lost.

I said nothing, but I waited. And then one night the feeling overcame me. I was in the Hudson's Bay store when an Indian came in from the north with a large pack of buckskin. As they unrolled it a dash of its insinuating odor filled the store. I went over and leaned above the skins a second, then buried my face in them, swallowing, drinking the fragrance of them, that went to my head like wine. Oh, the wild wonder of that wood-smoked tan, the subtlety of it, the untamed smell of it! I drank it into my lungs, my innermost being was saturated with it, till my mind reeled and my heart seemed twisted with a physical agony. My childhood recollections rushed upon me, devoured me. I left the store in a strange, calm frenzy, and going rapidly to the mission house I confronted my Father Paul and demanded to be allowed to go "home," if only for a day. He received the request with the same refusal and the same gentle sigh that I had too often been greeted with, but *this* time the desire, the smoke-tan, the heart-ache, never lessened.

Night after night I would steal away by myself and go to the border of the village to watch the sun set in the foothills, to gaze at the far line of sky and prairie, to long and long for my father's lodge. And Laurence—always Laurence—my fair-haired, laughing, child playmate, would come calling and calling for me: "Esther, where are you? We miss you: come in, Esther, come in with me." And if I did not turn at once to him and follow, he would come and place his strong hands on my shoulders and laugh into my eyes and say, "Truant, truant, Esther; can't *we* make you happy?"

My old child playmate had vanished years ago. He was a tall, slender young man now, handsome as a young chief, but with laughing blue eyes, and always those yellow curls about his temples. He was my solace in my half-exile, my comrade, my brother, until one night it was, "Esther, Esther, can't *I* make you happy?"

I did not answer him; only looked out across the plains and thought of the tepees. He came close, close. He locked his arms about me, and with my face pressed up to his throat he stood silent. I felt the blood from my heart sweep to my very finger-tips. I loved him. Oh God, how I loved him! In a wild, blind instant it all came, just because he held me so and was whispering brokenly, "Don't leave me, don't leave me, Esther; *my* Esther, my child-love, my playmate, my girl-comrade, my little Cree sweetheart, will you go away to your people, or stay, stay for me, for my arms, as I have you now?"

No more, no more the tepees; no more the wild stretch of prairie, the intoxicating fragrance of the smoke-tanned buckskin; no more the bed of buffalo hide, the soft, silent moccasin; no more the dark faces of my people, the dulcet cadence of the sweet Cree tongue—only this man, this fair, proud, tender man who held me in his arms, in his heart. My soul prayed to his great white God, in that moment, that He let me have only this.

It was twilight when we re-entered the mission gate. We were both excited, feverish. Father Paul was reading evening prayers in the large room beyond the hallway; his soft, saint-like voice stole beyond the doors, like a benediction upon us. I went noiselessly upstairs to my own room and sat there undisturbed for hours.

The clock downstairs struck one, startling me from my dreams of happiness, and at the same moment a flash of light attracted me. My room was in an angle of the building, and my window looked almost directly down into those of Father Paul's study, into which at that instant he was entering, carrying a lamp. "Why, Laurence," I heard him exclaim, "what are you doing here? I thought, my boy, you were in bed hours ago."

"No, uncle, not in bed, but in dreamland," replied Laurence, arising from the window, where evidently he, too, had spent the night hours as I had done.

Father Paul fumbled about for a moment, found his large black book, which for once he seemed to have got separated from, and was turning to leave, when the curious circumstance of Laurence being there at so unusual an hour seemed to strike him anew. "Better go to sleep, my son," he said simply, then added curiously, "Has anything occurred to keep you up?"

Then Laurence spoke: "No, uncle, only—only, I'm happy, that's all."

Father Paul stood irresolute: Then: "It is—?"

"Esther," said Laurence quietly, but he was at the old man's side, his hand was on the bent old shoulder, his eyes proud and appealing.

Father Paul set the lamp on the table, but, as usual, one hand held that black book, the great text of his life. His face was paler than I had ever seen it—graver.

"Tell of it," he requested.

I leaned far out of my window and watched them both. I listened with my very heart, for Laurence was telling him of me, of his love, of the new-found joy of that night.

"You have said nothing of marriage to her?" asked Father Paul.

"Well—no; but she surely understands that—"

"Did you speak of *marriage?*" repeated Father Paul, with a harsh ring in his voice that was new to me.

"No, uncle, but—"

"Very well, then; very well."

There was a brief silence. Laurence stood staring at the old man as though he were a stranger; he watched him push a large chair up to the table, slowly seat himself; then mechanically following his movements, he dropped onto a lounge. The old man's head bent low, but his eyes were bright and strangely fascinating. He began:

"Laurence, my boy, your future is the dearest thing to me of all earthly interests. Why, you *can't* marry this girl—no, no, sit, sit until I have finished," he added, with raised voice, as Laurence sprang up, remonstrating. "I have long since decided that you marry well; for instance, the Hudson's Bay factor's daughter."

Laurence broke into a fresh, rollicking laugh. "What, uncle," he said, "little Ida McIntosh? Marry that little yellow-haired fluff ball, that kitten, that pretty little dolly?"

"Stop," said Father Paul. Then, with a low, soft persuasiveness, "She is *white*, Laurence."

My lover startled. "Why, uncle, what do you mean?" he faltered.

"Only this, my son: poor Esther comes of uncertain blood; would it do for you—the missionary's nephew, and adopted son, you might say—to marry the daughter of a pagan Indian? Her mother is hopelessly uncivilized; her father has a dash of French somewhere—half-breed, you know, my boy, half-breed." Then, with still lower tone and half-shut, crafty eyes, he added: "The blood is a bad, bad mixture, *you* know that; you know, too, that I am very fond of the girl, poor dear Esther. I have tried to separate her from evil pagan influences; she is the daughter of the Church; I want her to have no other parent; but you never can tell what lurks in *a caged animal that has once been wild*. My whole heart is with the Indian people, my son; my whole heart, my whole life, has been devoted to bringing them to Christ, *but it is a different thing to marry with one of them.*"

His small old eyes were riveted on Laurence like a hawk's on a rat. My heart lay like ice in my bosom.

Laurence, speechless and white, stared at him breathlessly.

"Go away somewhere," the old man was urging, "to Winnipeg, Toronto, Montreal; forget her, then come back to Ida McIntosh. A union of the Church and the Hudson's Bay will mean great things, and may ultimately result in my life's ambition, the civilization of this entire tribe, that we have worked so long to bring to God."

I listened, sitting like one frozen. Could those words have been uttered by my venerable teacher, by him whom I revered as I would one of the saints in his own black book? Ah, there was no mistaking it. My white father, my life-long friend who pretended to love me, to care for my happiness, was urging the man I worshipped to forget me, to marry with the factor's daughter—because of what? Of my red skin; my good, old, honest pagan mother; my confiding French-Indian father. In a second all the care, the hollow love he had given me since my childhood, were as things that never existed. I hated that old mission priest as I hated his white man's hell. I hated his long, white hair; I hated his thin, white hands; I hated his body, his soul, his voice, his black book—oh, how I hated the very atmosphere of him!

Laurence sat motionless, his face buried in his hands, but the old man continued: "No, no; not the child of that pagan mother; you can't trust her, my son. What would you do with a wife who might any day break from you to return to her prairies and her buckskins? *You can't trust her.*" His eyes grew smaller, more glittering, more fascinating then, and leaning with an odd, secret sort of movement towards Laurence, he almost whispered. "Think of her silent ways, her noiseless step; the girl glides about like an apparition; her quick fingers, her wild longings—I don't know why, but with all my fondness for her, she reminds me sometimes of a strange—*snake*."

Laurence shuddered, lifted his face, and said hoarsely: "You're right, uncle; perhaps I'd better not; I'll go away, I'll forget her, and then—well, then—yes, you are right, it *is* a different thing to marry one of them." The old man arose. His feeble fingers still clasped his black book; his soft white hair clung about his forehead like that of an Apostle; his eyes lost their peering, crafty expression; his bent shoulders resumed the dignity of a minister of the living God; he was the picture of what the traders called him—"St. Paul."

"Good-night, son," he said.

"Good-night, uncle, and thank you for bringing me to myself."

They were the last words I ever heard uttered by either that old arch-fiend or his weak, miserable kinsman. Father Paul turned and left the room. I watched his withered hand—the hand I had so often felt resting on my head in holy benediction—clasp the doorknob, turn it slowly then, with bowed head and his pale face rapt in thought, he left the room—left it with the mad venom of my hate pursuing him like the very Evil One he taught me of.

What were his years of kindness and care now? What did I care for his God, his heaven, his hell? He had robbed me of my native faith, of my parents, of my people, of this last, this life of love that would have made a great, good woman of me. God! How I hated him!

I crept to the closet in my dark little room. I felt for a bundle I had not looked at for years—yes, it was there, the buckskin dress I had worn as a little child when they brought me to the mission. I tucked it under my arm and descended the stairs noiselessly. I would look into the study and speak good-bye to Laurence; then I would—

I pushed open the door. He was lying on the couch where a short time previously he had sat, white and speechless, listening to Father Paul. I moved towards him softly. God in heaven, he was already asleep. As I bent over him the fullness of his perfect beauty impressed me for the first time; his slender form, his curving mouth that almost laughed even in sleep, his fair, tossed hair, his smooth, strong-pulsing throat. God! How I loved him!

Then there arose the picture of the factor's daughter. I hated her. I hated her baby face, her yellow hair, her whitish skin. "She shall not marry him," my soul said. "I will kill him first—kill his beautiful body, his lying, false heart." Something in my heart seemed to speak;

it said over and over again, "Kill him, kill him; she will never have him then. Kill him. It will break Father Paul's heart and blight his life. He has killed the best of you, of your womanhood; kill *his* best, his pride, his hope—his sister's son, his nephew Laurence." But how? How?

What had that terrible old man said I was like? A *strange snake.* A snake? The idea wound itself about me like the very coils of a serpent. What was this in the beaded bag of my buckskin dress? this little thing rolled in tan that my mother had given me at parting with the words, "Don't touch much, but sometime maybe you want it!" Oh! I knew well enough what it was—a small flint arrow-head dipped in the venom of some *strange snake.*

I knelt beside him and laid my hot lips on his hand. I worshipped him, oh, how, how I worshipped him! Then again the vision of *her* baby face, *her* yellow hair—I scratched his wrist twice with the arrow-tip. A single drop of red blood oozed up; he stirred. I turned the lamp down and slipped out of the room—out of the house.

I dreamt nightly of the horrors of the white man's hell. Why did they teach me of it, only to fling me into it?

Last night as I crouched beside my mother on the buffalo-hide, Dan Henderson, the trapper, came in to smoke with my father. He said old Father Paul was bowed with grief, that with my disappearance I was suspected, but that there was no proof. Was it not merely a snake bite?

They account for it by the fact that I am a Redskin.

They seem to have forgotten I am a woman.

TOPICS FOR EXPLORATION

1. Whose point of view has Pauline Johnson used to tell her story? What effect does that have upon her narrative?

2. Discuss how the portrait of the missionary gradually unfolds in the story. How does the girl initially describe him? Why do the trappers call him "Saint Paul"? What does the missionary's behaviour reveal about him?

3. How has Johnson portrayed the incursion of missionaries into the Native community? How is the word "Blackcoat" symbolic of its sinister aspects? What steps did the missionaries use to dispossess the Cree children of their identity? What stereotypes were used to rationalize the "civilizing" mission?

4. Why does the girl's father allow her to be taken to the mission school? What does his reaction to the Blackcoat's Christian teachings reveal about the reception given to white men by Native people?

5. How is Laurence a victim of the missionary's double standard? Is Father Paul aware of his own hypocrisy? Why does he "distrust" Esther?

6. For Esther, what does the betrayal by white religion consist of? What lesson does she learn at the mission about being "a Redskin" and "a woman"?

7. Despite its indictment of Christian hypocrisy, the story relies heavily on Christian symbolism. What is the symbolic meaning of the "snake"? How appropriate is the allusion to the Garden of Eden in the story's title? Can it also be read as an allegory of betrayed trust in the relationship between Native people and whites?

Robyn Sarah

Robyn Sarah was born in 1949 and grew up in Montreal. She has published several collections of poetry, most recently The Touchstone: Poems New and Selected *(1992). "A Minor Incident" is taken from her first short story collection,* A Nice Gazebo *(1992).*

A Minor Incident

For a few years beginning around when I was twelve, my father worked for a Jewish organization, a branch of it devoted to fighting anti-Semitism. To his desk came samples of printed materials against which complaints had been lodged; he had to read these and decide what action, if any, need be taken—he was a sort of filter for hate literature. Sometimes he brought it home with him in the evenings. I remember a kind of pained face he'd have, like the face of someone who has been walking all day in shoes that are too tight, and whose feet have blistered; and he might call to me from his desk in the alcove, when I was doing my homework at the dining-room table: "Esther. Come here, I want you to see something. I want you to read this. Look, look what they say about us, terrible things ... look ..."

But I would not; instead I'd gather up my books without a word, and go to my room and shut the door, clenching and unclenching my hands; would he call me again? Would he insist? If he did, my mother might protest to him, in a low voice, in Yiddish which I did not understand; and he would reply audibly, in English, "She's old enough. She should see it. She should know."

I do not remember being told about the Holocaust, not when, nor by whom, though it must have been one of them my father or my mother, who told me, before it was called the Holocaust, before it had a name attached to it whereby it could be handled, contained, dismissed. I do know that only a few years elapsed between the times when, waking from nightmares, I was reassured that there were no wicked witches, that there weren't any monsters, that I didn't need to be afraid because there were no such things, they were just "made up"—and the time when I knew that men in uniforms, ordinary human beings, had dashed out the brains of babies against concrete walls before their mothers' eyes, and then shot the mothers dead; and that this was not a bad dream, not a made-up story, but was the truth and had really happened. Who could accept that and need to hear more? The one image contained the Holocaust for me; in it I felt my knowledge to be complete. The rest was numbers. Say it isn't true? Say it didn't happen *really*? No, it really happened. It happened over and over.

I know now, too, that the years when I lay awake in the dark, fearful of witches, were years when the full extent of the horror was still being uncovered; in our house, years of hushed conversations in Yiddish and rustling newspapers, radio babble, grownup talk behind closed doors. My grandmother was alive, then, and lived with us; I remember her room at the end of the hall, with a smell all its own that permeated everything in it, the maroon plush chair, the chenille bedspread, the patterned Indian rug. She had her own radio, an enormous one with a wicker front, on a shelf above the bed; she had hatboxes in the closet in which were hats of crumpled felt garnished with glazed wooden cherries, curled black plumes, pearl-tipped hat pins; in her closet, too, there hung old nylons stuffed at the bottom with cloves and dried orange peel; on her bureau was a glass bowl filled with rose petals. I remember that every once in a while, my mother would call her to the telephone in a tense, urgent tone, and with one hand to her heart she would go; the conversation that followed would be a trading of names, of people I did not know and of what I later realized were towns in Galicia; yes, she would say then, yes? No. No. No. And she would shake her head at my mother, who hovered listening. No. No. Her face would slacken, she would wish the caller good health in Yiddish, and good luck. "A different Charney," she would say, putting the phone down. "Not related." It was her brother she was hoping to hear from, or have news of. People with the same name, arriving in new cities, would do that then—look up the name in the telephone book, call each listing, seeking family connection, word of relatives. They would look up every spelling. Calls came to us from Charneys, Cherneys, Chierneys. To no avail.

Years passed before I understood the significance of those phone calls. That Gran hoped to hear from her brother, yes; but not why; not what might have become of him, what was more likely with each passing day to have become of him. Years, before I realized what had happened to Gran's sister, the one I knew I was named for.

The sister Gran only ever described to me as the small girl whose hair she, Gran, had braided each day, as she now braided mine: Esthie, Gran's littlest sister, still a young girl when Gran came to Canada. Years, before I connected the Holocaust with my family, in a moment of shocked comprehension. That was a connection they never made for me, and why was that? A question I've never answered. Why it took so long for me to make it myself is another. There are many such questions from my childhood. The question about Mrs. Howick is one.

When I was twelve my best friend was Rhoda Kendal, quiet like me, studious and shy. We were friends more by circumstance than by our choosing, both of us having transferred from other schools (I in fourth grade, she in fifth) at the age by which girls have formed tight bonds and cliques and are not easily receptive to newcomers. I made no friends in my first year at Wilchester School, and I knew what that felt like, so when Rhoda showed up in my class the next year and I saw her standing alone and diffident in the schoolyard, I took her under my wing. She was a sweet-natured girl with a round smooth face, placid features, and dove-soft black hair that waved. She had an air about her, among the harder-edged, more socially conscious girls, of still being a child, somehow untouched by sophistication; she seemed defenseless to me in her pleated, regulation tunic—a style the other girls, myself included, had discarded in favour of the 'A-line' pleatless tunic older girls at our school were permitted to wear.

My own defenses were already in place. Close on the realization that I would not be invited into the circle, at Wilchester, came the realization that I did not want to be. I signified this by fastening my pleatless tunic with the old regulation two-button belt, declining to purchase from the office the long, shiny-threaded sash the other girls rushed, thrilled, to trade theirs for. I continued to clump around in navy-blue Oxfords even after the principal, badgered by mothers of unhappy girls, conceded to allow an alternative, more stylish shoe. In this I differed from the two or three other loners in my class: Donna, the only Gentile girl; Brina who had a mysterious illness that absented her for weeks at a time; Jana who was cross-eyed and came to school with egg on her blouse. They, like the rest, opted for sashes and loafers, hoping thus to avoid becoming targets for whispering.

I for my part might be ignored, but I was not whispered about because my marks were too good. I did not strain for this. It was my luck, I was so constituted, that term after term, effortlessly, I led the class; and it was also my luck that Wilchester was a place where that counted.

Rhoda studied much harder than I did and got "Very Goods" and "Goods" where I got "Excellents." It was indicative of her nature that she did not in the least resent me for this, but wholeheartedly admired me and exulted in my successes as if they were her own. "Gee, you make me sick!" she might say, looking at my report card, but she couldn't stop smiling. The other girls who rushed over to compare their marks with mine, subject by subject, said flattering things to me, but their voices betrayed them, barely masking bitter envy.

As my marks protected me from being targeted, so being my friend protected Rhoda. By seventh grade we were inseparable. We spent recesses together, griping about Home Economics, discussing which girls were "boy crazy." On Saturdays we exchanged our books at the library and rode the bus home to her house or mine, giggling too loudly, dropping potato chips in the aisle. At the end of the day, we would walk each other "half-way home," and the half-way might stretch to all the way, then, "I'll walk you half-way home," till it was dark out and we were giddy with the silliness of it. Looking back on it, I think that if Rhoda had not come late to Wilchester and had not met me first of all, she might have become one of the crowd—she had it in her to fit in—whereas I, even had I not come late, would have remained singular and apart. But Rhoda had a loyal heart, and though she ditched her pleated tunic and succumbed soon enough to the sash and loafers, she was staunchly my friend and stuck by me.

Rhoda's parents had been in the camps. I didn't know this at the time; I'm not sure how I know it now. Somebody must have told me, long afterwards—perhaps my mother, perhaps Rhoda herself when we ran across each other again, years later, in graduate school. There was little to show it. They had a home like other homes in that neighbourhood, a brand-new, fashionable split-level, white rugs, sunken living-room, sofas in plastic slipcovers. It was much fancier than my parents' house; the hall floor was parquet instead of vinyl tile; the bedrooms had wall-to-wall carpeting. In the bathroom a basket by the sink contained coloured, scented soap puffs for visitors; I had to ask what they were. Everything was always immaculately clean and tidy; Rhoda and her younger brother and sister, who were twins, were generally not allowed in the living-room. It was a sharp contrast to my house, where a comfortable level of clutter prevailed and everything—furniture, flooring, fixtures—had a well-used, time-worn look.

I preferred for Rhoda to come to my house because I never felt entirely comfortable in hers. Her parents (when they were around for both worked), spoke Yiddish most of the time; their English was poor, formal, and thickly accented. About them I felt a foreignness, an apart-ness, that I could not read or gauge. Rhoda's mother was not friendly like mine. She would smile at me and say hello when we came in, but she never conversed with me or drew me out, as my mother did with the friends I brought home, and she never sat down to chat with us when we fixed ourselves snacks in the gleaming kitchen; instead she would retire to another room. Once, I confessed to Rhoda that I did not feel welcome in her house, that I thought her mother disliked me; but Rhoda, stunned, told me her mother liked me very much and was happy she, Rhoda, had me for a friend. "She's shy, Esther," she told me, "and she thinks her English is bad. Maybe she's afraid you'll laugh at her. I tell her all the time how brilliant you are—"

Of Rhoda's father I have only one clear memory, and it strikes me now as being an odd one. It is of a hot spring afternoon when I arrived at the house to call for Rhoda; we were going somewhere together, I don't remember where, and as I turned up the walk, Rhoda called to me from her bedroom window, "I'll be down in a sec, I'm just changing." To pass the time, I strolled around the side of the house to look at the lilacs, and came suddenly upon her father on a ladder in the driveway, shirtless, painting the garage door. He had a cap on, and for a moment I thought he was a hired worker; then he looked up from beneath the visor and smiled at me, an oddly warm, sad smile that crinkled the corners of his eyes. He was amused to see that I had not recognized him, and motioned me nearer. "Esther. So, Esther. You like my hat?"

I felt awkward and shy. It was the first time I had seen him alone, or exchanged more than a word or two with him. I can't remember the conversation we had there, in the sunny driveway, with faint breezes wafting the smells of lilac and wet paint; but I remember that the tone was kindly, gentle, sad, and oddly intimate. "It's hard, to be a Jew," I remember him saying to me in his European accent, slowly shaking his head (and my sudden, forlorn sense of discomfiture)—"You know what they say, Esther? It's hard to be a Jew."

What was the context? I cannot at all remember. And did this scene take place before, or after, the incident with Mrs. Howick? That, too, evades me.

Seventh Grade was at that time the final year of elementary school, a year in which teachers strove to prepare students for the comparative rigours to come. Our teacher, Mrs. Howick, was strict and uncompromising, but scrupulously fair. She was a short woman in her mid-forties—the bigger girls already had the edge on her—but she commanded respect in every fiber by the way in which she planted herself at the front of a classroom: square posture, legs placed slightly apart, chin erect, hands on hips. She wore pleated skirts, high-necked blouses, dark support hose, "sensible" shoes. No jewellery, no perfume—indulgences of the younger teachers on staff. Her hair, a nondescript light brown as yet unmixed with grey, was center-parted and cut short, it stood out a little from her face, giving her a severe yet slightly dowdy appearance.

I liked her well enough. She had a brisk, animated classroom style, could be salty, was not boring, gave a reasonable amount of homework, and expected us to deliver, without coddling. Her digressions, when she digressed, were interesting. She quickly recognized my abilities and acknowledged me matter-of-factly, without effusions; she also gave me to understand that it was the thoughtfulness of my answers, rather than the correctness, that she valued. "Think, think, think," she used to exhort us, "don't let anybody else do your thinking for you." Or sometimes, if she asked for a show of hands on who agreed with a particular answer: "What are you looking around at your neighbour for? I'm asking what *you* think! *You!* Never mind the others! Else you're nothing but sheep." Her words were often accompanied by so vigorous a tapping of her pointer against the blackboard or floor that the wooden stick would snap in two, the broken end bouncing off somebody's desk to the accompaniment of stifled giggles.

The comparing of marks, whenever a test was given back, was something that evoked equal vehemence from her. "Keep your paper to yourself. What do you care what *she* got? 'What did you get, what did you get?'" (she mimicked, in mincing tones). "Is that all that matters to you? Look at your *own* paper! *Read* the comments on it—do you think I write them to amuse myself? Look at your mistakes, *learn* something!" And shaking her head in exasperation: "It's marks, marks, marks, with you people—that's all you're interested in. Just like with your parents it's money, money, money. Who's got the most—isn't that true? Today it's marks, marks, marks, and when you grow up, it'll be money, money, money."

One afternoon in midwinter, as I was getting my books together to leave, she spoke to me from her desk in an uncharacteristically personal tone. "Esther, do you have a few minutes to spare? Please stay behind. I want to talk to you about something."

My heart lurched for a second, but my conscience was clear. Maybe she had plans for me for the school concert. Maybe she wanted me to help her with something. Wondering, I followed her out of the classroom—away from a group of girls who were staying for detention—and down the hall a distance. "Esther," she said then, in a confidential voice, putting a hand on my shoulder, "I don't know if you've heard that I've been accused of saying things against Jews." Her eyes looked straight into mine, transfixing me. I shook my head; I was tongue-tied.

"Esther," she repeated. "You're Jewish. You're my brightest student. Please tell me. Have you ever heard me say anything against Jews?"

Again I shook my head. My heart was pounding; I didn't know why. It flashed through my mind that I had never thought of Mrs. Howick as being non-Jewish, or as not being Jewish. I had never thought of the student body at Wilchester, a Protestant school, as being almost all Jewish, even though I knew that in our class, only Donna wasn't, and that on Jewish holidays the handful of students from all grades who showed up were pooled in one classroom and had Art all day; Donna had told us.

"Esther, you know what I say when people in the class start comparing their marks—that they want more marks just like their parents want more money? Tell me the truth. When I said that, did you ever think that I was speaking against Jews?"

No, I had not thought so, I said, completely taken aback.

"Good. I'm glad. Well, dear, some people have thought so. Your friend Rhoda mentioned it to her parents, and her parents complained. They brought it up at the P.T.A. meeting last week, and some parents were upset and called the principal." She tapped the squat heel of her shoe against the shining floor; I saw that the edges of her hair were quivering. "Esther, you know that it was *people* I was talking about, not just Jews, but the kind of person who is always wanting more than the next one; you know some people are like that, don't you?"

"Yes," I said. The tone of entreaty in her voice dismayed me.

"I wanted to ask *you*, because you're a very intelligent girl, and very mature, and because I know you and Rhoda are friends. Maybe you'll talk to her about it. Explain to her that I didn't mean it that way. Will you do that for me?"

I said, "I'll try," and she patted my shoulder, gratefully, and said, "Good girl," and then I left.

That was the end of it; there was no sequel. The episode blew over without further ado; presumably, apologies were made, and the matter was allowed to drop. I did talk to Rhoda, but I don't remember what we said—only that it was a little uncomfortable, a little strained, I think she felt pulled between respect for her parents and loyalty to me; that she neither challenged my opinion nor concurred; but I don't remember. I never mentioned the affair to my own parents, who had little use for the P.T.A. and doubtless had not attended the meeting in question. At the end of the year, Rhoda and I went off to separate high schools and gradually, as our lives diverged, lost touch with each other.

But I still sometimes think about Mrs. Howick. Though I shovelled it under at the time, I know that something opened up beneath me, that afternoon in the dim-lit school corridor, like a section of floor caving in. I see her plain, earnest, sometimes sardonic face; I remember that I liked her, and that she liked me. I hear her voice reiterating the offensive phrases and I wonder: Was it a slur, or wasn't it? And was it fair of her to ask me to decide? I could not argue with her observation as it applied to my school and neighbourhood: the kids were as a rule competitive and pushy for marks; the parents were typically brash, upwardly mobile suburbanites of the fifties. But what gave her the right to say it, and *for whom* was she saying it? "You people," she called us. And what was she asking me to uphold—the thoughtfulness of her statement, or the correctness of it? What unexamined premises of hers did my answer endorse? In retrospect I know that even as I gave her what she wanted, even as I said I had not taken her remark to be a slur, I began to wonder whether it had been; and over the years, off and on, I have gone on wondering.

At first what I wondered about was simple: if I liked her, how could she be an anti-Semite? But if she was an anti-Semite, how could I like her? Later, painfully, having allowed that both could be the case, I wondered which of us I had let down the most.

I remember coming late out of school, that winter dusk, and trudging across the empty schoolyard alone, over the bumpy, frozen crust of old footprints. Rhoda had not waited for me; there was no point, as we walked home in opposite directions. I remember how it began to snow lightly as I reached the gate, and how the snow fell thicker and thicker, in swift dizzying flakes, across my path home.

TOPICS   FOR   EXPLORATION

1. What does the first paragraph contribute to the unity of the story? What is "hate literature"? What is its origin and purpose? In what sense is Esther later cast in her father's role as described here?

2. Explain why to Esther the Holocaust "happened over and over." What does her grandmother stand for? What is the relationship between the first part of the story, discussing the Holocaust and its impact upon the narrator's life, and the "minor incident" she narrates later?

3. In what areas can Rhoda and Esther be compared? How are their families different? What is the cause of the differences? How is language an issue that causes Rhoda's mother to display "shyness"?

4. Why is Mrs. Howick accused of anti-Semitism? Why do Rhoda's parents construe her remark about the parents wanting "money, money, money" to be anti-Semitic?

5. Why can't Esther decide whether Mrs. Howick's remark was a slur? Who is the victim of this misunderstanding? The story's ending raises several questions. Why does the author leave them unanswered?

6. How is the purpose of education distorted by both Mrs. Howick's remark and Rhoda's parents' response to it?

Clark Blaise

Clark Blaise was born in North Dakota in 1940 and educated at the University of Iowa's Writers Workshops, where he later taught. He has also taught in Montreal and Toronto. He has written three short story collections, Tribal Justice, A North American Education, *and* Resident Alien, *and two novels,* Lusts *and* Lunar Attractions. *His essays and stories have been published in over thirty anthologies. Blaise is married to Bharati Mukherjee, and together they authored two books,* Days and Nights in Calcutta *(1977), about their experiences while visiting India in the early seventies, and* The Sorrow and the Terror: The Haunting Legacy of the Air India Disaster *(1987), an account of the explosion of an Air India jet in 1985.*

A Class of New Canadians

Norman Dyer hurried down Sherbrooke Street, collar turned against the snow. "Superb!" he muttered, passing a basement gallery next to a French bookstore. Bleached and tanned women in furs dashed from hotel lobbies into waiting cabs. Even the neon clutter of the side streets and the honks of slithering taxis seemed remote tonight through the peaceful snow. *Superb*, he thought again, waiting for a light and backing from a slushy curb: a word reserved for wines, cigars, and delicate sauces; he was feeling superb this evening. After eighteen months in Montreal, he still found himself freshly impressed by everything he saw. He was proud of himself for having steered his life north, even for jobs that were menial by standards he could have demanded. Great just being here no matter what they paid, looking at these buildings, these faces, and hearing all the languages. He was learning to be insulted by simple bad taste, wherever he encountered it.

Since leaving graduate school and coming to Montreal, he had sampled every ethnic restaurant downtown and in the old city, plus a few Levantine places out in Outremont. He had worked on conversational French and mastered much of the local dialect, done reviews for local papers, translated French-Canadian poets for Toronto quarterlies, and tweaked his colleagues for not sympathizing enough with Quebec separatism. He attended French performances of plays he had ignored in English, and kept a small but elegant apartment near a colony of *émigré* Russians just off Park Avenue. Since coming to Montreal he'd witnessed a hold-up, watched a murder, and seen several riots. When stopped on the street for directions, he would answer in French or accented English. To live this well and travel each long academic summer, he held two jobs. He had no intention of returning to the States. In fact, he had begun to think of himself as a semi-permanent, semi-political exile.

Now, stopped again a few blocks farther, he studied the window of Holt Renfrew's exclusive men's shop. Incredible, he thought, the authority of simple good taste. Double-breasted chalk-striped suits he would never dare to buy. Knitted sweaters, and fifty-dollar shoes. One tanned mannequin was decked out in a brash checkered sportscoat with a burgundy vest and dashing ascot. Not a price tag under three hundred dollars. Unlike food, drink, cinema, and literature, clothing had never really involved him. Someday, he now realized, it would. Dyer's clothes, thus far, had all been bought in a chain department store. He was a walking violation of American law, clad shoes to scarf in Egyptian cottons, Polish leathers, and woolens from the People's Republic of China.

He had no time for dinner tonight; this was Wednesday, a day of lectures at one university, and then an evening course in English as a Foreign Language at McGill, beginning at six. He would eat afterwards.

Besides the money, he had kept this second job because it flattered him. There was to Dyer something fiercely elemental, almost existential, about teaching both his language and his literature in a foreign country—like Joyce in Trieste, Isherwood and Nabokov in Berlin, Beckett in Paris. Also it was necessary for his students. It was the first time in his life that he had done something socially useful. What difference did it make that the job was beneath him, a recent Ph.D., while most of his colleagues in the evening school at McGill were idle housewives and bachelor civil servants? It didn't matter, even, that this job was a perversion of all the sentiments he held as a progressive young teacher. He was a god two evenings a week, sometimes suffering and fatigued, but nevertheless an omniscient, benevolent god. His students were silent, ignorant, and dedicated to learning English. No discussions, no demonstrations, no dialogue.

I love them, he thought. They need me.

He entered the room, pocketed his cap and ear muffs, and dropped his briefcase on the podium. Two girls smiled good evening.

They love me, he thought, taking off his boots and hanging up his coat; I'm not like their English-speaking bosses.

I love myself, he thought with amazement even while conducting a drill on word order. I love myself for tramping down Sherbrooke Street in zero weather just to help them with noun clauses. I love myself standing behind this podium and showing Gilles Carrier and Claude Veilleux the difference between the past continuous and the simple past; or the sultry Armenian girl with the bewitching half-glasses that "put on" is not the same as "take on"; or telling the dashing Mr. Miguel Mayor, late of Madrid, that simple futurity can be expressed in four different ways, at least.

This is what mastery is like, he thought. Being superb in one's chosen field, not merely in one's mother tongue. A respected performer in the lecture halls of the major universities, equipped by twenty years' research in the remotest libraries, and slowly giving it back to those who must have it. Dishing it out suavely, even wittily. Being a legend. Being liked and a little feared.

"Yes, Mrs. David?"

A *sabra:* freckled, reddish hair, looking like a British model, speaks with a nifty British accent, and loves me.

"No," he smiled, "I *were* is not correct except in the present subjunctive, which you haven't studied yet."

The first hour's bell rang. The students closed their books for the intermission. Dyer put his away, then noticed a page of his Faulkner lecture from the afternoon class. *Absalom, Absalom!* his favorite.

"Can anyone here tell me what the *impregnable citadel of his passive rectitude* means?"

"What, sir?" asked Mr. Vassilopoulos, ready to copy.

"What about the *presbyterian and lugubrious effluvium of his passive vindictiveness?*" A few girls giggled. "O.K.," said Dyer, "take your break."

In the halls of McGill they broke into the usual groups. French-Canadians and South Americans into two large circles, then the Greeks, Germans, Spanish, and French into smaller groups. The patterns interested Dyer. Madrid Spaniards and Parisian French always spoke English with their New World co-linguals. The Middle Europeans spoke German together, not Russian, preferring one occupier to the other. Two Israeli men went off alone. Dyer decided to join them for the break.

Not *sabras*, Dyer concluded, not like Mrs. David. The shorter one, dark and wavy-haired, held his cigarette like a violin bow. The other, Mr. Weinrot, was tall and pot-bellied, with a ruddy face and thick stubby fingers. Something about him suggested truck-driving, perhaps of beer, maybe in Germany. Neither one, he decided, could supply the name of a good Israeli restaurant.

"This is really hard, you know?" said Weinrot.

"Why?"

"I think it's because I'm not speaking much of English at my job."

"French?" asked Dyer.

"French? Pah! All the time Hebrew, sometimes German, sometimes little Polish. Crazy things, eh? How long you think they let me speak Hebrew if I'm working in America?"

"Depends on where you're working," he said.

"Hell, I'm working for the Canadian government, what you think? Plant I work in—I'm engineer, see—makes boilers for the turbines going up North. Look. When I'm leaving Israel I go first to Italy. Right away-bamm I'm working in Italy I'm speaking Italian like a native. Passing for a native."

"A native Jew," said his dark-haired friend.

"Listen to him. So in Rome they think I'm from Tyrol—that's still native, eh? So I speak Russian and German and Italian like a Jew. My Hebrew is bad, I admit it, but it's a lousy language anyway. Nobody likes it. French I understand but English I'm talking like a bum. Arabic I know five dialects. Danish fluent. So what's the matter I can't learn English?"

"It'll come, don't worry," Dyer smiled. *Don't worry, my son*; he wanted to pat him on the arm. "Anyway, that's what makes Canada so appealing. Here they don't force you."

"What's this *appealing*? Means nice? Look, my friend, keep it, eh? Two years in a country I don't learn the language means it isn't a country."

"Come on," said Dyer. "Neither does forcing you."

"Let me tell you a story why I come to Canada. Then you tell me if I was wrong, O.K.?"

"Certainly," said Dyer, flattered.

In Italy, Weinrot told him, he had lost his job to a Communist union. He left Italy for Denmark and opened up an Israeli restaurant with five other friends. Then the six Israelis decided to rent a bigger apartment downtown near the restaurant. They found a perfect nine-room place for two thousand kroner a month, not bad shared six ways. Next day the landlord told them the deal was off. "You tell me why," Weinrot demanded.

No Jews? Dyer wondered. "He wanted more rent," he finally said.

"More—you kidding? More we expected. *Less* we didn't expect. A couple with eight kids is showing up after we're gone and the law in Denmark says a man has a right to a room for each kid plus a hundred kroner knocked off the rent for each kid. What you think of that? So a guy who comes in *after* us gets a nine-room place for a thousand kroner *less*. Law says no way a bachelor can get a place ahead of a family, and bachelors pay twice as much."

Dyer waited, then asked, "So?"

"So, I make up my mind the world is full of communismus, just like Israel. So I take out applications next day for Australia, South Africa, U.S.A., and Canada. Canada says come right away, so I go. Should have waited for South Africa."

"How could you?" Dyer cried. "What's wrong with you anyway? South Africa is fascist. Australia is racist."

The bell rang, and the Israelis, with Dyer, began walking to the room.

"What I was wondering, then," said Mr. Weinrot, ignoring Dyer's outburst, "was if my English is good enough to be working in the United States. You're American, aren't you?"

It was a question Dyer had often avoided in Europe, but had rarely been asked in Montreal. "Yes," he admitted, "your English is probably good enough for the States or South Africa, whichever one wants you first."

He hurried ahead to the room, feeling that he had let Montreal down. He wanted to turn and shout to Weinrot and to all the others that Montreal was the greatest city on the continent, if only they knew it as well as he did. If they'd just break out of their little ghettos.

At the door, the Armenian girl with the half-glasses caught his arm. She was standing with Mrs. David and Miss Parizeau, a jolly French-Canadian girl that Dyer had been thinking of asking out.

"Please, sir," she said, looking at him over the tops of her tiny glasses, "what I was asking earlier—*put on*—I heard on the television. A man said *You are putting me on* and everybody laughed. I think it was supposed to be funny but *put on* we learned means get dressed, no?"

"Ah—*don't put me on*," Dyer laughed.

"I yaven't erd it neither," said Miss Parizeau.

"To put some*body* on means to make a fool of him. To put some*thing* on is to wear it. O.K.?" He gave examples.

"Ah, now I know," said Miss Parizeau. "Like bullshitting somebody. Is it the same?"

"Ah, yes," he said, smiling. French-Canadians were like children learning the language. "Your example isn't considered polite. 'Put on' is very common now in the States."

"Then maybe," said Miss Parizeau, "we'll ave it ere in twenty years." The Armenian giggled.

"No—I've heard it here just as often," Dyer protested, but the girls had already entered the room.

He began the second hour with a smile which slowly soured as he thought of the Israelis. America's anti-communism was bad enough, but it was worse hearing it echoed by immigrants, by Jews, here in Montreal. Wasn't there a psychological type who chose Canada over South Africa? Or was it just a matter of visas and slow adjustment? Did Johannesburg lose its Greeks, and Melbourne its Italians, the way Dyer's students were always leaving Montreal?

And after class when Dyer was again feeling content and thinking of approaching one of the Israelis for a restaurant tip, there came the flood of small requests: should Mrs. Papadopoulos go into a more advanced course; could Mr. Perez miss a week for an interview in Toronto; could Mr. Giguère, who spoke English perfectly, have a harder book; Mr. Coté an easier one?

Then as he packed his briefcase in the empty room, Miguel Mayor, the vain and impeccable Spaniard, came forward from the hallway.

"Sir," he began, walking stiffly, ready to bow or salute. He wore a loud gray checkered sportscoat this evening, blue shirt, and matching ascot-handkerchief, slightly mauve. He must have shaved just before class, Dyer noticed, for two fresh daubs of antiseptic cream stood out on his jaw, just under his earlobe.

"I have been wanting to ask *you* something, as a matter of fact," said Dyer. "Do you know any good Spanish restaurants I might try tonight?"

"There are not any good Spanish restaurants in Montreal," he said. He stepped closer. "Sir?"

"What's on your mind, then?"

"Please—have you the time to look on a letter for me?"

He laid the letter on the podium.

"Look *over* a letter," said Dyer. "What is it for?"

"I have applied," he began, stopping to emphasize the present perfect construction, "for a job in Cleveland, Ohio, and I want to know if my letter will be good. Will an American, I mean—"

"Why are you going there?"

"It is a good job."

"But Cleveland—"

"They have a blackman mayor, I have read. But the job is not in Cleveland."

"Let me see it."

Most honourable Sir: I humbly beg consideration for a position in your grand company ...

"Who are you writing this to?"

"The president," said Miguel Mayor.

I am once student of Dr. Ramiro Gutierrez of the Hydraulic Institute of Sevilla, Spain ...

"Does the president know this Ramiro Gutierrez?"

"Oh, everybody is knowing him," Miguel Mayor assured, "he is the most famous expert in all Spain."

"Did he recommend this company to you?"

"No—I have said in my letter, if you look—"

An ancient student of Dr. Gutierrez, Salvador del Este, is actually a boiler expert who is being employed like supervisor is formerly a friend of mine ...

"Is he still your friend?"

Whenever you say come to my city Miguel Mayor for talking I will be coming. I am working in Montreal since two years and am now wanting more money than I am getting here now ...

"Well ..." Dyer sighed.

"Sir—what I want from you is knowing in good English how to interview me by this man. The letters in Spanish are not the same to English ones, you know?"

I remain humbly at your orders ...

"Why do you want to leave Montreal?"

"It's time for a change."

"Have you ever been to Cleveland?"

"I am one summer in California. Very beautiful there and hot like my country. Montreal is big port like Barcelona. Everybody mixed together and having no money. It is just a place to land, no?"

"Montreal? Don't be silly."

"I thought I come here and learn good English but where I work I get by in Spanish and French. It's hard, you know?" he smiled. Then he took a few steps back and gave his cuffs a gentle tug, exposing a set of jade cufflinks.

Dyer looked at the letter again and calculated how long he would be correcting it, then up at his student. How old is he? My age? Thirty? Is he married? Where do the Spanish live in Montreal? He looks so prosperous, so confident, like a male model off a page of *Playboy*. For an instant Dyer felt that his student was mocking him, somehow pitting his astounding confidence and wardrobe, sharp chin and matador's bearing against Dyer's command of English and mastery of the side streets, bistros, and ethnic restaurants. Mayor's letter was painful, yet he remained somehow competent. He would pass his interview, if he got one. What would he care about America, and the odiousness he'd soon be supporting? It was as though a superstructure of exploitation had been revealed, and Dyer felt himself abused by the very people he wanted so much to help. It had to end someplace.

He scratched out the second "humbly" from the letter, then folded the sheet of foolscap. "Get it typed right away," he said. "Good luck."

"Thank you, sir," said his student, with a bow. Dyer watched the letter disappear in the inner pocket of the checkered sportscoat. The folding of the cashmere scarf, the draping of the camel's hair coat about the shoulders, the easing of the fur hat down to the rims of his ears. The meticulous filling of the pigskin gloves. Mayor's patent leather galoshes glistened.

"Good evening, sir," he said.

"*Buenas noches,*" Dyer replied.

He hurried now, back down Sherbrooke Street to his daytime office where he could deposit his books. Montreal on a winter night was still mysterious, still magical. Snow blurred the arc lights. The wind was dying. Every second car was now a taxi, crowned with an orange crescent. Slushy curbs had hardened. The window of Holt Renfrew's was still attractive. The legless dummies invited a final stare. He stood longer than he had earlier, in front of the sporty mannequin with a burgundy waistcoat, the mauve and blue ensemble, the jade cufflinks.

Good evening, sir, he could almost hear. The ascot, the shirt, the complete outfit, had leaped off the back of Miguel Mayor. He pictured how he must have entered the store with three hundred dollars and a prepared speech, and walked out again with everything off the torso's back.

I want that.

What, sir?

That.

The coat, sir?

Yes.

Very well, sir.

And *that.*

Which, sir?

All that.

"Absurd man!" Dyer whispered. There had been a moment of fear, as though the naked body would leap from the window, and legless, chase him down Sherbrooke Street. But the moment was passing. Dyer realized now that it was comic, even touching. Miguel Mayor had simply tried too hard, too fast, and it would be good for him to stay in Montreal until he deserved those clothes, that touching vanity and confidence. With one last look at the window, he turned sharply, before the clothes could speak again.

TOPICS FOR EXPLORATION

1. Is Norman Dyer a sympathetic character? How would you describe his self-image? Are there any ironic touches in Clark Blaise's portrait of Dyer?

2. Characterize Dyer's attitude to Montreal, to the States, to his French-Canadian and immigrant students. What does the internationality of Dyer's clothing suggest? How does it correspond with his upward mobility? How does his clothing contrast with that of his Spanish student Miguel Mayor?

3. What is Dyer's motive for teaching nightschool English? What are some of the rewards? Compare his reasons for being in Montreal with those that brought his students there. How does he essentially differ from them?

4. Why does Dyer, who is American, distrust the attitudes commonly associated with Americans? Why does he like to think of himself as "a semi-permanent, semi-political exile" in Montreal?

5. Why is a country that does not enforce the learning of its language "not a country," according to Mr. Weinrot?

6. In the last paragraph, Dyer thinks that "Miguel Mayor had simply tried too hard, too fast, and it would be good for him to stay in Montreal until he deserved those clothes, that touching vanity and confidence." Comment on the idea of "deserving" expressed here. Is Dyer displaying a double standard here?

Carol Geddes

Carol Geddes is from the Tlingit Nation in the Yukon. She graduated from Concordia University and has worked for the National Film Board. She has made several films, including Doctor, Lawyer, Indian Chief. *Her writing and films often describe the problems that aboriginal women face in both Native and white society. "Growing Up Native" was first published in* Homemaker's Magazine *in 1990.*

Growing Up Native

I remember it was cold. We were walking through a swamp near our home in the Yukon bush. Maybe it was fall and moose-hunting season. I don't know. I think I was about four years old at the time. The muskeg was too springy to walk on, so people were taking turns carrying me—passing me from one set of arms to another. The details about where we were are vague, but the memory of those arms and the feeling of acceptance I had is one of the most vivid memories of my childhood. It didn't matter who was carrying me—there was security in every pair of arms. That response to children is typical of the native community. It's the first thing I think of when I cast my mind back to the Yukon bush, where I was born and lived with my family.

I was six years old when we moved out of the bush, first to Teslin, where I had a hint of the problems native people face, then to Whitehorse, where there was unimaginable racism. Eventually I moved to Ottawa and Montreal, where I further discovered that to grow up native in Canada is to feel the sting of humiliation and the boot of discrimination. But it is also to experience the enviable security of an extended family and to learn to appreciate the richness of the heritage and traditions of a culture most North Americans have never been lucky enough to know. As a film-maker, I have tried to explore these contradictions, and our triumph over them, for the half-million aboriginals who are part of the tide of swelling independence of the First Nations today.

But I'm getting ahead of myself. If I'm to tell the story of what it's like to grow up native in northern Canada, I have to go back to the bush where I was born, because there's more to my story than the hurtful stereotyping that depicts Indian people as drunken welfare cases. Our area was known as 12-mile (it was 12 miles from another tiny village). There were about 40 people living there—including 25 kids, eight of them my brothers and sisters—in a sort of family compound. Each family had its own timber plank house for sleeping, and there was one large common kitchen area with gravel on the ground and a tent frame over it. Everybody would go there and cook meals together. In summer, my grandmother always had a smudge fire going to smoke fish and tan moose hides. I can remember the cosy warmth of the fire, the smell of good food, and always having someone to talk to. We kids had built-in playmates and would spend hours running in the bush, picking berries, building rafts on the lake and playing in abandoned mink cages.

One of the people in my village tells a story about the day the old lifestyle began to change. He had been away hunting in the bush for about a month. On his way back, he heard a strange sound coming from far away. He ran up to the crest of a hill, looked over the top of it and saw a bulldozer. He had never seen or heard of such a thing before and he couldn't imagine what it was. We didn't have magazines or newspapers in our village, and the people didn't know that the Alaska Highway was being built as a defence against a presumed Japanese invasion during the Second World War. That was the beginning of the end of the Teslin Tlingit people's way of life. From that moment on, nothing turned back to the way it was. Although there were employment opportunities for my father and uncles, who were young men at the time, the speed and force with which the Alaska Highway was rammed through the wilderness caused tremendous upheaval for Yukon native people.

It wasn't as though we'd never experienced change before. The Tlingit Nation, which I belong to, arrived in the Yukon from the Alaskan coast around the turn of the century. They were the middlemen and women between the Russian traders and the Yukon inland Indians. The Tlingit gained power and prestige by trading European products such as metal goods and cloth for the rich and varied furs so much in fashion in Europe. The Tlingit controlled Yukon trading because they controlled the trading routes through the high mountain passes. When trading ceased to be an effective means of survival, my grandparents began raising wild mink in cages. Mink prices were really high before and during the war, but afterwards the prices went plunging down. So, although the mink pens were still there when I was a little girl, my father mainly worked on highway construction and hunted in the bush. The Yukon was then, and still is in some ways, in a transitional period—from living off the land to getting into a European wage-based economy.

As a young child, I didn't see the full extent of the upheaval. I remember a lot of togetherness, a lot of happiness while we lived in the bush. There's a very strong sense of family in the native commu-nity, and a fondness for children, especially young children. Even today, it's like a special form of entertainment if someone brings a baby to visit. That sense of family is the one thing that has survived all the incredible difficulties native people have had. Throughout a time of tremendous problems, the extended family system has somehow lasted, providing a strong circle for people to survive in. When parents were struggling with alcoholism or had to go away to find work, when one of the many epidemics swept through the community, or when a marriage broke up and one parent left, aunts, uncles and grandparents would try to fill those roles. It's been very important to me in terms of emotional support to be able to rely on my extended family. There are still times when such support keeps me going.

Life was much simpler when we lived in the bush. Although we were poor and wore the same clothes all year, we were warm enough and had plenty to eat. But even as a youngster, I began to be aware of some of the problems we would face later on. Travelling mission-aries would come and impose themselves on us, for example. They'd sit at our campfire and read the Bible to us and lecture us about how we had to live a Christian life. I remember being very frightened by stories we heard about parents sending their kids away to live with white people who didn't have any children. We thought those people were mean and that if we were bad, we'd be sent away, too. Of course, that was when social workers were scooping up native chil-dren and adopting them out to white families in the south. The con-sequences were usually disastrous for the children who were taken away—alienation, alcoholism and suicide, among other things. I knew some of those kids. The survivors are still struggling to recover.

The residential schools were another source of misery for the kids. Although I didn't have to go, my brothers and sisters were there. They told stories about having their hair cut off in case they were carrying head lice, and of being forced to do hard chores with-out enough food to eat. They were told that the Indian culture was evil, that Indian people were bad, that their only hope was to be Christian. They had to stand up and say things like "I've found the

Lord," when a teacher told them to speak. Sexual abuse was rampant in the residential school system.

By the time we moved to Whitehorse, I was excited about the idea of living in what I thought of as a big town. I'd had a taste of the outside world from books at school in Teslin (a town of 250 people), and I was tremendously curious about what life was like. I was hungry for experiences such as going to the circus. In fact, for a while, I was obsessed with stories and pictures about the circus, but then when I was 12 and saw my first one, I was put off by the condition and treatment of the animals.

Going to school in Whitehorse was a shock. The clash of native and white values was confusing and frightening. Let me tell you a story. The older boys in our community were already accomplished hunters and fishermen, but since they had to trap beaver in the spring and hunt moose in the fall, and go out trapping in the winter as well, they missed a lot of school. We were all in one classroom and some of my very large teenage cousins had to sit squeezed into little desks. These guys couldn't read very well. We girls had been in school all along, so, of course, we were better readers. One day the teacher was trying to get one of the older boys to read. She was typical of the teachers at that time, insensitive and ignorant of cultural complexities. In an increasingly loud voice, she kept commanding him to "Read it, read it." He couldn't. He sat there completely still, but I could see that he was breaking into a sweat. The teacher then said, "Look, she can read it," and she pointed to me, indicating that I should stand up and read. For a young child to try to show up an older boy is wrong and totally contrary to native cultural values, so I refused. She told me to stand up and I did. My hands were trembling as I held my reader. She yelled at me to read and when I didn't she smashed her pointing stick on the desk to frighten me. In terror, I wet my pants. As I stood there fighting my tears of shame, she said I was disgusting and sent me home. I had to walk a long distance through the bush by myself to get home. I remember feeling this tremendous confusion, on top of my humiliation. We were always told the white teachers knew best, and so we had to do whatever they said at school. And yet I had a really strong sense of receiving mixed messages about what I was supposed to do in the community and what I was supposed to do at school.

Pretty soon I hated school. Moving to a predominantly white high school was even worse. We weren't allowed to join anything the white kids started. We were the butt of jokes because of our second-hand clothes and moose meat sandwiches. We were constantly being rejected. The prevailing attitude was that Indians were stupid. When it was time to make course choices in class—between typing and science, for example—they didn't even ask the native kids, they just put us all in typing. You get a really bad image of yourself in a situation like that. I bought into it. I thought we were awful. The whole experience was terribly undermining. Once, my grandmother gave me a pretty little pencil box. I walked into the classroom one day to find the word "squaw" carved on it. That night I burned it in the wood stove. I joined the tough crowd and by the time I was 15 years old, I was more likely to be leaning against the school smoking a cigarette than trying to join in. I was burned out from trying to join the system. The principal told my father there was no point in sending me back to school so, with a Grade 9 education, I started to work at a series of menial jobs.

Seven years later something happened to me that would change my life forever. I had moved to Ottawa with a man and was working as a waitress in a restaurant. One day, a friend invited me to her place for coffee. While I was there, she told me she was going to university in the fall and showed me her reading list. I'll never forget the minutes that followed. I was feeling vaguely envious of her and, once again, inferior. I remember taking the paper in my hand, seeing the books on it and realizing, Oh, my God, I've read these books! It hit me like a thunderclap. I was stunned that books I had read were being read in university. University was for white kids, not native kids. We were too stupid, we didn't have the kind of mind it took to do those things. My eyes moved down the list, and my heart started beating faster and faster as I suddenly realized I could go to university, too!

My partner at the time was a loving supportive man who helped me in every way. I applied to the university immediately as a mature student but when I had to write Grade 9 on the application, I was sure they'd turn me down. They didn't. I graduated five years later, earning a bachelor of arts in English and philosophy (with distinction)....

Today, there's a glimmer of hope that more of us native people will overcome the obstacles that have tripped us up ever since we began sharing this land. Some say our cultures are going through a renaissance. Maybe that's true. Certainly there's a renewed interest in native dancing, acting and singing, and in other cultural traditions. Even indigenous forms of government are becoming strong again. But we can't forget that the majority of native people live in urban areas and continue to suffer from alcohol and drug abuse and the plagues of a people who have lost their culture and have become lost themselves. And the welfare system is the insidious glue that holds together the machine of oppression of native people.

Too many non-native people have refused to try to understand the issues behind our land claims. They make complacent pronouncements such as "Go back to your bows and arrows and fish with spears if you want aboriginal rights. If not, give it up and assimilate into white Canadian culture." I don't agree with that. We need our culture, but there's no reason why we can't preserve it and have an automatic washing machine and a holiday in Mexico, as well.

The time has come for native people to make our own decisions. We need to have self-government. I have no illusions that it will be smooth sailing—there will be trial and error and further struggle. And if that means crawling before we can stand up and walk, so be it. We'll have to learn through experience.

While we're learning, we have a lot to teach and give to the world—a holistic philosophy, a way of living with the earth, not disposing of it. It is critical that we all learn from the elders that an individual is not more important than a forest; we know that we're here to live on and with the earth, not to subdue it.

The wheels are in motion for a revival, for change in the way native people are taking their place in Canada. I can see that we're equipped, we have the tools to do the work. We have an enormous number of smart, talented, moral Indian people. It's thrilling to be a part of this movement.

Someday, when I'm an elder, I'll tell the children the stories: about the bush, about the hard times, about the renaissance, and especially about the importance of knowing your place in your nation.

TOPICS FOR EXPLORATION

1. According to Geddes, what contradictions are involved in growing up Native in Canada? Why does she think that exploring these contradictions is necessary and fruitful?

2. What advantages does Geddes identify that compensate for the "sting of humiliation and the boot of discrimination" felt by Natives in Canada?

3. Discuss the impact of white civilization upon the way of life of Yukon Native people. What different means of survival have they been trying to adopt? What problems do they face?

4. What conditions existed in the schools in Whitehorse? What methods did the white teachers use to humiliate Native students? How has this treatment affected Native self-esteem?

5. What was the turning point for Geddes in reclaiming her sense of self-worth?

6. What are the "plagues of a people who have lost their culture"? How does the self-government movement offer "a glimmer of hope"?

7. Contact between white people and Native people is usually seen as a one-way process, with the dominant white culture imposing its norms upon the Natives. How does Geddes visualize the possibility of influences running in the opposite direction? What traditional Native values could enrich white lives as well?

Isabel Vincent

Isabel Vincent is the South American correspondent for The Globe and Mail, *based in Rio de Janeiro. This selection was originally published in* The Globe and Mail *in December 1990.*

Finding a Nationality That Fits

We started to become Canadian the day my mother got her first pair of pants.

They were gray-green gabardine with a high waist, and came wrapped in tissue paper in an Eaton's box. My mother reluctantly modelled them for my brother and me, all the while declaring that she couldn't imagine ever feeling comfortable with the stretchy cloth hugging her hips. Portuguese women didn't wear pants, only the *canadianas* dared wear anything so revealing. But in the same breath she'd rationalize that she spent too much money not to wear them, and besides they'd probably be warm in the winter.

That was in 1975, a few years after my family had made the big break and moved from the poor immigrant enclave of Kensington Market to the more upscale neighborhood of North York, where pockets of European immigration were just beginning to emerge. We were pioneers in a way. My father had been among the first wave of Portuguese immigrants to Canada in the early fifties, working a bleak stretch of railroad near Port Arthur—now Thunder Bay, Ont.—to earn enough money for my mother's passage across the Atlantic. My mother arrived sea-sick in Halifax in 1955, and took a slow train to Toronto, where she joined my father in a roach-infested flat on Nassau Avenue in the Market.

My mother still speaks of those early *sacrifícios*: living in a cold climate with cockroaches and mutely shopping for groceries, pointing out items to a local shopkeeper because she couldn't speak English. Her language skills were so tenuous that she once interpreted a greeting from an Orthodox Jew who lived in the neighborhood as an offer to buy my brother.

In those days, Toronto police used to disperse small crowds of Portuguese men who lingered too long outside cafes. Despite a burgeoning group of immigrants, there were few Portuguese speakers, even in the market.

But by 1975, the market became a Saturday-morning diversion for us, a place to shop for salted cod and fresh vegetables. To the hearty Portuguese immigrants who still worked in the factories and construction yards, and rented windowless basements in the market, we were on our way up. After all, there were very few Portuguese families north of Eglinton Avenue. Although we lived in a mostly Jewish and Italian neighborhood, we were finally becoming Canadian. Or so I thought.

I learned English in my first year of school. Multiculturalism was just beginning and hyphenated Canadians were beginning to flourish. I played with Italian-Canadians, Lithuanian-Canadians and Chinese-Canadians, but at that time nobody—especially suburban 7-year-olds—seemed able to pronounce "Portuguese-Canadian," so I told people I was Greek; it was easier to say. My brother went even further, changing his name to something faintly Anglo-Saxon, so his teachers and classmates wouldn't get tongue-tied around those sloshy Portuguese vowels and embarrass him. It seemed a very practical idea at the time, and I reluctantly followed suit.

But we still had problems, and didn't seem to belong. We never quite fit into the emerging Portuguese community, growing up around the parish of St. Mary's Church and the Toronto branch of the popular Benfica soccer club on Queen Street West. We were strangely aloof with our compatriots, most of whom had emigrated from the Azores, and whose guttural form of Portuguese we had difficulty understanding. My brother and I balked at heritage-language classes and remained passive spectators at the annual religious processions.

But if we had trouble dealing with our peers in downtown Toronto, in North York we were not much better off. My mother and aunts spoke disparagingly of the *canadianas*, Canadian women who (they were sure) knew nothing about how to keep a clean house or cook a decent meal. My mother taught me to cook and sew, and she and my aunts teased my brother, saying someday he'd marry a *canadiana* and would end up doing all his own housework.

For all her predictions, my mother was delighted to find out that she had been wrong. My brother, a physician, did marry a Canadian, but he doesn't do much of the housework. These days, my mother's biggest problem is pronouncing the name of her new grandson, Matthew Loughlin MacLean Vincent.

As I grew older I developed a nostalgia for my Lusitanian past, and tried desperately to reintegrate into the community. But I soon grew to hate the hypocrisy of some of my compatriots, most of whom were immigrants who chose to spend several years working in Canada, only to retire to the Portuguese country-side and build their palatial retreats with the fat pensions they collected from the Canadian government. Like my father, who learned English quickly and severed ties with his homeland, I became a staunch Canadian. I could sing *The Maple Leaf Forever* before I was 10, and spent my childhood years in French immersion. I became so good at masking my heritage that a few years ago when I applied for a job at a Toronto newspaper I was turned down because I was perceived as being too Anglo-Saxon.

"If you were ethnic, I'm sure they would have hired you on the spot," the wife of the paper's managing editor told me a year later.

But for most of my life being Portuguese seemed to me a liability. And then my mother bought that important first pair of pants. For a while it seemed that my life had changed. I was proud of my mother: she was becoming like all of the other mothers in the neighborhood.

But my excitement was short-lived. A few days later, she decided they just wouldn't do. She carefully wrapped them back up in the tissue paper, placed them in the cardboard Eaton's box, and returned them to the store.

TOPICS FOR EXPLORATION

1. The motif of Isabel Vincent's mother's first pair of pants functions as a framing device here. In what way does it highlight the major differences between the author and her mother?

2. What range of responses to her new country does Vincent register among different generations of Portuguese immigrants? What is the significance of moving from Kensington to North York?

3. Vincent doesn't feel quite Canadian, but she also feels estranged from the Portuguese community. Why? What methods has Vincent used to "Canadianize" herself?

4. What is the irony that Vincent is turned down for a newspaper job because she is perceived as too Anglo-Saxon?

5. In her school years and then in her career, has the author perceived her ethnicity as an obstacle, an asset, or both? Does she ever resolve the ambiguity of her feelings about her ethnic heritage and her desire to belong to the WASP establishment?

6. The title of this essay may suggest that nationality is something that can be fitted and changed at will, like an article of clothing. Does the rest of the essay maintain that view?

SUGGESTIONS FOR
FURTHER STUDY

1. Compare the account of the Holocaust given by Robyn Sarah's fiction with the factual narrative by Miriam Rosenthal in Unit One. How is the experience different for Sarah's narrator, who has only heard about that tragedy, and for Rosenthal, who witnessed it firsthand? How is it similar?

2. What have the effects of Christian missionaries been upon Canadian Natives? Compare the role of missionary schools in Pauline Johnson's story and Carol Geddes's essay.

3. What are "mixed messages" sent to Natives by white culture? How do they affect young people's self-image? Compare the treatment of this problem in the works by Carol Geddes and Pauline Johnson.

4. Compare the images of the teachers presented in the stories by Clark Blaise and Robyn Sarah. How is private morality confused with their professional ethics and purpose as educators? Does Rosalba, also a teacher, in Genni Gunn's story (Unit Three), ever make a similar error?

5. What role does education play in the process of assimilation of immigrant children? Compare Isabel Vincent and the protagonist of Garry Engkent's story (Unit Three) as "products" of the Canadian education system. In what ways has school alienated them from their roots?

UNIT FIVE

DRIFTING APART: GENERATION GAP

INTRODUCTION

Children often choose to define themselves in opposition to their parents. A gap that opens between generations can be filled with recriminations, regrets, indifference, guilt, or sadness. The stress of this estrangement, though necessary for maturation, is increased if the parents are immigrants who cherish the traditional "home culture" they bring with them while their children, by contrast, adopt the assimilated or dominant culture of the new country. Parental preferences in language, food, and religion, and the cultural memories the parents transmit, may be met with distrust and left behind. Later, perhaps, they may be appreciated. Sometimes the parents, consciously or not, perhaps pressured by cultural and educational demands or economic needs, encourage their children to yield their ethnic language and customs and to embrace, to a lesser or greater degree, the opportunities for success offered by conforming to the majority culture. However they are expressed, the generational changes cannot be avoided.

Each cultural group responds to the defection of its children in different ways that are specific to itself. In Frank G. Paci's story "Mancuso's and Sons," the father is determined to pass on the Italian family tradition of bread baking that threatens to be interrupted. The symbol of craft passed from father to son is disturbed by the son's injury, which does not permit him to support the arduous profession of baking in the old manner, and by the mother's stubborn refusal to allow her "weak" son into apprenticeship.

Maara Haas applies humour to a serious situation involving a conflict between Baba Podkova and her daughter Anastasia. The old Ukrainian refuses to change her eccentric ways even though her old world mannerisms irritate and embarrass Anastasia, who has social aspirations of her own. In fact, Haas shows that Anastasia's upper-class pretensions are a phony pose, no less ridiculous than Baba's strange behaviour, which at least reflects her authentic personality. The conflict over assimilation, which tears apart two generations of the immigrant family in the story, remains unresolved although Baba achieves a sort of moral triumph in the end.

In a more contemporary setting than Haas, Ann Jew in her story also describes a generational conflict in an immigrant family clashing over the issue of interracial dating. Three generations of the Chinese family presented by her demonstrate different stages of detachment from their traditional culture. The young narrator falls in love with a white boy and consequently faces a confrontation with her parents. Hurt by their intolerance, she finds peace and comfort at the bed of her invalid grandmother.

In an autobiographical essay, Rudy Wiebe pays an oblique tribute to his late father while probing the philosophical, biological, and historical meanings of fatherhood. Combined with the vivid recollections of his Mennonite childhood are Wiebe's reflections on cultural change. His writing constitutes an attempt to bridge the gulf between himself and his immigrant father, whose absences have had such a profound effect on Wiebe.

The father-son relationship is also at the centre of Eva Stachniak's story. It deals with a reunion between the father and the son, whose estrangement from each other—originally caused by their conflicting political views—has only deepened after the son's emigration to Canada. Always a staunch communist, the father at the end of his life tries to reach out and justify himself in his son's eyes. The rift between them, however, cannot be closed. Casualties on the battlefield of history, they both return to their separate lives.

Confrontations between the generations cannot be resolved by the capitulation of either side; inevitably, there will be a drifting apart as each generation defines itself anew, against the values of the previous one and in response to the needs of its environment. Nevertheless, as the authors in this Unit have shown, the memory of these rites of passage can continue to explain us to ourselves and our children.

Tara's Mother-in-law:

What kind of place you've brought me to, son?
Where the windows are always closed
And the front door it is always locked?
And no *rangoli* designs on porch steps
To say please come in?
How can you expect Lakshmi to come, son?
You think she'll care to enter
Where the same air goes round and round?
She "the lotus-seated consort
    of him who reposes
    on the primeval ocean of milk?"
You think they'll bless this food
    three days old
    you store in cans and ice-cupboard?

Son, son, it gives me great joy
to see you so well settled,
children and wife and all.
Though my hairs do stand on end
When your wife holds hands with men
And you with other men's wives.
But I am glad, son, I really am
That you are settled good good
And thought to bring me all the way
To see this lovely house and car and all.

But I cannot breathe this stale air
With yesterday's cooking smells
going round and round
Son, cooking is an everyday thing
Not a Sunday work alone
And son, cooking should smell good
The leaping aromas
    of turmeric and green coriander,
    and mustard seeds popped in hot oil
    that flavour food, not stink up the air.

Open the windows, son.

I am too used to the sounds
    of living things;
Of birds in the morning
Of rain and wind at night,
Not the drone of furnace fan
    and hiss of hot blasts
    and whoosh whoosh of washing machine.

Open the windows, son,
And let me go back
    to sun and air
    and sweat and even flies and all
But not this, not this.

—*Uma Parameswaran*

Uma Parameswaran came to Canada from Madras in 1966 to study at the University of Winnipeg. The poem reprinted here was published in Shakti's Words: An Anthology of South Asian Canadian Women's Poetry, *edited by Diane McGifford and Judith Kearns (1990).*

Frank G. Paci

Frank G. Paci was born in Italy in 1948 and came to Canada in 1952. He was an English teacher for several years in Sault Ste. Marie and Toronto. In 1988–89 he was writer-in-residence at York University. He has published three novels, The Italians, Black Madonna, *and* The Father; *three other novels are awaiting publication. His works are characterized by a thematic consistency: they all explore the life of Italian immigrant families, especially the impact of immigration upon their self-image and personal well-being. "Mancuso's and Sons" has been taken from* The Father, *first published in 1984.*

Mancuso's and Sons

In the kitchen his father spoke to him like a grownup as he was having his coffee.

"I started to work when I was nine years old," he said in Italian. "My father owned the only bakery in the town in the Abruzzi. We only made large loaves of rough bread that weighed 4 kilos. Large loaves taste better because they take longer to bake, and therefore more flavour and aroma are in the oven. Then, after I got my papers as a master baker, I made my special kind of bread. The people in the town called it *Orestepane*. Bread named after me, you understand. When my father had to stop working because of arthritis I was the only baker there. If I didn't bake bread no bread was sold. But then, in the army in Rome, the officers made me make lighter pasty bread I didn't like. We called it black bread because of the black shirts. Then, when I was a prisoner of war in North Africa, I almost went crazy because I didn't have anything to do most of the time. Many soldiers went crazy, Stefano. It was a bad time. Our nails didn't grow and our hair fell out because we didn't have any vitamins. Friends of mine died of starvation and pneumonia and jaundice—much worse than your hand."

Stefano sipped his cocoa and listened intently. He had never heard his father speak so long, except for the time they went fishing at Echo Bay. Stefano didn't ask any questions. He was content just to listen. "How can the fish bite a worm that talks so much," he recalled his father saying.

His father wore a white short-sleeved shirt and white pants. They were immaculately clean and looked soft from repeated washings. Every third day Maddelena washed a batch of his whites. They hung like cut-outs on the line: shirt, pants, shirt, pants.

His father's black hair glistened with brilliantine. He had a handsome face, with smooth pale skin and a cleft on his chin. Stefano had heard his mother say jokingly that the only reason she married him was that he looked like Valentino and her father. He had never seen Valentino, but his grandfather, whose picture was in his parents' bedroom, did look a little like his father. Oreste, though, had gentle and kind eyes. Stefano had rarely seen him angry. Even when he had to discipline them Stefano could tell his heart wasn't in it. Maddelena had to goad him into using his belt. When he hit, though, it hurt.

Oreste was his most cheerful in the mornings when he was in the bakery whistling or singing while baking bread with Amelio. "Bread can't grow," he'd say, "under the hands of a sad man." Then he'd go on delivery in the Ford station-wagon. Besides fishing, he liked to play cards with his friends at the Marconi Hall, just a couple of houses up the street.

"People are funny here," Oreste would say, shaking his head. "They don't like their work at the steel plant. In Italia life is more important, you understand. To work is to live."

When they finished their breakfast they went through the side door of the kitchen and into the storage-room of the bakery. Oreste had told him the bakery had been built just after the First World War. The previous owner had been old Giuseppe, the Marchegian. Stefano was too young to remember much of him, except that he used to give him pieces of bread. His dad worked in the bakery alongside the old man until Giuseppe had to retire. There was no-one in his family to take over the business, so it had passed into Oreste's hands. Afterwards, for almost a year, the old man couldn't stay away from the bakery. Oreste would let him come and help out. Giuseppe passed on all his methods and treated Oreste like a son. When the old man died his father closed the bakery for three days. He hung a black wreath on the door and stayed at the Marconi for a long time.

At the front of *Mancuso's and Sons* was the shop where Maddelena sold the bread. The loaves were piled just behind the large plate-glass window and behind the counter. They made an assortment of crusty breads in various sizes. Above the counter was a sign with the varieties sold and the prices. His father's specialty was a large loaf with a shiny brown crust and a long cut on the top.

Behind the storage-room it was like a cave. There was a large hearth oven made of bricks on one side and a long counter on the other. Except for a small mixing-machine everything was done by hand.

Oreste explained a few details about the nature of dough and how it had been left to rise during the night. In a few minutes Amelio DiLabio came through the back and they were ready to start. Amelio was a short squat Calabrian who was the only other person working with his father. As soon as Amelio saw him his face lit up.

"*Bravo*, Stefano! You learn the business now, hey?"

Stefano smiled and stood to the side. Oreste took out a white paper cap from his back pocket and put it on. Stefano saw his father turn his face away for a moment, as if he had something in his eye. Then he made the sign of the cross.

Amelio was beaming. "*Vieni qui*, Stefano. I show you how to light the oven."

After he lit the oven he said, "The oven is the most important part of the bakery, Stefano. This is an old oven made of bricks, see. The stone inside is important for the taste. We make our bread just like the Romans did thousands of years ago."

Stefano listened in awe.

Oreste said, "People were making bread before they could write."

Afterwards they dumped a large pan of dough onto the counter and started to make bread. Amelio cut chunks of dough and weighed them on a flat scale while Oreste shaped them into loaves. They worked fast without talking, conscious of his presence. Then Amelio started to whistle. He had such a sharp clear whistle that Stefano took notice of him more closely.

In no time it was very warm in the small room. The clean yeasty smell of the dough was strong and made Stefano a little giddy. He looked at the sliced dough with the small bubbles at the side. Something made him reach out to touch it.

Amelio laughed heartily. "Good, hey. Just like the body of a woman. You'll know soon."

He had close-cropped brown hair and a ruddy face, with broken veins all over—and reminded Stefano of a cartoon character.

"Your father and I," Amelio went on, his face, lighting up like a Christmas tree, "we bake bread for a long time. The best bread in the West End.... in the country. And this dough—" he brought the end of his cupped fingers to his lips and kissed them with an exaggerated show of emotion—"I say it to you right now, is better than any woman."

Oreste laughed. "Better than any woman you know, that's for sure."

Throwing his head back like an opera singer, Amelio suddenly broke into song. "*Oy Marie, Oy Marie ...*"

"Stefano," his father called out to him. "Come up here beside me."

Stefano watched closely as his father kneaded the hunks of dough. His hands worked fast at the beginning—punching down the roughness, poking and rolling the unformed chunk and sprinkling flour over it. But as the loaf began to take final shape he slowed down and took greater care. Stefano noticed the long tapering fingers of his father's hands. Whitened with flour they moved with slow, deft movements, as if caressing the dough. At the end he dipped a small brush in a jar that contained a yellowish liquid and brushed the top of each loaf.

"This is my secret method," his father said proudly. "It is responsible for the special crust of *Mancuso's and Sons.*" He paused as he took a knife and cut a long slash on top of each loaf. "Crust is the soul of the bread, figlio mio. Never forget. In this country they don't believe in crust."

"Daddy, what's in the jar?"

Oreste looked attentively at him and smiled. But he didn't answer.

Carefully he placed each loaf on a tray. Every so often Amelio put the loaves into the oven on a flat wooden board with a long handle shaped like a paddle. In a while there was a delicious smell in the room.

"See how it's done, Stefano," Oreste said. "You have to touch it a certain way. With the heel of your palms. Then the fingers. Add a little flour. Don't let it get too pasty. But just right. There, see. There's nothing better to eat in the world than bread. But good bread, not the stuff they make over here. Like those soft mushy rolls and the hamburger buns and the sliced paste they call sandwich bread. *Mannaggia America,* they don't know bread at all in this country!"

Stefano was surprised by his father's outburst. Amelio laughed good-naturedly, but Oreste gave him a long look and cursed a few times in Italian.

Finally his father put a hunk of dough in place and said, "Try it yourself, Stefano. Put some flour on your hands first."

All activity stopped. It didn't take him long to realize why. Since his accident his mother had fussed over him so much he hadn't been allowed to do much of anything. Certainly not to play games with the other kids. Or to work in the bakery.

With his left hand he cautiously started to knead the dough. His ears burned with embarrassment. He could feel their eyes on him. It made him so self-conscious of his deficiency he wanted to run and hide. Only the persistence of some inner voice kept him rooted to the spot. The dough was tougher than he thought. He couldn't put much pressure on it with one hand alone. Awkwardly he brought his deformed hand up to the counter and used it to keep the roll in place.

"*Bravo*, Stefano!" his father cried out.

Stefano turned and saw the fierce look of joy on his father's face.

"*Bravo!*" Oreste cried out again, shaking his fist in the air.

Stefano returned the look. His heart was bursting with happiness.

Soon he was shaping the tough dough into something resembling a loaf of bread. Amelio started to sing again and his father whistled as he went about his business. Without any further need of instruction Stefano continued making loaves. When he had four done he stepped back and surveyed his work.

"Ready for the oven?" Amelio called out.

Stefano didn't know what to say.

"Brush them first," his father instructed.

Stefano dipped the brush and coated his loaves with his father's secret formula. It had an eggy smell.

"Here," Amelio came up to him. "This is what we did in the old country with our very first loaf." He rolled two long sticks of dough.

"Which one is your first?" he asked Stefano.

Stefano indicated the smallest of the four loaves. Amelio very carefully made an S and an M on top with the sticks of dough.

"Now you'll know," his father said, taking a towel and mopping his forehead. "We keep the first loaf to remind us of the care we put into it. So that every one after will have the same care."

They were standing in silence when his mother appeared on the scene. She was in her blue robe. Her long red hair was uncombed.

Stefano looked at her in triumph. He was about to show her the loaf he had made when he noticed the way she was regarding Oreste. Amelio stepped back and looked after the oven. Oreste looked at the floor.

His mother came up to him and took his hand. She didn't even notice what he had done. She was looking all along at Oreste, not at him.

"I told you, didn't I?" his mother said in an angry tone.

Oreste looked up bewildered.

"Aw, Maddelena, what harm will it do?" he said.

"He's too delicate, I told you."

"When I was nine—"

"Oh, shut up, when you were nine!" she lashed out at him.

Stefano had to hold himself back from crying. She was holding his good hand so firmly that she was crunching the knuckles.

Oreste shook his head and gave Stefano a pitiful look.

"He has to learn sometime," he said with annoyance.

"Learn what?" she snapped.

"To work with his hands."

"*Ma, stai zitto, ignorante!*" she yelled at him. "Can't you see?"

Stefano's ears burned with embarrassment. No-one looked at him. He put his deformed hand behind his back.

He could feel his mother trembling with rage. He tried to break free of her hold, but she only held him tighter, hurting his hand. Oreste kept silent, staring at the floor like a student who had done something wrong at school.

"Daddy," Stefano pleaded, as if his father needed a little coaxing.

But Oreste wouldn't look up to face him. Stefano couldn't understand why he didn't just speak out and tell her to go back in the kitchen where she belonged. They had work to do.

"Daddy," he called out again.

He was afraid to say anything more in case the fish wouldn't bite.

But before anything else could happen his mother whisked him out of the bakery and into his bedroom. His clothes were removed and his hands washed of flour. He was put back to bed. Somehow he was too numb to cry.

When he came home from school that day he found a loaf of baked bread in his room. It had a shiny crust with his initials on the top. He kept it hidden for seven days until his mother found it and threw it away because it had hardened into stone.

TOPICS FOR EXPLORATION

1. Oreste relates his life experiences to the theme of baking bread. How is the baking of bread symbolic of the heritage passed from father to son? Consider the legacy of old Giuseppe to Oreste and the situation of Stefano and his father.

2. In a way, the narrative shows Stefano's initiation into the traditional art of baking bread. Try to reconstruct the steps he has to learn in the process of bread making.

3. Stefano's injury is a central theme in the story. Why is it important for Oreste that his son learn to bake bread? Why is it important to his mother that he *not* bake?

4. Characterize the father/son relationship in the story. What do you think it was like prior to the episode described here? Why is there a gap between them? How is a new bond formed between them?

5. What traditional view of gender roles does the family in the story represent? Why does the mother come between her husband and her son?

Maara Haas

Maara Haas is a writer, storyteller, and performer. Her collection of short stories, The Street Where I Live, *was written and narrated for CBC Radio. She has performed in productions for the National Film Board and Manitoba Theatre Centre. The story included here was first published in the collection* Made in Manitoba: An Anthology of Short Fiction *(1990).*

The Green-Roses Kerchief

There's more to the story of Baba Podkova than Burtzik the dog, planting corn in your front yard or gallstones in a pickle jar, though all of them have something to do with that fateful night in January of 1930 and the note on the pillow.

The whole of north-end Winnipeg went out in search of Baba Podkova, the old blind collie sniffing for clues—much good that was—you could put a raw steak or sliver of turnip on his nose, he couldn't tell which was which.

How it turned out goes back to where it really began, starting with the green-roses kerchief and hoity-toity Anastasia, Baba Podkova's only child, who married upper-crust River Heights, the army big shot Colonel General Reginald Fortescue Brown, Esquire.

Baba Podkova was happy enough to live with herself and the dog Burtzik, better company than Mr. Podkova, her cold-storage husband, an egg candler with cold cement feet and the habit of spitting up phlegm in the kitchen sink.

When God in His mercy shortened her husband's miserable life with killing gallstones, she respectfully placed the gallstones on the oak sideboard under the calendar picture of the crucifixion and went on living.

Haggling for sour salt at the Farmers' Main Street market, smoking her garlic sausage in the backyard kiln or weeding between the stalks of corn on the house side facing the sun, there was no mistaking Baba Podkova's knobby head in the green-roses kerchief tied under her chin.

Late into the night Baba and Burtzik sat together, sharing the earphone plugged to the crystal radio set, holding their breath as the creaking door opened and closed on THE SHADOW.

The fly in the butter was Anastasia, who wanted her mother upper-crust and pushing her to change her name, cut off your leg if the shoe doesn't fit.

"You simply have to bend with the times," her daughter scolded. "You know Woyblansky, our garbage man? He changed his name to Webb and what do you think? He's running for mayor. Why do you have to live in this rotten shanty? You could live like a lady in River Heights. Learn to play bridge, meet cultured people. You really should think of buying yourself an English hat instead of wearing that immigrant babushka. You look as if you just got off the boat from Europe. Neighbours are whispering your daughter is neglecting you, leaving you here unprotected, all alone. Suppose a thief, an escaped convict, a strangler even, was on the loose from Stony Mountain?"

Baba Podkova usually closed the doors in her ears to anything Anastasia said, but she got to worrying about the thief who might break into the house one night and steal the gallstones in the pickle jar, the last remains of her suffering husband.

So the next fine day Baba packed her things and left her house in the care of a neighbour who promised to bank the boxstove with a shovel of coal once a day to keep the water pipes from bursting.

What little I learned of the time that Baba Podkova spent in her daughter's house isn't good. The River Heights bylaw stopped her from smoking garlic sausage in the back garage. When she hit the health inspector with the leg of a chair, her son-in-law, Colonel General Reginald Fortescue Brown, Esquire, threatened to drum her out of the district with a bloody show of artillery and the Union Jack in flying colours.

River Heights is different, alright. It's hard to believe that the people out there grow nothing but grass on their property, just to watch it grow and cut it down till it grows again, but it's not a story that Baba Podkova could invent. Or could she? Another thing—the colonel's hound, German Shepherd Somerset Wagstaffe Masefield Reginald Brown, retired from the British Intelligence Secret Service, would have nothing to do with a commoner civilian like Burtzik the dog.

From her daughter's side, life with Baba Podkova was even worse. Rattling around in the upper-crust mansion like a dried-out pumpkin shell, Baba took up smoking Old Chum tobacco, rolling her own. Anastasia hid the Chanticleer papers for the cigarettes, but being Ukrainian and always resourceful, Baba tore out the onionskin papers from the first editions in the colonel's den and smoked her way through all of Dickens and Thackeray.

Introduced by her daughter as Mrs. Cove, Baba Podkova brought out the stones in the pickle jar: "And this is my husband. How do you do."

Or she came to tea in her green-roses kerchief and black felt boots, acting like a dummy, pointing to herself: "Me Ukrainian off da boat," whispering aside to a horrified guest, "I'm a prisoner here."

Anastasia finally laid down the law. Tomorrow Baba would have to renounce her green-roses rag, she would have her hair cut and frizzled at the Tip Top Beauty Parlour, and be Canadian.

The rest you know, aside from the note her daughter found pinned to her pillow:

Dear Anastasia and Mr. Colonel.
I am not hiding my green-roses kerchief.
I am not hiding anymore who I am.
I am going by foot to Czechoslovakia.
Don't try to follow me.

And where do you think they found her? In the most expected place, of course. Clutching her ancient wicker suitcase containing the two-ton family Bible, three dozen hard-boiled eggs for the journey, there she was, on the steps of the old St. Nicholas church three blocks from home—the miracle of the green-roses kerchief blooming like a spring garden in the midst of the swirling winter snow.

TOPICS FOR EXPLORATION

1. Describe Baba Podkova. What do we learn about her life? What are some of Baba's habits that she continues to practise after leaving her homeland?

2. How does the author describe Baba's daughter Anastasia, her husband, and her home in River Heights?

3. Do you think Baba is resisting her daughter's wishes that she become more Canadian? What actions prove it? How does Baba get her revenge?

4. What are some comic moments in the story? Is the author making fun of Baba Podkova? or Anastasia? or the Colonel? Are there any differences in the comic treatment of these characters?

5. The daughter in the story seems embarrassed by her mother. What causes her to feel this way? What part of her own culture is the daughter trying to deny or hide?

6. There is a conflict of values in the family described in this story. Evaluate both viewpoints. Does Baba Podkova have the right to remain who she is while staying in her daughter's home? Does Anastasia have the right to demand that her mother change her ways?

Rudy Wiebe

Rudy Wiebe was born in 1934 and grew up in a Mennonite community in Saskatchewan. From 1967 to 1992, he taught English and creative writing at the University of Alberta. He published his first novel in 1962, and in 1973 his historical novel, The Temptations of Big Bear, *won him the Governor General's award for fiction. In 1994, he won a second Governor General's Award for* A Discovery of Strangers. *His most recent book is* River of Stone: Fictions and Memories.

Father, Where Are You?

When I was a child, my parents were classic, western Canadians: immigrant homesteaders. With their children they were trying to build a livable farm out of a poplar-covered quarter section of land. The fact that they, as 1930 refugees from the Soviet Union, had to choose the stony bush near Turtle Lake, Saskatchewan, during a worldwide depression, made their work all the harder. I was the family baby and so had the privilege of watching the others without doing much myself, but as I grew older, one thing puzzled me. My father was rarely at home. And if he was, it was not for long.

A few early memories of him remain. Of him setting up a tent for us one summer evening because our log house—he and my two brothers built it, I was born in it—had to be fumigated with formaldehyde to kill the lice that kept moving in from the bush; father made an enormous fire from our lousy straw mattress that blazed up against the towering thunderheads and the dark house, its windows and log cracks and doors stuffed tight with grass. Of him walking so easily into the yard and beating a strange range bull, who had terrorized us all afternoon roaring about the yard, over the head with a poplar stick until the beast fled like a whipped cur. Of his beautiful tenor rising above all the men's voices behind me in our small church.

Lovely memories indeed; nevertheless, for most of my childhood he seemed to be missing. And it was in that very church where the most powerful image of my childhood was impressed upon me in every hymn, sermon, prayer, and Bible reading: God is our Father. Tenderly He cares for us, nurtures, teaches, comforts, but also punishes hard if necessary. When I began school, every day all 27 children together addressed Him, aloud, that father, and the prayer for me went far beyond word recitation into something powerfully searching: "Our Father, which art in heaven, Hallowed.... " In my child's mind the possible picture of "father" shifted, fluid as fish in the spring creeks. The questions "Where is he?" and "Where is He?" slid in and out of each other, wavered into one.

By the third grade, I had read a shortened version of *The Odyssey*. It begins with the boy Telemachus asking passing strangers whether in their travels they have seen his father, who left home 10 years ago. With such an absence, he says, "It is a wise child indeed that knows its own father."

Those famous words memorialize the profound mystery that has forever surrounded the facts of fatherhood. The facts of motherhood are plain: this is the child that she carried within herself, to which she gave birth at such a time and in such a place, and which she now feeds. The facts of fatherhood, however, seem not to exist. The instant of begetting is unknown to anyone; the begotten child grows hidden in the mother's body, and the man (the father?) can at best be an attentive watcher at its birth.

In my case, as a child I had no sense of a mother or a father's activities before my birth because I was taught unambiguously that children were "a gift from God." I never made any connection between the farm births of animals and the appearance of new babies in our small community where everyone came to church on Sunday. Animals gave birth, sometimes in a bloody, horrible mess as I once saw my brother pull a calf from a cow, but children were a divine gift; rocking me against her warm, huggable body, my mother told me that again and again. I was told nothing about human sexual behavior, certainly never stumbled on any, and, as the youngest in the family, I never saw my mother grow pregnant. For all I could imagine, babies arrived all pink-faced from God up in Heaven, beautifully wrapped in their Sunday cap and blankets exactly the way they were carried in their mothers' arms into the church babyroom.

HAVE WE NOT ALL ONE FATHER? HATH NOT ONE GOD CREATED US?

MALACHI 2:10

A mother (my mother) was a mother because she was always there, caring for her child (me) and never once leaving home (as I did not). A mother was someone who, as I discovered with amazement from a nursing woman who lived nearby, could unbutton the top of her dress and silence her screaming baby by holding it against her bare skin, which bulged there like some marvellous, glowing fruit. And answer your staring question with complete calm:

"He was hungry, and so he's eating."

"What's he eating?"

"Milk."

And when you ask, ever more astonished, "Where's it from?" can answer, "Me, it comes from me." And show you a milky nipple to prove it.

Which of course makes perfect sense, since your mother is always feeding you too, though in different ways. And when you ask her about this strange arrangement Mrs.— has for feeding her baby, she explains that's the way all infants are fed, but that you're too big, you already have teeth to chew potatoes and meat and can sit in a chair at the table and drink the milk warm from cows.

O, as a child I understood what a mother was very well; she displayed most of the characteristics ascribed to God. So what was a father?

The Second World War was being fought then, and it provided for many missing fathers. Mine was not one of them. The world war he had fought was the first of this century, not as a military combatant but as a conscientious objector. The Czar allowed Russian Mennonites an extended term of alternative service (usually hospital or forestry work) in lieu of compulsory military training, but in 1914 my father was barely home from three years of that when the Great War broke out and he was conscripted again. He spent another three years in the forests of Siberia until the Russian government fell; in the resulting chaos of civil war, he disguised himself in a soldier's uniform and rode freight trains back to his home village. By 1940, after 10 years in Canada, he was too old for so understandable a form of "missing" as military service, even if he had accepted it. Which I know now he never would have.

I know now, and knew even then, the ostensible reason for his being away so much. He was "working out," as we called it. In the spring, he would clamber over the wooden planks of one of those tall, square-cabbed trucks, vintage 1928, to breathe dust 300 gravel miles to Swift Current, Saskatchewan, or 400 to Nemiskam, Alberta, where the big farmers hired laborers for their huge War Effort crops. By the middle of summer, he would be working his way north with the harvest, pitching bundles onto the hayracks (field pitcher: the toughest job on the crew) for hauling to the giant threshing machines, and as he approached home he would sometimes return for a Sunday and leave immediately after with his own rack and team (he could earn up to $3.50 a day that way). Eventually the enormous steam tractor, blasting woodsmoke, would drag the threshing machine into our yard and manoeuvre it against our granary. If he had threshed long enough, he would have earned the price of threshing our own small crop. It seemed our bush clearing was always the last on that long harvesting trail north, a circumstance about which my mother complained bitterly as rain and then snow increased.

But with that late return, my father would remain home only until the winter settled in; by early November he would harness our two best horses to the heaviest working sleigh, heap it with hay and oat bundles, and drive north to the sawmills near Paradise Hill, or even as far as Cold Lake, Alberta. He would skid logs out of the bush with the team, and always be home for Christmas, but after New Year's he would be gone again to the mills if there was any work; during the war there always was.

I THINK A CHILD SHOULD BE ALLOWED TO TAKE HIS FATHER'S OR HIS MOTHER'S NAME AT WILL ON COMING OF AGE. PATERNITY IS A LEGAL FICTION.
JAMES JOYCE. LETTER. 18 SEPTEMBER, 1905

My mother and brother (beginning in his teens) farmed our homestead, and I have since learned that my father worked away from home so much not only to earn money to keep that bush farm barely alive. Nor was he lazy, far from it; he was physically very strong and he worked longer, harder, than anyone I have ever known. But long ago my mother told me he hired out because he was a man who did not make good decisions. This was not only so in Canada, she said; it had been that way in Russia too. It seemed he could not anticipate, seemed unable to foresee consequences. He worked tirelessly at the most thankless jobs, but though he knew a great deal about farming, he could not make the myriad, small decisions necessary to build up a marginal farm in Canada. He worked best when told what to do. He was not, it seems, a leader.

Many, perhaps most, men aren't. And why the elementary physical ability of being able to impregnate a woman, why a momentary sexual spasm of uncertain time and always unknown effectiveness, should, somehow, direct the qualities of human leadership toward the male remains an unfathomed mystery to me. In our family our mother was the leader; we all knew that. The Judeo-Christian teaching of God as Father, man as head, made little sense in my family. God always away? God told what to do and doing it? We were biblically wrong, all upside down or inside out, reversed, faintly freaks.

For me this was a private matter, and I would no more have admitted it than go about naked in public. But I longed to be "normal," as I believed other families to be, and what concerns me now is the contradictory understanding of "father" I grew up with. It was not my father who guided me into the great mysteries of life. Death? The whole community gathered together for the arrival of death. Since before I can remember, I saw the profiled bodies of people I had known alive lying uncovered on the steps of the church, a surround of relatives weeping about the coffin while someone took pictures that I would see above the family table when we went there to visit. Sex? I was to eventually have my nose (as it were) rubbed into the mechanics of human sex through the conjunction of a giant stallion, the mare I usually rode to school, and a snickering neighbor boy somewhat older than myself. The mechanical facts as presented to my eight-year-old eyes seemed to me so savagely brutal that for as long as I could I refused to believe them; the humane facts, of course, required more time than that.

My father did not punish me; he was absent too much, and my mother did not trust him not to overdo it when he was present. Nor did he advise me about my life's work. True, his example taught me the value of hard physical work, especially after we left the homestead in Saskatchewan to my brother and moved to a small town in Alberta where he worked for the rest of his life as a farm laborer. But he could tell me nothing about growing up in Canada; he was over 40 when he arrived here and never understood more than the most minimal of spoken English.

YOU MUST DEAL WITH THE MEMORY OF A FATHER. OFTEN THE MEMORY IS MORE POTENT THAN THE LIVING PRESENCE, IS AN INNER VOICE COMMANDING.... AT WHAT POINT DO YOU BECOME YOURSELF? NEVER, WHOLLY, YOU ARE ALWAYS PARTLY HIM.

DONALD BARTHELME, THE DEAD FATHER

Such a gulf between father and child is, I believe, no longer unique to immigrants; most families experience it today. The technological revolution has made much of men's traditional work obsolete; more importantly, the social revolution of personal and racial rights, women's rights, and individual moral value has, I believe, made implausible our traditional Judeo-Christian patterns of authority.

Whether we know it or not, for most western men the problem is this: because we can no longer say in the traditional Judeo-Christian way, "This is what God says. Now do it," therefore men also can no longer say, "This is what I (the father, the man) say. Now do it." How can a father establish his role today?

As far as I can see, there is nothing inherent in the male that would give him primacy over the human race. In fact, his momentary and invisible role before birth, his secondary role after (he can at best feed the mother who must feed the child), makes him naturally subordinate to the female. Brute strength alone cannot, I believe, confirm his dominance with humanity, any more than can the early Jewish idea of fatherhood, based on Yahweh, a sort of perfect Middle Eastern desert patriarch. It seems to me that no thoughtful man facing the 1990s can believe in such an image of himself as "father". Such a certain male confidence is today a fatal delusion. The ideas of "a self-evident, worldwide male superiority", of "my belief (or race, or nation) is stronger than yours and I'll kill you to prove it": such traditional male western thinking can no longer hold our fragile, entangled global humanity together. Probably not even until the twenty-first century.

> MY FATHER IS GATHERED TO HIS FATHERS,
> GOD REST HIS WRAITH!
> AND HIS SON
> IS A PAUPER IN SPIRIT, A BEGGAR IN PIETY,
> CUT OFF WITHOUT A PENNY'S WORTH OF FAITH.
>   A.M. KLEIN, "CHILDE HAROLD'S PILGRIMAGE"

Which returns me to my original question: "Father, where are you?" The cemetery where his body was buried 14 years ago tells me nothing, but perhaps my memories of him, filtered now through my own sometimes sad 30-year experience as a father, can discover a little.

Unlike the God I heard thunder (with the voices of men only) in church, my father never gave me specific instructions. On the other hand, despite the disasters of his life, he lived his 86 years with a humble grace I think about more and more. For him there was work: whatever you must do (he rarely had any choice), no matter how miserable, you did it as well as you possibly could. There was also life: you killed animals for the necessity of food, but otherwise life was sacred. I never saw him touch a gun; he did not want one in the house, because "A gun can do only one thing."

Finally, for him there was faith: faith in the God revealed in the German Bible, which he studied with absolute devotion, and faith in his family. He was anchored by and, especially in later life, anchored in turn my mother; together they lived through 61 years. And he believed in his children.

For example, he was amazed that I, the child of peasants, should be successful at university. He could not read my writing (it was all English to him), but when my first novel, *Peace Shall Destroy Many*, highly critical of the patriarchal Mennonite community, caused a Canada-wide controversy in the church, he defied the preachers and supported me. He laughed with delight that a child of his could create such an uproar among all those "big men," as he called them, and he never doubted that I had written a "good book."

It seems to be that physical birth itself establishes a woman's primary claim as "mother." What kind of a mother she becomes, of course, is defined by her continuing life with or without the child she has borne, but the almost total irrelevance of the man in that very birthing gives him no such irrefutable beginning. He can only begin and must continue to prove himself "fatherly" by the way he lives. When I now look at pictures of my ageing father, I see a resolute, determined, occasionally intense, and almost defiant face, characteristics that, as a child, I do not remember seeing.

It cannot be the defiance of autocratic, patriarchal command, because none of his children experienced his life that way. It can, I think, only be the resolute defiance of a humble life lived, despite great difficulties, with some firm, certain convictions he never tried to force on anyone, not even his own children. It seems to me now that he was a very good father to have had in the twentieth century. Perhaps even for the twenty-first.

TOPICS FOR EXPLORATION

1. What are Rudy Wiebe's early memories of his father? What connection did he make between his own father and the father-figures in the Bible and *The Odyssey*?

2. Why is fatherhood in Rudy Wiebe's perception surrounded by mystery? How does the fact of fatherhood differ from the facts of motherhood?

3. Why did the author grow up with the contradictory understanding of "father"? Why did he think as a boy that his family was not "normal"?

4. In what different ways has the author's life been affected by his father's prolonged absences? Does Wiebe see the gulf between fathers and children as specific to immigrant families? In what sense have "our traditional Judeo-Christian patterns of authority" become obsolete?

5. Why does the author reach a conclusion that his father was "a very good father to have in the twentieth century"? From the perspective of his own maturity, what redeeming qualities is Rudy Wiebe able to discover now in his father's life?

6. Rudy Wiebe's essay is punctuated with brief quotations from the Bible and different writers. Read these inserted passages and comment on their relation to the main text.

Anne Jew

Anne Jew is an English graduate of the University of British Columbia. She has published fiction and criticism in many journals, anthologies and newspapers. Her film work has been produced by the National Film Board and she is currently writing her first novel.

Everyone Talked Loudly in Chinatown

Lately I have been walking home from school in the sunshine with Todd. It's October and the leaves have turned, though the temperature hasn't changed since the end of August. My father says the reason for this is there were two Junes in the Chinese calendar this year. I wonder if that makes this year thirteen months long or if one month is left out to fit it into the regular calendar. But I don't ask. He would launch into a long, boring explanation of the history of the Chinese calendar and say it was superior to the Western calendar. If it was anyone else, I would probably ask.

Todd is very good looking. All the girls at school think so, and it makes me feel good when they turn to look at us walk down the hall together. Sometimes on our walk home we stop at the park to sit on the swings and talk. Actually Todd talks a lot and I listen. He usually describes his daily visit to the vice principal, the cars he wants, and the bands he likes. There is a Led Zeppelin logo drawn onto the back of his jean jacket in black felt pen which kind of bothers me.

"Have you ever really listened to their lyrics? They just make so much sense." It's his favourite band.

I try hard to stay interested in what he says and ask him questions, but mostly I end up nodding my head and saying, "Uh huh, uh huh." He doesn't seem to mind my quietness though. His eyes are clear blue, almost like glass, and it's hard to describe the feeling I get when he looks at me. My whole body feels like it's melting to the ground, and I'm always surprised to see that it hasn't.

Today Todd walks me to the beginning of my block as usual and then crosses the street to go on. My mother would start to ask questions if she saw us together.

As I enter the house, I pass my grandmother's room to go upstairs. She is lying in there dying. I throw my bag into my room and head into the kitchen. I take out a bag of chips from the cupboard and pour a glass of orange juice and join my brother in the living room where he is watching a rerun of "The Brady Bunch." It's the one where Jan refuses to wear her glasses and smashes into the family portrait with her bike. After a while I forget about the Bradys and start to daydream about Todd.

The next thing I know, my mother is waking me up to feed my grandmother, whose hands shake all the time so she can't do it herself. My brother and I take turns every night.

I stand by the window in the kitchen waiting for my mother to put the food onto the dinner tray. I draw hearts encircling Todd's initials and mine on the steamed glass.

"Hey, what are you doing?" she asks. I quickly wipe away the evidence.

"Nothing."

Her dinner is basically the same every night—soup, rice with water, steamed vegetables, salted fish and a thermos of tea. When I go into the room, she is sleeping with the quilt drawn up to her chin, which is usually how I find her now. Before, my mother would move her to an armchair by the window where she could watch people walk by or she would watch the new television set my father bought for her. Her favourite shows were "The Roadrunner" and "The Beverly Hillbillies," both which I couldn't stand. She would point and laugh and mumble something in Chinese. She didn't understand them, but I think she liked their movements. Now she stays in bed, too weak to get up.

She looks really old. I think she's almost eighty-four, but no one knows for sure. They didn't have birth certificates in China then, and she had to lie about her age when she came over to Canada. Her skin is bunched up like fabric and it just kind of hangs from her cheekbones. But it feels thin and soft. I touched it once when she was asleep. Her hair is grey and white and oily. It's combed back, making her forehead look like a shiny grapefruit. The lobes of her ears have been stretched by the weight of gold earrings I have never seen her take off. She is hardly moving. She almost looks as if she were dead already.

"Grandmother, it's time to eat rice."

She briefly opens her eyes and then closes them again.

"Grandmother, it's time to eat rice," I repeat a little louder.

She opens her eyes again, and I bring the tray closer for her to see. She starts to sit up, and I put down the tray to help her. After I prop her up onto some pillows, I tuck a paper napkin into the neck of her pyjamas and begin to feed her. I really hate doing it and I always want it to be over as soon as possible. Luckily she has been eating less and less. I have been begging my mother to do it instead, but so far she hasn't given in.

"You're not the one who has to bathe her and change the sheets. Don't be so bad. You are the only one she has treated well. She is going to die soon anyway."

My mother can't wait for my grandmother to die. She is always telling my brother and me how she was treated like a slave by Grandmother when she first married my father.

"Why didn't you stand up for yourself?" I ask.

"Oh, you don't know what it was like then."

We start with the soup. The spoon makes a clanging noise as it knocks against her teeth, sending a shiver through me. She still has all of them, which is amazing since my mother already has false front teeth. She doesn't chew the food very much though. It stays in her mouth a while, and then she makes a great effort to swallow. I try to show her how to chew by making exaggerated movements with my mouth, but she just ignores me. She finishes the soup, and we start on the rice in water. Some of it dribbles out of her mouth, so I have to scrape it off her chin and spoon it back in like I'm feeding a baby. I feel disgusted and guilty and I don't know why. I also feel guilty for not spending more time with her and for not wanting to spend more time with her. Todd would die if he knew I had to do this.

She is a grown-up who has always taken care of me, but now I have to take care of her. It bothers me. She used to be different.

When I was little, she would take me to Chinatown every week-end. We would go to a small pastry shop at the corner of Pender and Gore. I would have a Coke and a coconut bun while she had tea with the owners. I had to call them Uncle and Auntie although they weren't related to us. They spoke to each other about the people they knew: who was dying, who was dead, whose daughter-in-law was lazy. They drew out their words into sighs and shook their heads at the misfortunes of others. Sometimes they would comment on me, looking at me as if I couldn't see or hear them.

"Look at that high nose. She doesn't look Chinese."

"She is such a shy cute girl."

I usually watched the customers, the bell tinkling above the door as they came and went. Most were short, chubby women with unmade faces and hair. They always looked tired and reminded me of my mother. They carried plastic shopping bags with different shop logos on them in Chinese characters, and their children would run around them as they tried to order. They would scream out their orders and at their children at the same time.

There were also old stooping men with brown spots on their faces and the odd gold front tooth, and old women with straight grey hair pinned back over their ears. The old people were always buried under layers of clothing no matter what season it was.

Each time we left, the owners would give me a box of barbecued pork buns to take home.

"Lin, thank Uncle and Auntie."

"Thank you Uncle and Auntie."

"What a cute girl."

My grandmother was very popular in Chinatown. While we shopped we would be stopped every few feet by her acquaintances. Everyone talked loudly and waved their arms. I couldn't understand why they had to be so loud. It seemed uncivilized. She also took me to visit her friends and I would occupy myself with extra game pieces while they played mah-jong.

But as I started to grow up, I stopped going to Chinatown with her, where it was too loud, and then I stopped spending time with her altogether. I started to play with friends who weren't loud and who weren't Chinese. This upset my mother. She was suspicious of all other cultures. My best friend for a long time was a German girl who lived up the block. Everything was neat and orderly at her house, and her mother was a quiet, pleasant woman who offered me green apples from their tree. My mother only bought red ones in Chinatown.

Grandmother eats the rest of the rice and some vegetables and then motions me to stop. I wipe her mouth and chin and help her to lie down again. She closes her eyes, and I turn out the light and climb the stairs to my own dinner.

On our walk home from school the next day, Todd asks me to see a movie with him. I lie to my parents and tell them I am going with my girlfriend Sandra. She swears not to say anything to anyone. Todd pays for the movie and popcorn, and we sit in the back row of the theatre. He puts one arm around me, balances the bucket of popcorn on his knee, holds his drink between his legs, and eats and drinks with his other hand. I am impressed. I usually gorge myself on popcorn, but I feel compelled to eat one kernel at a time.

Halfway through *The Great Santini* and after we've finished the popcorn, Todd offers me a Certs. Then after a while he turns to me and kisses me on the lips. He opens his mouth on mine, and not knowing what to do, I open my mouth. I feel his tongue moving around in my mouth, so I move my tongue around in his. He still tastes faintly of popcorn under the flavour of the Certs. Just as I'm becoming used to the new sensation, he stops and kisses me on the lips and turns back to the movie. I can feel saliva clinging to the edges of my mouth, and not wanting to wipe it away with my hand, I press my face into his shoulder, hoping his shirt will absorb the moisture. It works.

As we leave the theatre, Todd takes hold of my hand. I am quickly beginning to fall in love.

"Now that was a great movie. That Robert Duvall guy is one harsh dude. What'd you think? Did you like it?"

"Yeah, I thought it was quite good."

"Yeah, it was great."

My hand feels good in his, but his strides are twice as long as mine, so our mismatched rhythms make us bounce along instead of walk. By now I am truly in love and I let him take me all the way home. Only the living room light is on, so we sit in the darkness of the carport in the back. Todd kisses me again and we move our tongues around. I am lost in the kissing until a car's headlights shine at us as it pulls into the driveway.

"Oh my God! It's my mother!"

I grab Todd's arm, and we run to the front of the house.

"Go! Hurry up!" He quickly kisses me and runs up the block. I stand around debating whether to go inside or escape to Sandra's house. I finally decide to go in. My mother and father are standing in the living room.

"How can you be so fearless! Going out with a white boy!" screams my mother.

My father walks up to me, his eyes wide with anger, and slaps me on the face. Automatically, I slap him back. He is stunned and I take the opportunity to run into my room. I expect him to come charging after me, but I am left alone for the rest of the night. It is only when the last light is turned out that I start to cry.

When I wake up hours later, my eyelashes are clumped together with dried tears. I didn't draw the curtains, so the moon shines into my room. Everything looks calm and quiet covered in moonlight. It comforts me. Todd, my father—it seemed to happen so long ago.

Only the hum of the fridge can be heard as I creep out into the hallway. I slowly climb down the stairs to my grandmother's bedroom.

I imagine the sound of movement as I enter, but I stop and there is nothing. It is dark, so I feel my way over to the window and draw the curtains back a little. She is so still in the moonlight. I go to her and touch her face. It is soft, but cool. The shadows make it look almost ghostly. I take her hand, bony and fragile, and find she has no pulse. I drop it instantly and stand back to look at her. She is dead, I think. I stare at her face expecting it to move, but somehow it looks peaceful. I take her hand again, kneel beside the bed, and rest my head against her. Soon I am asleep.

TOPICS FOR EXPLORATION

1. Characterize the narrator's relationship with Todd. Why do they feel they have to keep it a secret from her parents?

2. How does Lin (the narrator) describe her grandmother? What is her mother's attitude toward the grandmother? Why does Lin feel "disgusted and guilty" while feeding her grandmother?

3. What does Lin remember of her visits to Chinatown as a young girl? How close was she to her grandmother at that time? How has Lin's attitude toward her culture changed as she started to grow up?

4. What takes place during Lin's date with Todd? What happens between them that triggers a family crisis at home? Why does her father slap her? Why does she slap him back?

5. Why does Lin go to her grandmother's room after the fight with her parents?

6. Discuss different gender roles represented by the characters in the story. How important are cultural and generational differences in understanding specific gender roles assumed by the daughter, mother, father, grandmother, and the daughter's boyfriend in the story?

Eva Stachniak

Eva Stachniak came to Canada in 1981; she has a Ph.D. in English from McGill University. She teaches at Sheridan College. The story published here first appeared in the journal Fiddlehead *(Winter 1994).*

Fatherland

H e walks through the street slowly, his eyes lingering over the grey buildings, over the signs of passing time. In his memory the apartment buildings stand along the sidewalk in a straight, disciplined row. When he was little, he leaned from his bedroom window to watch the army compound across the street. It was the guns, slim metal tubes mounted on the wooden handles, that excited him most. From his safe haven he surveyed the daily rituals of the soldiers who did not care for childish games. In their world everything was real: the guns, the uniforms, and the enemy they would track and shoot.

He thinks that now the buildings are short, slack, and lifeless. His eyes register small rectangles of windows, warped frames of beige doors, cracked plaster exposing raw, concrete walls. Something is missing, he thinks, and this unexplained absence troubles him. "The trees," he remembers, as he walks along. "The trees are gone." A whole row of old chestnuts disappeared. The rustling carpet of autumn leaves he used to trudge through, thrilled by their uncountable multitude. The chestnuts he used to pick up, pluck out of their green, spongy flesh, his fingers tracing their shiny, brown shells. He carried them in his pockets for days, just to fumble through the possibilities of shapes he could give them.

He doesn't recognize anyone here. His friends, one after another, did not return from their summer jobs in the West, their exchange programs, their feigned pilgrimages to Rome where, after the guided tour of the Vatican they ended up in refugee camps. He watches the women. His eyes cling to their chapped knuckles, bulging from the weight of canvas bags. Short, thick legs quivering, covered with nets of livid veins. He cannot locate them in his memory. He cannot recall the trajectory of change. His own mother died almost twelve years ago, a few months after he left for Canada. "She died in agony," his father wrote on a thin leaf of airmail paper which rustled in his hands as he opened it. "Her only wish was to see you before she died."

He used to come back home late into the night, defying the stillness of the street, smashing it with the truculent beat of his heels. But once he reached his apartment, he pressed the keys into his palm, silencing the clinking noise, gently pushing the squeaking door. His mother always woke up, a phantom emerging from the darkness, her face flushed with worry.

"You're not hungry? ... You should be wearing something warmer for this time of the year ... Is everything all right?" He did not answer. Her soft, pleading voice, her uncomprehending love, angered him even more than her fearful warnings, "Shhh ... you will wake HIM up."

His father's voice caught up with him in the daylight.

"What would you do without socialism? Spread manure on some rich man's fields! Or do you think you are too smart for that!" He tried not to listen, but the voice grew stronger. "Do you think anybody bothered, anybody wanted me to learn, to have what you have?" The thin doors to his bedroom opened wide. "But even then I loved my country! And I am proud of it." The voice was right above him now, exploding into his ears. "PROUD OF IT. Do you hear me!"

He did fight back. He took part in student protests. He went to clandestine meetings where he added his signature to the manifestos and petitions. He read underground pamphlets, listened to Radio Free Europe, The Voice of America. Whenever he heard of a crushed demonstration, arrested dissidents, he threw the news in his father's face: "Is this the country you want me to love?"

"Lies! All lies!" his father shouted then. "Spread by traitors and CIA agents." He watched his father's hands, the fingers folding slowly, the white skin stretching over the sharp crown of his knuckles.

"So my son, too, wants their dirty dollars?" He knew the mocking tone by heart. He knew what would follow. "As long as you live in my house you will show respect for your Fatherland!" "Fatherland!" he yelled back, slamming the door to his room. "That's it! Your land. With no place for me."

One day he came home with his hand hanging limp along his body, his right arm swollen, gushing with pain. He got caught in a real fight. He could feel how hard police batons were. A series of dry, crackling shots pierced the sky. He was their enemy, their target. And it didn't even start out as a protest. He was with his friends. They were leaving a jazz concert; they were excited, happy. Someone started singing. Someone else joined. Men in grey uniforms emerged from the night like giant, stalking cats, invisible but for their flashing eyes. He tried to run away. Sharp blows slowed him down, brought him to the ground. He crawled home, his face clenched in pain, swearing that he would never let them do it again.

But then, in his room, alone with the pulsating pain, he gave in to the waves of hopelessness. Hopelessness that whispered to him that nothing will ever change, that he will just waste his life in endless fights, suffocate in bitterness. He thought he knew what a drowning man must know, breathing in the heaviness of water, drawn into the rocky bottom, to the slow, murky darkness, among the wrecks, the ruins, which must have once started as different shapes.

His father's letters arrived every month. Small, shapely script followed in neat, even rows. "So my son is a traitor. He prefers to beg for crumbs at the tables of the rich than to endure the honest poverty at home." No word was ever crossed out; there was no place for doubt. He threw them into the fireplace, watched the pages go black, turn into square leaves of ash. Then he carefully printed his father's name and address on long, white envelopes and stuffed them with colourful pictures of his own son, the still, mute story of a new life.

The street has a new name now, a shining blue plaque with large white blocks of letters. The discarding of the name of a minor communist hero does not surprise him. Now his father lives on Cherry Street! Years ago, when he was growing up here, his friends took him to the attic of an old apartment building, just a block away from where he is now. There, in the dust, he saw boxes of old German records from before the war, the black disks with their silenced, unknown sounds locked into the grooves. They carried the boxes with them into the street, shattered the black discs against the walls, jumped on them in triumph, their shoes crushing the thick, black plastic. The things they used to find in these attics! Old banknotes, stamps with the arrogant face of Adolf Hitler. He climbs the stairs, slowly, step by step, his heart racing forward.

At the door he stops and waits.

When he is ready, each knock is deliberate and clear so that his father can hear him. For years he swore he would never come back here. No matter what, he said. He was still terrified by "the immigrant's dream."

His Polish friends called it that, for the same nightmarish vision sought them out, no matter where they emigrated to. In the dream he was back in Poland, knowing that this time he could not leave. Lost in the maze of long corridors, he ran from one office to another, stopping uniformed officials, pointing to his name in a Canadian passport, the passport which was to make him special, immune to their claims. All he could hear was a mocking laughter, exploding from distorted lips, echoing in the grey rooms. He would wake up drenched in sweat, his hands searching for his wife's warmth, slowly convincing himself that it was only a dream.

The door squeaks, the familiar sound, but quieter, less annoying than he remembers. He watches the old man his father has become, his body still erect but thinner, his face sharper, bonier. He is slower, too, he thinks, as his father shuffles to the living room, clearing his throat.

"Remember anything?" his father's voice urges him to make an effort, to think of himself in this familiar space, growing older, fighting battles over every poster he wanted to hang on the walls, trying to make room for himself in the solid space that was so very much his father's.

"It is all so different," he finally ventures. "You changed so much." He does not know what to say. His father does not help, just watches. "The walls are all different. This table ... I don't remember it. Must be a new one."

"When you left," his father's voice is sharp, "I gave your things away. I couldn't look at them." He turns his face. "It was a mistake. You should have things which make you remember!"

"Please, Dad. Really! It doesn't matter!" He watches his father's hands as the old man brings in a bottle of vodka and carefully pours two drinks. The crystal glasses were his mother's pride. He can see the veins, the outline of the bones. He would like to cover his father's hand with his, to stop the trembling.

"It matters. I was wrong. I threw away your past." The smooth, transparent surface of vodka quivers dangerously. The glasses are too full.

"Dad, I couldn't live here, no matter what. It's not your fault." His voice is quiet. Slow. Soothing.

"It is my fault. I shouldn't have thrown away your past. You have to remember." His father turns around to face him again. "Tomorrow I will take you to see your mother's grave."

They hold their glasses in hand, firmly, and drink their vodka in one gulp, squinting from the painful burning in the throat, waiting for the warmth to take over, to make them forget. "What was bad was not intended," his father mutters the old, soothing incantation, refilling the empty glasses. The old saying takes on a new life. They drink to it. He nods, relieved. That's what he wants, now. No more arguments. No accusations. His father would not understand, anyway. His heart is weak; he should take it easy.

"So what are you doing with your time, Dad? What have you been up to?" he jokes.

His father is silent for a long while. "I've been thinking a lot," he says, slowly, each phrase punctuated by silence. "About what you told me before you left. How you don't care why I joined the communists. That all I did was to build your prison. No, no ... don't deny it. That's what you said."

"Forget what I said, Dad. It was twelve years ago. I was angry." He leans toward his father, his hand presses hard on his father's fingers. The trembling stops.

"I can't forget." His father looks at him; his face is still too serious, too pale.

"I've written my memoirs. I explained everything. For you and for Marek. So that my only grandson would understand why I did it. When you leave, I'll give you my memoirs."

They sit together for a long time, afterwards, in a room swept clean of meaning, of his memories. Only the shape is the same, the blueprint for the world he has left behind. His mother would have kept his old things, hidden, and she would have brought them to him, secretly, at night. But even her traces are gone.

They talk about friends, the sad procession of death's warnings. Operations, heart attacks, pain, fear, cancer. "They did not even operate, just opened him up and closed. Too far gone." His father's cheeks are flushed now, warmed by vodka. "Young men are dying now. Your old friends. Remember Robert? Only forty years old. Heart attack! Too much has happened, too much." He listens to his father's voice, his monotonous accounts, his litany to their common roots, the few faces he can't even remember any more. But he nods anyway. He knows these are his father's fears.

On the plane a thin notebook in hard, brown cover lies on his lap for a long time. He opens it slowly and begins to read. *My life, my memories written in 1990, for my son and my grandson in Canada.*

He turns the page, impatiently. *These are the thoughts of a man who has always loved his country,* he reads. *They may not be always accurate for I have tried to describe from memory what happened to me during my lifetime.* The little notebook is covered with rows of neat, even handwriting. It has a page of contents with all the important places in his father's life: Makow, the small village in Southern Poland where he was born, Warsaw, Wroclaw.

I was born in 1924. My father owned a small farm, but the land really belonged to his late wife, and after his death would legally belong to my half-brother. My mother and I had nothing ... He reads about the childhood of hard work and poverty.

When the war broke out I saw people who were running away, trying to escape the German army. They came through our village, often with nothing to eat, no place to go. German pilots liked to fly over these columns of refugees and shoot with their machine guns. And then I saw them go back where they came from. Germans were everywhere. There was no escape. The word "escape" is crossed out. Right above it he reads the word "refuge."

I saw young men, women and children marched to concentration camps. But I am not a writer, and I cannot describe how it really looked. He turns the pages, all neatly numbered, organized into short, uniform chapters. *The most beautiful thing during the war was that people forgot their differences, and together fought against the Nazis. Without that unity we wouldn't have survived.*

His eyes slide over a dry list of his father's distinctions, his years of pride. *In 1944 I was mobilized to the new Polish army.... In 1946 I became a communication officer.... In 1952, when my son was born, I was the commander of the first Warsaw platoon and in the fall of the same year I was offered a position as the commander of the newly created division in Wroclaw. A great distinction for a 28 year old, from a small village, a son of poor peasants.* The dates he remembers, the strikes, show trials, the waves of student protests, the crushing of the Prague Spring, do not appear in his father's diary.

In May, 1965, I joined the Communist party. This decision helped me to be a better soldier and gave me a chance to have more to say about matters which touched me directly. I had no problems arriving at this decision. For many years I fully accepted the materialist view of the world, and I still do.

Before he left his father pointed to the empty yard in the back of the apartment building. When he was growing up, he played there with his friends. They played soccer, basketball. The ball ploughed through the ground, tearing off the tufts of grass. Their bodies collided in mid-air; sweaty, red faces screamed in victory. The old soccer field is now an empty square of sandy space, surrounded with benches and borders of autumn flowers. "That's where my grandson should be running now," his father said.

Canada was a good country to take my son in, to give him a good job. I will not say one bad word against it. If my son had to live among strangers, he picked well. But when young people leave it is the blood of the nation that leaves, the best blood. I was not bringing my son up for Canada. I do not want to live in the world where a son does not love the land of his father.

When he was leaving, his father said he wanted to go back to his village. To walk in the fields in the morning, to feel that cold strength of the wind.

I was an ordinary man who took what fate brought him, not trying to escape his destiny. A man who would never leave his Fatherland to serve one which gives him more comfort. I want to say this to my grandson, to my future grand-grand children in Canada: the love of your country is the most beautiful, the most important, the most sacred feeling in the world. Do not give it up. For anything.

He closes the notebook and looks out, beyond the small oval of the airplane window, toward the immaculate sea of white clouds, toward the purity of snow-white stalagmites. He thinks of a never-ending field of ice, a pure shield of crystal coldness, an impenetrable lid over the world below. A smiling stewardess rolls in a large trolley with drinks. He asks for vodka. He holds the glass in his hand for a long time, its coldness slowly giving in, dissolving in his palm.

He will keep the notebook for his son.

TOPICS FOR EXPLORATION

1. What changes in people and places does the protagonist of Eva Stachniak's story notice upon his return to Poland? What memories are triggered by familiar sights?

2. Why did politics get in between the father and the son? What two polarized political attitudes do they represent?

3. What was the mother's role in the family? Whose side did she take in the conflict between the father and the son?

4. Why did the son choose to emigrate to Canada? How did the father feel about his son's decision? What messages were sent through the father's letters?

5. During their reunion, are there any changes revealed in the father? Has there been any change in the son after all these years?

6. What does the son learn from his father's memoirs, which he reads on the plane? Why will he keep the notebook for his own son?

7. Does the concept of "fatherland" have different meanings for the son and the father?

SUGGESTIONS FOR FURTHER STUDY

1. Compare the use of foreign words and expressions by Isabel Vincent, Frank G. Paci, and Garry Engkent (Unit Three). Portuguese, Italian, and Chinese vocabulary respectively appears in the texts written by these authors, usually without translation. What functions do foreign phrases have in their texts?

2. Compare the mother-daughter relationship in Maara Haas's story and Isabel Vincent's narrative (Unit Four). Both mothers resist their daughters' wishes for them to become Canadianized. How do the daughters respond?

3. Both Paci's narrative and Genni Gunn's story "The Middle Ground" (Unit Three) explore the effects of cultural origin upon the children of immigrant Italian parents. What do the two selections have in common with regard to parental authority, childhood self-determination, and the willingness of both parents and children to compromise?

4. Compare the effects upon their children of the fathers in Rudy Wiebe's memoir and Eva Stachniak's story. How is the "mystery" of the father in Wiebe's narrative and Stachniak's story portrayed? How do the two fathers differ? In what sense does each of them become a significant "other" for his son?

5. Isabel Vincent (Unit Four) describes her mother's difficulty of "letting go" of a cultural habit or custom. How does this compare with the parents' insistence on the preservation of tradition in the stories by Frank G. Paci and Anne Jew?

6. How is cultural specificity of gender roles expressed in two stories by Chinese writers, Anne Jew and Garry Engkent (Unit Three)? What distance between parent and child is created by cultural and generational differences in their attitudes to gender?

MAPS OF MEMORY: PLACES REVISITED

INTRODUCTION

In voyages from the old world to the new and from the past to the present, the old world of the past is not abandoned; it resides in memory of place: its intimate geography, the particular images of times past, and the experiences lived there. Sometimes "the map of memory" is all that remains, if the actual landscape has been destroyed by violence or utterly transformed by time. Those who remember have themselves changed in their journey from the past. Although scenes from childhood that they revisit in memory might be bathed in a nostalgic glow, when they revisit them in fact with adult perceptions, the collision of memory and actuality can often result in bewilderment, alienation, or even anger.

A vivid reminiscence about a formative landscape, now lost to time and change, can still affect the adult narrator. The importance of Frobisher Bay to the Inuit author Alootook Ipellie, as a crossroads of the north and a crossroads of his personal landscape, is the substance of his essay "Frobisher Bay Childhood." The impact of white culture in terms of money, food, and entertainment is strong, but the values of Inuit culture nonetheless remain sound in this warm and humorous recollection. The famous French-Canadian author Gabrielle Roy has a similar response to her childhood experiences in the French settlement of Saint-Boniface, Manitoba. For Roy, like Ipellie, her childhood town on the prairies was a meeting place for the immigrant populations of the world; this experience of "the disparity of the species" has had a lasting effect on her views as a writer. Roy writes of the "divided love" of the Québécois who have transported their culture to other parts of Canada, but can never forget their roots. Finally, the landscape of Manitoba itself—the hills, the prairie, the horizon—have a significance for Roy which she cannot abandon.

The losses of the past and the alienation of the present occur in C.D. Minni's fiction. The main character tries without success to regain, even reconstruct, the past. Minni recognizes the changes that time has made in the Italian-Canadian real estate mogul Vitale and in the landscapes of his youth. After a painful separation from his Canadian wife and a twenty-three-year absence from Italy, he returns to the Rome of his university days and the hill village of his youth, trying to recapture their vitality in himself, but the choices of his adult life have placed them beyond his reach.

Harold Horwood takes us on a journey to Newfoundland, back to the 1950s. He offers a satirical look at some of the transformations that the province was undergoing after it had joined Canada in 1949. At the same time, he reveals the unique folklore of Newfoundland, which is best reflected in the language of its inhabitants.

Visits to the scenes of childhood can often provoke a troubling clash of memory and present experience. This can lead to disenchantment, despair, or rage. Dionne Brand's narrator, in "St. Mary's Estate," revisits the plantation where she was born. Her memory enlivens the scenes of her visit where her grandfather had been overseer for twenty years. The contrast between black poverty and white affluence on this former slave plantation—the blacks crowded into slave barracks even today, and the white mansion inhabited only two months a year—sharply renews the latent resentments of her childhood. Things have not changed as much as they should.

The maps of memory may be accurate or faulty; they may survey landscapes that never existed or that have been reshaped by time. Without them we could not orient ourselves in the past or retrace the way that has brought us here. If we lose or misread our memory of the places of our past, we can sometimes lose our direction in the present.

Travelling Song

A spirit
travelling on the wind
touched me
with its song
opened the door
swept me upward
I looked
saw stars
and desert red
painting paths
on lonely stretches
of land
for once
alone
with quietness
there is beauty
there

In the distance
a soft light
cast shadows
from a window
come back
come back

I will come home
bringing star designs
and desert paint
a quiet song
to sing
when the travelling song
ends

I will have things
to take out
and give you
before
I leave
for the silent
place

—*Jeannette Armstrong*

Jeannette Armstrong is Okanagan, and resides on the Penticton Indian Reservation, where she was born. She is director of the En'owkin International School of Writing. Her visual and artistic works have been recognized through several awards in Canada. Her published works include two children's books, one of which won the Children's Book Centre "Our Choice" award, a critically acclaimed novel, Slash *(1987), and a collection of poetry,* Breath Tracks *(1991). She has collaborated with renowned Native architect, Douglas Cardinal, on the book* Native Creative Process, *and recently edited a collection of essays,* Looking at the Words of our People: First Nations Analysis of Literature. *Her other creative works include two produced video scripts, three produced poetry music and collaborations, of which "Indian Women," on the Cargo Record release* Till the Bars Break, *was nominated for the Canadian Juno award. She has performed a story telling mini-series on Vision TV called "Arts Express." Works in progress include a music art video collaboration of South American and Okanagan Indigenous Musicians and Artists, and a new novel.*

Alootook Ipellie

Alootook Ipellie, a talented Inuit writer and graphic artist, was born in 1951 in Frobisher Bay (now Iqaluit) in the Northwest Territories. He was educated in Iqaluit, Yellowknife, and Ottawa, where he now lives. He has worked as a CBC announcer and producer, and has been editor and contributor to different Inuit magazines, including Inuit Today *and* KIVIOQ Inuit Fiction Magazine.

Frobisher Bay Childhood

When anyone asks me where I was born, I usually answer, 'Frobisher Bay,' but I never can tell them exactly where my birthplace was. I always say, 'Somewhere down the bay.'

But Frobisher Bay is the place where I grew up. My most vivid childhood memories are still strongly rooted in this town. It is the place where I suffered my set-backs and experienced my triumphs. Although they may not know it, the people I grew up with are still dear to me. They really are an extension of my own life. For this reason I will always come back to Frobisher no matter where I live on this earth. Sometimes, one's roots are sacred to a person.

I remember the first time I went to school. It was in a small red and white metal building, which was the Anglican Church at that time. I was about eight years old then, and we had only one teacher— she was a lady. It was a chilly winter day with the sun shining from the sky above. I had no idea why we were called together in the church. The first day we played a few games and it was cold inside, so we had our parkas on. Round and round we went holding hands together, until finally the game was all over. It was actually the first day of my education; the *Quallunaaq* feeling had entered my heart.

I cannot say exactly how I felt at the time, but I am quite sure I enjoyed it. I remember there was a machine inside the church that made a noise; I found out later that this sound came from a round disc inside a box with a top that opened and closed. I learned that the discs were records and that the box was a 78 r.p.m. record player with a handle on the side that you had to wind in order to make it play. This was very new to me at the time and another extraordinary addition to my knowledge of the new things the white man was bringing to our little town.

Many of the essentials for living came in by freight ships when the ice broke up in late July. The sight of these great vessels entering the world where we lived made thrills go through our hearts. If a ship came while we slept, the elders wasted no time telling us the news.

'Wake up boys, there is a big umiak anchored in the bay.' We got up, rushed out the door, and looked at the enormous vessel that was already unloading its cargo into the barges.

Our ship that came to Frobisher was the Hudson's Bay Company ship, bringing the year's goods to the stores. When it arrived, most of the Inuit in town went to help unload the barges. This was during high tide and everyone worked as a unit, just like a circus setting up the big tents and other things to get ready for the opening night. There was laughter among the people, a sign of happiness which never seemed to stop as long as the ship stayed. The way they worked together was truly beautiful; they reminded me of a large family. No matter how old or young they were, they were there carrying things, big or small, both day and night.

At low tide, when there wasn't much work to do, the Hudson's Bay Company staff members brought out hot tea and pilot biscuits for everyone. We were hungry by then and as soon as the paper cups were handed out, we scrambled to reach into the large teapot as if it was our last chance. It was a thrill to be among these people; my own Inuit brothers and sisters. I looked at them as truly wonderful human beings, enjoying their day together. But soon there would be a time to end all this when the ship left to go to other settlements in the North. It was time now to get paid.

This was a day of joy, when everyone lined up to receive their money. It was usually only a dollar for each day and night that they helped in the unloading of the cargo. Even a few bills satisfied them, although they had worked hard for at least a whole week. There were no feelings of being underpaid or cheated; they merely took what they were given. And the very same day, most of them were completely broke again. They loved to spend money on goods of all kinds. Fascination was in their eyes when they saw certain things for the first time, and they thought to themselves, 'I must buy this thing—it is so beautiful and different.'

In those days I remember that the United States had an Air Force base in Frobisher Bay. We, as Inuit kids, would go over to their base to wait outside their kitchen in hopes of being offered something to eat. We often succeeded and the smell of their food was like nothing that we had ever smelled before.

There came a time when at least once a day I would start to dream of having tons and tons of *Quallunaaq* food right in our little hut. Even if all of the food could not go in, I would think of becoming a genius at storing food and somehow get it all in there.

One day when a group of us were just outside the Hudson's Bay store in the base area, a number of guys came out of the store and got in their jeep. As the jeep started up one of them threw us what looked like paper money. We scrambled for it like hungry pups ... only to find out that it was play money made for the game of Monopoly. We looked up at the guys on their jeep and they were laughing their heads off. We nearly cried in disappointment.

I can remember one day I picked a fight with one of the students at lunch hour. The boy was one of those who was always causing trouble with other children and teachers. I distinctly had the feeling that I could beat him easily that day. I was feeling very strong and all my friends cheered me on. It was as if we were fighting for the heavy-weight boxing championship of the world. All the kids made a 'ring' around the two of us and we crashed into each other without a bit of hesitation, fists flying and muscles bulging from our arms! We grabbed each other's parkas and wrestled to the ground and up again. We swung our arms like sledge-hammers towards the opponent's head and made noises like only fighters made! I heard the crowd around us shouting words of encouragement and it was clear that the majority were rooting for me. It was important that I did not suffer a defeat in front of my friends. I fought hard but in the end, I received a bleeding nose and cried. Luck was not with me that day and it was good that my old friends were still my old friends. I never fought again after that.

There was a community hall in Apex Hill, which is about three miles from Frobisher Bay, and I remember they used to have a free movie for everyone on Sunday nights. Those of us who did not have very much money to throw around could not pass up the chance to see a full length movie free. So we would walk to Apex and back to see the shows that were often filled with action.

When the first movies came to our land, a whole new world was introduced to the Inuit. Our eyes would open up in fascination when the lights went out to start a movie. When the first frame appeared on the screen, we started to live in a world of fantasy.

The walks back home were as entertaining as the shows. Everyone got a big kick out of what they saw and amused themselves by reminiscing about the action-filled parts of the movie. Some of us would re-enact the roles of the movie stars and we had fun entertaining each other.

When we got back to Frobisher after the movie we'd find a deck of cards and start playing. My group of buddies played cards at least once a week like 'hard-nosed' gamblers. We would take our places and decide who was to deal the cards first and then go on to the serious business of winning as many games as we could. There was no cheating, and we played until one of us won everything the other players had.

What we were playing for were pictures of Hollywood stars.

Probably every kid in town had a movie idol in those days and pictures of these movie stars were considered as valuable as any good wristwatch or bicycle. So we never missed an opportunity to look through any magazines and newspapers that we could find around town. If we happened to find one good picture of John Wayne or Tony Curtis, it was as if we had found a gold nugget worth at least a couple of hundred dollars. Photographs of stars from western movies were without a doubt the most sought after because they were worth the most at the card table.

Next came the sword-clanking stars like Kirk Douglas or Steve Reeves. And there were the strongmen—like Tarzan, Hercules and Sampson. They were big heroes when I was an Inuit child. The photographs of clowns like Jerry Lewis, Bob Hope and the Three Stooges were also popular. So were Laurel and Hardy, and that timid knee-shaking character, Don Knotts.

The quality and the size of the pictures were very important. A good photo of John Wayne was worth two poor ones of the same star. Colour pictures were worth a few times more than black and white—no matter what condition they were in. The pictures of the stars in newspapers were considered good bargains but they were not as crisp as the magazine pictures and did not last long. Most of us could not get photographs from magazines so we had to resort to movie advertisements in the newspaper and newspapers were very scarce in our town in those days.

I can remember many times when my pockets would bulge with magazine photographs after a successful day of playing cards. They were valuable to me, so I could not afford to leave them around at home where they would not last for two minutes. I took great care not to crumple them. If I did, they would not be worth much when we started playing cards. So they were a bit of trouble to me because I could not move around the way I wanted to, and sitting down was always a problem. If I sat down many times during the day, I would find out that some of the faces of the movie stars were completely wiped out because of all the rubbing they were going through. A picture without a recognizable face was worth not a penny at the card table.

Clipping out photographs of movie stars was 'big business' for us as Inuit children. A good collector would naturally be considered the one to beat at the card games that would last for several hours. If he happened to be a little greedy about his collection we had all the more pleasure when we won his precious pictures.

These are a few memories of my childhood in Frobisher Bay. Life in the Arctic is changing fast and Frobisher has changed along with its people. If Frobisher has a distinct character today, it is that it has become 'home' to many Inuit from other communities in the North. On any given day in Frobisher you might meet an Inuk who had come from a town as far away as Port Burwell in the east or from Tuktoyaktuk in the west. There were Inuit from Northern Quebec, from the High Arctic, from the Central Arctic or the Keewatin. Today there is no surprise in meeting an Inuk from Alaska or even from Greenland, on the streets of Frobisher Bay. Who knows, maybe one day we will begin to see whole families coming in from Siberia to live in Frobisher Bay!

TOPICS FOR EXPLORATION

1. For whom has Ipellie written this autobiographical sketch? How much will his audience know about his subject? What is his purpose in discussing his childhood in Frobisher Bay?

2. In one of the opening paragraphs, the author says that "one's roots are sacred to a person." How does his essay support this statement?

3. How much space in this essay is devoted to showing the contacts between the Inuit and *Quallunaaq* (white people)? What was the Inuit experience of money? How did the Inuit entertain themselves?

4. What is the significance of the fistfight?

5. For Ipellie, Frobisher is the crossroads of the North. Why does its sense of space have a big impact on his view of the North?

6. Analyze the relationship between the loose structure of this story and the working of memory on which it seems to rely.

Gabrielle Roy

Gabrielle Roy, a distinguished Canadian writer, was born in 1909 in Manitoba, and moved to Montreal when she was thirty. She received several literary awards, including the 1957 Governor General's Award for Rue Deschambault *(translated as* Street of Riches*), the Prix David (1971), the Molson Prize (1978), and the Canada Council Prize for Children's Literature (1979). Among her other books are* Bonheur d'occasion *(translated as* The Tin Flute*), the first Canadian work to win a major French literary award, the Prix Fémina;* La Petite Poule d'eau *(translated as* Where Nests the Water Hen*);* Alexandre Chenevert *(The Cashier);* La Montagne secrète *(The Hidden Mountain);* La Rivière sans repos *(translated as* The Windflower*); and* Ces enfants de ma vie *(translated as* Children of My Heart*). Gabrielle Roy died in 1983. "My Manitoba Heritage," first published in the review* Mosaic, *was translated by Alan Brown.*

My Manitoba Heritage.

I

My maternal grandparents came from a little, lost region in the foothills of the Laurentians, north of Montreal. One fine day they left everything that had been their life to answer the call of the West and become homesteaders in Manitoba. They were no longer young—they had reached middle age, in fact—and it was a decision with no return, and a tremendous adjustment in their lives.

They travelled by railway, and then from St. Norbert, which at the time seems to have been a kind of caravanserai for French-Canadian settlers heading south, they started off one spring morning in their wagon filled to the ridge-pole, across the wild plain, following a faintly marked trail toward the rolling Pembina mountains. According to my grandfather, their irregular profile was supposed to console his wife for the loss of her native hills—but the very opposite happened: the sight of these pretentious little humps was to sharpen her regret at ever having left the steep slopes of her youth. This was the beginning of generations of divided love in our family, divided between prairie and mountain: a heartbreak, as I wrote in *The Road Past Altamont*, but also an inexhaustible source of dreams, of confidences, of leavings and "travellations" such as few people knew to the extent we did, a family that was horizon-bound, if there ever was one. And of course it is in their divided loves that artists and others find their hurts and treasures.

At the time of our family epic, my mother was a lively girl with a vivid imagination. Any voyage would have delighted her, for she had never been away from home, except for the occasional jaunt with her father from St. Alphonse to the big market on the square in Joliette. How can one imagine the effect of the prairie opening out before her without end and without reserve, wide as the sky which until then she had seen clipped by the crests of hills like the disconnected curves of a jigsaw puzzle. Now here was a sky that stretched all the way across from one sweet horizon to the other.

She never recovered from her emotions during that trip, and would tell about it all her life. To the point where my own childhood also fell under its spell, as my mother launched again into the old story, holding me on her knees in the big kitchen rocking chair; and I would imagine the pitching wagon and the accompanying rise and fall of the horizon as in a ship at sea.

Later, when I read Chekhov's *The Steppe* I felt myself in exactly the same atmosphere as in my mother's story. Everything was there: the rapture at the sight of the great, flat expanse of land, inviting as an open book and yet obscure to the mind; the touching unexpectedness, in this monotonous unfolding landscape, of the least sign of human presence—in the Russian story the windmill, visible from so far and for so long; in my mother's version, the roof of a house appearing at last in the distance of this uninhabited country—and even the feeling that this elusive horizon, constantly calling, constantly retreating, was perhaps the symbol and image of the ideal in our lives, or of the future as it appears to the eyes of our youth, full of promises that will always be renewed.

Once at their destination, which my grandmother called the "barbarian lands," although a number of her compatriots were already established there, she and my grandfather went about the task common to all settlers: recreating what they left behind.

Soon they had their steep-roofed houses, their sculptured cabinets, their bench beds, their kneading troughs and their spinning wheels; with their speech, still pure and picturesque in those days, their "Jansenist" faith, as people would say now, forgetting perhaps to what extent its severity was tempered by the shy tenderness of their hearts; with the grim cross in dark wood on the bedroom wall, but also the gaiety of their violins; and with all these and their memories and traditions, they built on this land in Manitoba, to the sound of the wind and the high, rustling grass, a new parish similar in all things to innumerable villages in Quebec.

My grandfather, the moving spirit behind this venture, I knew only through stories, which perhaps distorted his true face as much as they revealed it, as each raconteur painted him in his own image. Yet I often find him alive in myself at those odd moments of the soul when we seem to be acting in perfect liberty in our dreams and wanderings, but are really closely in harmony with the spirit of some ancestor. It is perhaps through him that I am still so deeply moved by the great elusive horizon, and especially the setting sun, from which came the clearest call.

My grandmother's tall figure hovers over my first memories like the grain elevators of the west, those towers rich in wheat and aroma and the magic of my childhood.

If she lived now, amid the preoccupation with self-fulfilment for women, my grandmother would likely be director of some big business or heading up a Royal Commission on the status of women. In her day, her talents were fully occupied from dawn till dusk making soap or cloth or shoes. She also concocted herbal remedies, dyes for her cloth and splendid designs for her rugs. I believe there still exist a few pieces of her homespun linen as resistant as her own willpower. In that "barbarous land" she succeeded in ruling, seldom giving in to it but often bending it to her own strong nature, having as little as possible to do with all these foreigners around her, these English and Scots, but re-baptizing in French all things and places they had named before her arrival.

For example, the neighbouring village of Somerset, where she had to go for her more serious shopping: on a fine autumn day she'd be sitting high in her buggy, reins in hand, looking very fine in her black bonnet and wide skirts spread across the width of the seat.

"Well, good-bye. I'm going shopping in *Saint-Mauricette*."

What would she have thought, she who created saints whenever she felt like it, of this age of ours which has unmade them by the dozen? Or of this ecumenism which has the audacity to bring together what she saw fit to keep asunder?

On second thought, I imagine she would have ended up rejoicing, not at the diminution in the communion of saints but at the growth in that of the believers.

II

The eldest daughter of this proud woman was my mother, and she lived, so to speak, in order to conciliate the opposing tendencies of her parents, from whom she inherited qualities in equal doses, for she was frightened yet infinitely attracted by the unknown. The longer she lived the more her self-confidence won out over her circumspection. In her were best united our family's two fond attachments: for Quebec, where she was born and of which she had the treasury of memories that only a child's ardent imagination could have kept safe; and for Manitoba, where she had grown up and loved and suffered. Perhaps the most successful lives are those that seem destined to bring about a meeting of such neighbouring ways which otherwise would run parallel forever. It seems to me now that her life was spent in trying to bring things together. First and foremost, her poor children who were so different in character; then the neighbours; and, finally, everyone. She lived in love for what was, is and will be.

Toward the end of her life, sick and very old but still full of the great wish of her life to see the sites and beauties of the world, she was anxious to make a farewell visit to Quebec to see some distant cousins again, she said, to call on this one or that one; but I suspect that the real purpose of her trip, perhaps unknown to herself, may have been to climb to the top of a Laurentian hill to listen to the wind in a tall pine, just to see if it sang as it had when she was a child.

In the little cemetery of Saint-Mauricette, I have also seen her, her face sad and serious, suddenly bend down angrily to pull out a weed from the grave of my grandmother, who in her lifetime had never tolerated a weed either in her flower beds or in her existence.

The place to which you go back to listen to the wind you heard in your childhood—that is your homeland, which is also the place where you have a grave to tend. Though I chose to live in Quebec partly because of the love for it which my mother passed on to me, now it is my turn to come back to Manitoba to tend her grave. And also to listen to the wind of my childhood.

Long before it was time for my mother's grave, before marriage, before the time for bearing children, when love was, for her, like the beautiful Manitoba horizon, a prospect of the most delightful mirages, a man was already making his way toward her through the years, following the mysterious paths of fate: he, too, had left Quebec, emigrated to the States, and in a variety of jobs had forged an experience as broad as life. A self-made man, he was now on the verge of returning to Canada, but via Manitoba.

They must have met at one of those evenings when Quebecers got together, evenings loud with singing, with memories, and talk about old Quebec. Perhaps on that first evening my father, who was gifted with a fine voice, charmed the girl with one of those old ballads I myself later heard him sing: *Il était un petit navire*, or *Un Canadien errant*, sad, sweet songs to which he brought a disconcerting sincerity, as if they were a barely veiled admission of his own uprooted state.

They liked each other, this dark-haired girl with the sparkling eyes, the soul of gaiety, and the blond man whose blue eyes were heavy with an indefinable melancholy, as if the struggle to educate himself and rise above the fate of so many like him at the time had made him over-sensitive to unhappiness.

They married, as people did then, for life, for better and for worse, accepting in advance the children God would choose to "send" them. Not only would they accept them, they would exhaust themselves to give them a better life than they themselves had had, richer and more enlightened. What was more, and as if this effort was not enough, they intended to transmit intact to their children the ancestral faith and language which in those days went together.

But against what odds! A material existence which by itself was difficult to ensure; children which it would have been more reasonable not to have; and now this stubborn determination, in the face of common sense in a continent where almost everyone spoke English, to preserve those words that bear from one generation to the next a people's continuity, a people's soul. The surprising thing is that they met this challenge perhaps better than their descendants who are in many ways infinitely better off.

III

My father had become a civil servant, assigned to settling immigrants on the virgin lands of Saskatchewan and, later, Alberta, a task which he carried out admirably, full of a paternal care for these bewildered souls whose confusion he understood from his own bitter times of test and sacrifice before he managed to achieve his present level. My parents had eleven children. Three died young. The elder ones were already scattered when I came into the world, the "last little one," as I was called for a long time. This was in Saint-Boniface, in the short street called Deschambault, whose gentle rusticity I tried to convey in my book *Street of Riches*. Did I succeed? Is it possible to record in a book the spellbinding powers of childhood, which can put the whole world inside the tiniest locket of happiness?

We lived with our backs to the town—a very quiet little town, serious, going about its business, its loudest noise being the church and convent bells—and facing the open spaces. These "open spaces" were nothing but lots which faded off into brushland and, for me, prefigured the truly open prairie. In places it was interrupted by small circles of trees, often stunted oaks which for as long as I can remember made me think of the chance encounter of travellers crossing the plain, who had gathered 'round for a moment to swap their news. The fact that the oaks stayed on the same spot day after day, and that their circle was never altered, did not hinder my fancy: they were people telling their stories of the world and all that they had seen and done.

In fact, Deschambault Street was a place where one lived one-third in France, one-third in Quebec, and to a great extent in our own personal fancies which changed with the seasons or the arrival of a new neighbour, or perhaps took shape from our contemplation of the infinite spaces that began where the street ended.

Saint-Boniface breathed, prayed, hoped, sang and suffered in French, but it earned its living in English, in the offices, stores and factories of Winnipeg. The irremediable and existential difficulty of being French-Canadian in Manitoba or elsewhere!

Yet it was perhaps at this time of my childhood that French life in Manitoba was at its purest, in a fever of discussions, demonstrations and visits of encouragement from Quebec, and a fervour which did not succeed in destroying the obstacles. The draining-off to Quebec of our educated young people, who found no way of living in French, had not yet reached its peak; it was to result later in a cruel impoverishment of our community. On the contrary, we received almost constant reinforcements from Quebec, in small groups: a new notary, a new teacher, a printer, a doctor. Some help also came from France. When, in 1928, I went to take over my first class in the little village of Cardinal, it happened that at least half my pupils were from Brittany or the Auvergne. For me it was as if I had spent that year in the *Massif central* or some retreat in the Morbihan. I had every opportunity to learn certain richly regional expressions. How marvellous, when one went to teach in a village, to receive more than one gave! The same was true of Notre-Dame-de-Lourdes, Saint-Claude and other predominantly French Manitoba villages.

Whether their origins were humble or elevated, these immigrants of French nationality or language, Walloon, Italian, a few Flemings, as they mixed in among us, enriched our French life and culture with vitality and a most distinctive originality.

Strange as it may seem today, I owe to Manitoba the good fortune of having been born and raised in a Francophone area of exceptional fervour. No doubt it was the fervour of a frail group fraternally united in its numerical fragility and its threatened ideal to build a common front.

I suppose that this enthusiasm, like a wick turned too high, could not burn forever. But its light was there—long enough to illuminate some lives.

IV

As soon as the Red River was crossed and we were in Winnipeg, it was another world. Even today the crossing of the Provencher Bridge from Saint-Boniface to Winnipeg is for me like going from the particular to the general. I know that the contrast between the two is less marked; but in those days, almost without noticing it, we made the transition from our life, somewhat turned inward on itself, to the manifold, strange, torrential and nostalgic human flood that made up Manitoba's population and came from all parts of the earth. This was the second marvellous gift I received from that province: to have glimpsed while still very young the pied disparity of the species— along with the realization that we are basically very much alike. Without having to travel, I could see the peoples of the earth parade before my eyes. I had only to stroll through the Canadian Pacific railway station to see women in white kerchiefs, their gaze so distant it was surely fixed on the other end of the world; or whole families with their bundles, their eyes dulled with boredom, sitting in a circle on their trunks, waiting for lord knows what; or patriarchs with long beards, wrapped in strange capes, followed by their families in Indian file along the wide sidewalks, as if they were picking their way through a mountain pass. I have said these things time and again, and can do no more than say them again every time I write about Manitoba, because for me the sight of these bewildered people, which the province offered me when I was very young, has become inseparable from my feelings about life.

At first my mother was startled and fascinated by this motley crowd of humanity that flowed almost past our door. In comparison to their lives, our own now seemed settled and secure, at least with some roots, she liked to emphasize. But the fascination was stronger than her mistrust. Soon she took her youngest children by a Red River cruise boat to see the Ukrainians at St. Andrews, and from the deck we would watch, perhaps a little ashamed, as the women, gleaning, trying to straighten their aching backs, would shield their eyes from the sun to stare at us, the do-nothings who had no better way to spend their time than watching others work. She also took us to see the Icelanders in Gimli; or we would simply cross the narrow River Seine, a stone's throw from home, to hear the mass "in Belgium," as we used to say.

The *Arabian Nights* of my childhood were made up of these excursions into Little Wallonia, Little Ukraine, Little Auvergne, Little Scotland, Little Brittany, wherever they were in Manitoba, and also the nearly exact replicas of Quebec scattered over the plain. This already, no doubt, gave me that un-anchored feeling, the drifting sensation of casting loose from habit which, with the slight anxiety it produces, is unequalled for making us want to see and seize and hold everything new, if only for a moment.

My father, home from long expeditions among the settlers, always brought fresh news about "his" unruly Doukhobors, "his" quiet Ruthenians, "his" devout Mennonites. His settlements now extended almost to Medicine Hat, each more surprising than the last, so that you'd think his tales were taken from certain pages by Gogol. This is perhaps why, when in later years I read *Dead Souls*, I was not as astonished as some western readers. Tchitchikov's adventures seemed somehow familiar to me. What was comical, singular and improbable was just as familiar to me as the dull, believable and everyday aspect of life. I even had to learn to tone down certain elements of the reality that lay behind some stories so that people wouldn't think I was overdoing things shamelessly.

This brings me to the essential thing Manitoba brought me. My father's stories, the little trips we took with my mother, the Manitoba backdrop where the faces of all the peoples of the world were to be seen, all this brought the "foreigner" so close to me that he ceased to be foreign. Even today, if I hear a person living only a few miles away described as a "stranger," I cannot help feeling an inner tremor as if I myself had been the victim of an insult to humanity.

Either there are no more foreigners in the world, or we are foreigners all.

But the most enduring thing Manitoba gave me was the memory of its landscapes. I have travelled quite a lot. Occasionally I have been happy elsewhere and managed for a moment to feel at home in the gentle range of the Alpilles, or, odder still, in a certain small village in Epping Forest, Essex, where I ended up one day by utter chance; and there's a corner of the Isle of Rhodes, in Lindos, where at times I thought I might like to live, among the bougainvilleas and the women all in black seen against the whitest walls in the world, and the little interior gardens made of simple pebbles arranged with such grace that they compose exquisite mosaics.

At last it was the St. Lawrence, the link with our most remote Canadian past, but still a living, moving sea lane, always flowing toward the future. I live near enough to the river to see it from my window at all times, and I never grow weary of it, especially in the country, in Charlevoix, where it is twenty-two miles wide and comes and goes in regular, ample tides like the beating of creation's very heart. The "sea" drops, as they say here, and my own heart knows a kind of letdown; it rises, and my sad being finds a fresh departure.

But all these are adult loves, reflected on and sought after. My childhood love is the silent sky of the prairie, fitting the soft, level earth as perfectly as the bell cover on a plate, the sky that could shut one in, but which, by the height of its dome, invites us to take flight, to fly to freedom. My love encompasses the special silhouette, two-walled, of our grain elevators, their blue shadow like a cutout against a sky blurred with heat, the only thing on a summer day that reveals from afar the existence of the villages on this flat immensity; the mirages of those torrid days when the dryness of roads and fields throws up from the horizon illusory waters trembling between land and sky; the small clumps of trees, the bluffs gathered in a circle as if to chat in the desert about the wide world; and the infinite human variety of that countryside.

When I was young in Manitoba, one of our favourite outings was a trip to Bird's Hill. What was so attractive about it then? From the level plain there arose, for no apparent reason, a singular, long, sandy crest, the shore, one would have said, of some ancient lake, dry for centuries and turned to land, grass and market gardens, except in certain parts where brush allowed the persistence of wild life, and where one heard the plaintive cry of birds. No doubt it was a former strip of water left behind by the Sea of Agassiz since that immemorial time when Manitoba, almost entirely under water, was not even a dream. We would stay there, full of respect and astonishment. Perhaps we had an inkling that this strange crest of sand was uniting ages before our very eyes, the ages we call "past," those yet to come, the new, the old, those that persist, those that overturn, those we think dead, those we call "today," and that all these times were in truth no more than a second on the great dial.

Bird's Hill is perhaps my most sacred memory of Manitoba: on the shore of long-vanished waters, these ancient fossils, these dreams of youth, this unshakeable confidence in the far-off horizon.

You know how it fools us, this Manitoba horizon! How many times, as a child, have I set out to reach it! You always think you're about to arrive, only to see that it has retreated slightly, kept its distance once again. It is really a great signpost of life which an invisible hand mockingly maintains beyond our reach. As we get older, we grow a little discouraged and we even suspect that there is a supreme ruse behind all this, that we will never reach the horizon's perfect curve. Sometimes, however, we feel that others after us will undertake the same mad venture and that this horizon, still so far away, is the circle of mankind, full and united at last.

TOPICS FOR EXPLORATION

1. What is the "divided love" Gabrielle Roy's family has experienced that she considers in her second paragraph? What is the effect of the two images, the prairie and the mountains, on her imagination? How do these two geographic representations reflect the opposing qualities in her grandparents?

2. Roy's account catches the archetypal appeal of the experience of pioneers and homesteaders. How does she manage to add an almost epic dimension to her family history?

3. What cultural features do the Québécois transport with them to Manitoba? How do they recreate "what they have left behind"? What legacy do they pass from one generation to the next?

4. What is the "irremediable ... difficulty of being French-Canadian in Manitoba or elsewhere"?

5. From what parts of the world did inhabitants of Saint-Boniface come? In what way has Roy's early exposure to a culturally diversified environment changed her attitude to such words as "homeland," "foreigner," or "stranger"?

6. Roy often compares her experiences to literature—her own and others'. How do these literary allusions associate Saint-Boniface with the scattered cultures of the world?

7. What other places in the world does Roy compare with her "childhood love," the Manitoba landscape? How does Bird's Hill typify the primordial quality of Manitoba? What does the horizon symbolize for Roy?

C.D. Minni

C.D. Minni was born in 1942 in Bagnole del Trigno, Italy, and grew up in Vancouver. A writer, critic, and editor, in 1985 he published a collection of short stories based on the theme of immigrant adaptation to the new country, titled Other Selves. *He also edited an anthology of Italian-Canadian Writing,* Ricordi: Things Remembered *(1989) and co-edited* Writers in Transition: The Proceedings of the 1st National Conference of Italian-Canadian Writers, *which appeared in 1990. C.D. Minni died in 1989. The story included here is reprinted from* Ricordi: Things Remembered.

Changes

By three o'clock, Friday, Vitale had talked to his last client. He locked up his office early.

"Goodbye, Miss Elliott."

The girl looked up from her typewriter, squinting through large, rimless glasses. "Goodbye, Mr. Di Pietro, and *bon voyage*."

Outside, it was snowing again, goose-feather flakes. Traffic moved sluggishly, but he had plenty of time to catch his flight. He had packed the night before. The two suitcases waited, like orphans, in the middle of the front room.

The house was empty, silent. He almost expected to find another note by the telephone. *No point in discussing the reasons again. Jennifer.*

He phoned Tina, his sister, to check up on his kids; they were out in the snow. She must have held the receiver up to the window, for he could hear their yelling.

Not to worry, she said.

He dialed for a taxi.

The Calgary airport was bustling, but Toronto that evening was bedlam: baggage, children, tearful relatives. There were embraces as the CP Air flight was announced. Half the city's Italians, it seemed, were going back for Christmas.

By three o'clock, Monday, he was on the train to Rome. He had decided not to spend time in Milan after all; the city had few memories for him. He'd been there scarcely one year, the ink still wet on his lawyer's diploma, before Canada and family ties had lured him away.

It was drizzling and cold when he came out of Rome's Stazione Termini. Several Fiat cabs were parked under the street lamps. The driver of one solicited him as he stood in the rain.

"*Tassi?*"

Vitale ran for it. The driver threw his suitcases into the back and flipped the meter lever to "on." He was a paunchy man, his hat askew, a cigarette hanging from his lips.

He was taking a roundabout way to their destination to increase his fare, but Vitale didn't mind the tour; that was what he had come for. *A rest, the doctor said. A change of scene.*

They passed the Coliseum and headed towards the Sant' Angelo bridge. Vitale looked up at the archangel over the circular fortress that had once been Hadrian's tomb and was almost relieved to see it there, in the moonlight.

By the time they reached Piazza Trilussa, in the Trastevere district, the rain had stopped. The driver let him off at the fountain. Vitale looked for other remembered landmarks. The statue of the poet Trilussa still leaned on one elbow. Beyond the square was a walled sidewalk along the river, where he saw the student walking; above, the skyline was crowded with bell-towers and cupolas.

He picked up his suitcases and walked the rest of the way to the *pensione*. Twenty-three years, but he recognized the owner; he was the same small, bald man, his remaining hair gone completely white.

Vitale asked for Room II, if possible.

The owner—Vitale remembered his name now, Carlo, and the wife's, Luisa—seemed surprised. *Certo*, certainly. It was the off season. He could have almost any room.

Vitale signed the register with his gold-plated fountain pen, asked after the Signora Luisa.

The owner peered over his glasses at this *americano* in a white cowboy hat. Vitale explained that he had roomed there as a student at the university before emigrating.

"Ah, *sì*." The old man rummaged in the attic of his memory. "I seem to remember...." But he didn't, probably had him confused with someone else. Luisa, he said, was dead these three years.

He took a key and came around to help him with his suitcases.

Entering his room was a step into the past. The same venetian blinds, flowered wallpaper, cracked mirror. The same Modigliani print on the wall. He opened the bathroom door, and yes, found the student, soaking in the tub. The hot water relaxed him; it made him drowsy.

The knock on the door startled him—"Is anyone home?" And a woman's teasing laugh, clear and high-pitched. Luisa.

Dead, these three years.

"*Scusa*," the owner apologized, looking at the towel around his midriff, the wet footprints on the ceramic floor. "*Scusa*, your receipt."

Vitale dressed again and went out, looking for the small *trattoria*, where the student always ate, settling his account at the end of the month. *O Cavalluccio*. A white stallion pranced above the big, spiked, double doors, three steps down from the pavement.

The proprietor put a flask of white Frascati in front of the law student, and took his order: *il piatto caldo*, the cheap, hot pasta dish. He was only a postman's son and had to be careful with his meagre allowance.

Where was the guitar player who used to go from table to table, singing ballads for the price of a meal?

He wore a red sash from which hung a tin cup. Strangers were his best patrons, and he had already spotted the blond girl with the young law student. It was the first time he had brought her there.

"*La biondina?*"

She gave her name, Elvira, and Vitale threw a coin into the cup.

The man strummed his guitar, found the right key, and burst into a somewhat bawdy song about a girl named Elvira and unrequited love. Vitale had heard it before. The lyric was always the same; only the name of the girl changed. It never failed to produce smiles around the room, however.

That night he dreamed. He was riding in a horse cab with a girl—Elvira? Jennifer? He couldn't be sure in the dark. She was angry. They had been fighting again.

"Is it something I've done?"

"No," she whispered, face averted. She did not want entanglements. "Try to understand."

He didn't.

Instead he took the job in Milan to forget, and then in Calgary, farther away.

Vitale lay awake a long time, thinking of Jennifer—all the times she had called him too conservative, a fascist. *I've changed, he pleaded. Changed? she screamed with a laugh he didn't like. Only on the outside!* He had tried to understand, really had, couldn't, then would lose his temper.

He was out early, sipped a coffee in a bar, then took a taxi to the university. It was deserted for the holiday. He walked most of the morning around the campus—a thin student with a green scarf, shoulders hunched against the cold.

He paused under the leafless trees, blew on his hands, then turned for the law library. It was open. He went in, and found Elvira at a table, surrounded by books.

He sat and just watched her: elbow poised on the table, the head inclined long-lashed to the page, left hand absently sweeping back her blond hair, which she wore long, over her thin, blue shoulder. She loved the law with a passion, she said.

One of the sacrifices of the move to Canada had been his career. He'd gone into real estate, made money, but.... He shrugged. He'd done it for his family, of course. Jennifer had never denied that he had been good to her. *But only with things!*

In the end, however, she had asked just for her car, her potted plants, and some money. He thought of her living with that man, that yuppie.

The librarian was staring at him. He became conscious, suddenly, of his attire—cowboy hat and high-heeled boots. Could she help him? No, no, he was just leaving.

He was due in Villa on Thursday.

He took the first afternoon bus and settled to read a newspaper. Across the aisle from him sat two fat women bundled in overcoats. One had a raffia bag on her lap, a veritable cornucopia from which she drew mandarins, biscuits, and candy to bribe her two small boys on the seat behind.

The bus climbed higher into the Apennines, the driver leaning on his horn at every hairpin curve. It stopped to let a flock of sheep cross the road. The landscape was bleak—grey fields, leafless trees, smoke from farm chimneys. Grey, stone villages, and in the distance the snow-covered peaks of La Majella (height: 2797 metres, the mountains here as rugged as the Alps).

He must have dozed over his newspaper, for the bus was over the watershed now and was descending. It began to rain, flat drops on his windshield. He waited for the first glimpse of Villa, like a black and white postcard: stone towers and ramparts against a metallic sky.

The bus continued to descend towards the river, and then climb again, through olive groves, over a stone bridge, past the tiny cemetery with its twin pines, and into town.

It was already dusk. Street lights blinked on. The station was by the post office. A small crowd had collected to meet the bus. As he waited for his suitcases, hat under one arm, someone asked if he was the telephone inspector; they were waiting for the telephone inspector.

In the post office, a blind man sold lottery tickets from a booth. Men in galoshes smoked or argued politics. A radio blared.

His father was at one of the wickets, a tall, spare man in a faded, brown jacket, white mustache, and eye-shield. They embraced. It attracted attention. He was recognized, surrounded. Someone pumped his arm. Luigino, Villa's soccer champion. Did he know. . . ? Of course, they'd gone to school together. They laughed that he'd been mistaken for the inspector. In that *cappellaccio,* hat!

They walked home together, he and his father, and he described his trip and gave news of the rest of the family. (All of them well. They send their love.) His heels caught on the cobblestones, and he stumbled. His father offered to take one of the suitcases. No, no, he'd manage.

His mother came from the kitchen when she heard voices, dry-ing her hands on her apron, face flushed from the stove. She was baking. An aroma of vanilla and liqueurs filled the house. She hugged him. How was he? Was he hungry? She sliced a thick piece of *panettone* while his father fetched up a decanter of wine, fresh from the keg. As if he were a boy again, home from school.

They knew he would be coming alone and did not ask about Jennifer and the children. He was grateful for that, as he sat there happily watching his mother bake.

After dinner, the house filled with relatives and neighbours. His father brought up another decanter of wine, and they drank, gos-siped, and joked into the night.

He was tired when he went up to bed, but content. He fell, for once, into a dreamless sleep.

He woke to the cries of a vendor in the street below. Morning. He threw back the heavy quilt and went to the window. Through the slats in the wooden *persiane,* shutters, he could see the street. A fierce wind rattled a tin can along the cobbles, and a few old women in thick black shawls were on the way to church, shoulders bent against the cold.

He showered, then plugged in his electric razor. His eyes met, like strangers, in the mirror as he combed his still luxuriant shock of black hair. In school, he'd been called Vitalis. Later, when he told Jennifer, she thought the story was funny.

Dressed, he went down for breakfast, pausing on the stairs when he heard voices.

Esaurimento nervoso, nervous breakdown. *Ma il perche?* The reason? And his mother's angry retort: what kind of woman leaves her children?

They changed the subject when he entered. His mother had prepared hot bread rolls with orange jam and tiny cups of espresso. It was snowing on the mountains all around them, his father said, and rubbed his hands together.

After breakfast he went out. He wandered towards the heights above the town, the oldest part. He passed through the gate, all that remained of Villa's walls, and entered the Middle Ages. The tortuous streets narrowed and climbed in steps, but cobbles had been replaced like missing teeth, and the centuries sand-blasted from the rough, stone exteriors of houses. He looked up, at new wooden shutters and iron balcony railings painted green or red or blue.

He no longer knew these streets, and they did not seem to know him.

What was he looking for?

Half-way up, he reached a small square with an arcade of shops. They were closed, but he saw in windows clocks and boots, souvenirs and postcards, fruit and cheeses. At the far end, where a street descended from the castle, was Café Villa. An ancient vine grew from the dirt floor and, in summer, spread a canopy of cool foliage over the outdoor tables. The student sat in the shade, sipped iced coffee and watched village girls fetching water from the public fountain at the centre of the square, copper urns expertly balanced on their heads, gay-coloured dresses blown by the wind.

The café was closed. He stopped only a minute there, sitting at a table on the concrete floor below a plastic covering. He looked at the fountain. The water was turned off.

Above him was the ruin of the castle. He was surprised to find an iron picket fence around it and surprised that the gate was secured with a padlock. A sign advertised the times of tours. From April to October only.

But, as in a dream, he was through the gate—a 12-year-old running through the courtyard in games of tag or war, or searching for secret passageways and hidden treasure.

Somehow these memories had become more precious as he grew older. *Changed? Only on the outside!*

He turned right, following a street from the parapet of which he could look down on the roofs of the town, smoke billowing from chimneys, and farther along found the shortcut, a steep flight of stairs carved into the granite of the mountain, which brought him down.

His mother had prepared a heavy afternoon meal, and the three of them lingered at the table companionably until his father glanced at his wrist-watch and stood up; he was due at the post office.

Vitale fetched his overcoat too. He strolled down to the main piazza. The afternoon was already dark enough for the street lights to blink on. In a gift shop, he bought a Pulcinella toy, the clown dressed in a green court jester's outfit and mounted on wheels so that it clapped a pair of cymbals as it moved. For his son. And a doll dressed in a traditional peasant costume for his daughter. He had these wrapped and packed to mail but, crossing the square to the post office, changed his mind; he'd bring them back himself.

It began to snow.

On the way home, the student heard the *zampognari* even before he turned the corner. He came upon a scene like an antique greeting card: the pipers playing carols in the yellow puddle of a street lamp, snow falling. A crowd had gathered around them, and people stood in doorways and at windows.

Each Christmas the pipers left their herds on the lonely, windy hills of Abruzzi and came down into the streets of towns. They were dressed in traditional shepherd costumes—short black capes, vests and leggings of sheepskin, and rawhide shoes with thongs around the legs and curled-up, pointed toes. They travelled in twos. One played a *zampogna* or kind of primitive bagpipe; the other a reed instrument like an oboe.

They held out their hats for tips, picked up coins thrown from windows, then moved on, followed by children.

His parents' house was full of family and friends. His mother had set up a side-table with *hors d'oeuvres*, bread, rolls, and wine bottles. Carols played from the stereo. He played the polite host, opening bottles, pouring wine, making himself useful with a towel on his shoulder. He was given small parcels to take back to mutual friends in Calgary. The slowness of the mails, you know. But why was he leaving so soon? In three days? He had just arrived.

Tired of explaining the reasons—his kids, his office, the difficulty of getting flight reservations around New Year—he was glad to escape to midnight mass. It was, he reflected, his first time in a church in years. At some point he had stopped going—too busy buying, selling, winning.

When he returned, the house was silent. In the kitchen embers still glowed in the fireplace. Bottles were empty, dishes stacked. He tiptoed upstairs. Yes, the game had been different. He had set out to win by the new rules, and he had won big. He lay in bed and counted his assets: two hotels, one paid for; a ski lodge; 453 acres of land; a half-share in a movie theatre; a pub; and a fine restaurant.

He was back in Calgary for the New Year. The invitation to the party was among the pile of letters, cards, and flyers inside his door.

He went.

The guests were his usual friends—accountants, agents, builders. The conversation ranged from business to sports to politics. It got louder as the liquor flowed.

A woman said something about Reagan's Star Wars programme. He recognized her vaguely, replied politely.

He was passed another Scotch.

How was his holiday?

It seemed, now, as if he had never been away.

"Five minutes," someone called.

"Four!"

Andy Williams was on TV from Times Square.

They began the countdown.

Outside, horns and banging pots.

She kissed him. There was liquor on her breath.

He left early.

Drunk, he made his way back to his car. He had parked on the road at the side of the house, and across the driveway the subdivision ended in empty fields and, beyond, the prairie.

He stumbled on the snowbank.

Something moved ahead of him. A small animal? He raised himself on one knee and reached out to grab it, but it moved away. He chased it, but whenever he got close, it jumped away from him.

He flailed his arms, stumbled, fell in the knee-deep snow.

He was unsure what it was, as it escaped across the prairie, or even if it had been there at all.

TOPICS FOR EXPLORATION

1. What is the purpose of Vitale's visit to Rome at Christmas? What does he hope to find after twenty-three years of absence?

2. Traversing space for Vitale also means traversing time. Several times he sees "the student" (his former self) in familiar settings. What does the use of time shifts contribute to our understanding of the protagonist?

3. Vitale's journey to his hometown, Villa, is a journey to the past; his parents treat him "as if he were a boy again, home from school." What present problem intrudes upon the nostalgic happiness?

4. Compare the modest home of his parents to the "assets" he has accumulated in Canada. Think as well of the contrast between the Christmas party in his parents' home and the New Year's party in Calgary. Vitale "had set out to win by the new rules, and he had won big." What has he lost?

5. The whole narrative is based on Vitale's point of view, yet we learn very little about his emotions. Evaluate his relationships with others—his wife Jennifer, his children, and his parents. What are the possible reasons for his mid-life crisis? Does he really undergo any "changes" in the course of the story?

6. How effectively does the final scene bring out a sense of emptiness and futility in Vitale's life? What does the "small animal" he sees on the snowdrift represent? Is there any attempt to solicit the reader's sympathy for Vitale?

Harold Horwood

Harold Horwood was born in St. John's, Newfoundland, in 1923. He has taught creative writing at different universities, including the University of Western Ontario, where he was writer-in-residence in 1976–77 and the University of Waterloo, 1980–83. He has published extensively in such areas as fiction, poetry, history, biography, as well as numerous articles for magazines and literary journals. His article printed below was written in 1959, ten years after Newfoundland joined Canada.

Fumigating the Map

The Island of Newfoundland is justly famous for place names with a punch. Famished Gut is an example. And Rogue's Harbour. There are also Horse Chops and Hole-in-the-Wall, not to mention Sally's Leg and Virgin's Arm, all named in the distant past by sailors and fishermen with a sense of humour.

But the Post Office Department is doing its best to abolish these salty place names and to substitute such masterpieces as Port Elizabeth and Fairhaven. The improvement will be obvious, I am sure, to any fair-minded reader. We Newfoundlanders are all in favour of these improvements. We do not want to live in Hole-in-the-Wall. We want to live in Parkdale. It sounds so nice and sanitary.

We feel that if the Canada Post Office succeeds in getting rid of all the old place names we will be much the better for it. We are even prepared to help them out by supplying them with a list of old names that they've never heard of yet. At least, we are pretty certain that they have never heard of them, since they have never managed to deliver any mail there. Devil's Thumb, for instance. I'll bet they've never delivered a letter to Devil's Thumb in all their born days.

And then there's Fom. That isn't really the way you spell it. On the map it is spelled "Femme", but everyone who lives there calls it Fom, so Fom it must be. There's a story about Fom:

An American yacht with a fishing party was plying along the northern inlets of Fortune Bay one evening, and tied up to a stage head in a small cove. The island offshore was known as Petticoat Island, but the Americans didn't know that. The yachting skipper accosted the first baccy-chewing character he met on the stage.

"Hello," he greeted. "Where are we? What do you call this settlement?"

"Fom," said the baccy-chewer, casting a speculative eye at the weather.

"OK," said the American. "We want to send a message home. Where's the telegraph office?"

"Fifteen miles out the bay," said the native, adding that they usually rowed there in a dory.

"Post office?" said the American hopefully.

"One over in English Harbour East," the fisherman explained. "Ye must've passed it comin' along shore."

"No telegraph, no post office, no roads!" the American exclaimed. "Do you have radios here?"

"Well," the fisherman drawled, "they's a couple. But we don't turn 'em on much. Can't get the stations up in St. John's, and them Canadian fellers never seems to have any news worth while."

"Well!" exclaimed the American. "You people in Fom are really cut off from the world, aren't you?"

"S'pose so," said the fisherman.

"Why," continued the yacht skipper, "if New York burned down tonight you wouldn't know anything about it!"

"That's true, I s'pose," the fisherman admitted, "but then," — and he paused to squirt a philosophic stream of baccy juice over the stage head—"if Fom burned down you fellers up in New York wouldn't know anything about it, either!"

You will agree that we can't have places like Fom in this day and age. The sooner they are changed to Fairhaven the better.

Our greatest misgivings are on the subject of the speed with which the Post Office is forging ahead. As a prominent politician once remarked, officialdom should never move faster than the public, but we are afraid the Post Office may be a step or two ahead of common usage here and there.

In fact, public confusion has reached the point described in an old folk tale from one of the recently renamed harbours of Fogo Island.

The tale concerns George Coles, one-time "king" of the little settlement of Hare Bay, just as his friend Henry Nipper was the unofficial "king" of neighbouring Shoal Bay.

One night after an evening of old-fashioned square dancing during which the moonshine can went round many times and everybody got very jolly, George fell asleep in his boat, tied to his own stage, in his own harbour. Some of the younger element, with a taste for practical jokes, towed the boat, George and all, to Shoal Bay, and tied it up to the stage owned by Henry Nipper.

Imagine George Coles' consternation when he awoke in the cold and chilly light of dawn, a little shaky perhaps, in the wrong harbour, tied to the wrong stage! His reported remarks have become a classic of Newfoundland folklore:

Who be I and where be I?
Be I Jarge Coles or bain't I?
Or be I Henry Nipper?
Be I in Hare Bay or be I in Shoal Bay?
Or have the devil got I?

The Canada Post Office will see my point, I'm sure. If things continue at their present pace we shall all, before long, be as badly off as George Coles. We won't know whether we are in Hare Bay, Shoal Bay, Ice Tickle or Happydale Acres.

I have sometimes regretted the fact that the men who originally named the Newfoundland coves cannot be present today to see how we are improving on their work. The men who built the villages of Heart's Content and Seldom-Come-By, the sailors who named Pushthrough and Run-By-Guess, the old castaway who, with a grim laugh in the teeth of fate, named Black Joke Cove—I regret that they cannot come back to see the job which the Canada Post Office is doing on those places now. They would if they could, I'm sure.

We have one other little word of censure:

Among the host of lovely names with which the Post Office is redecorating the map there are a few—just a few—which strike some of us as being a doubtful improvement. We do not refer to such names as Sunnydale and Pleasantview (nobody with a pint of good red Canadian blood in his veins could object to such strikingly original names as those). No, rather we refer to such names as Pickersgillville, a settlement in Bonavista Bay named after that eminent Canadian statesman John Whitney Pickersgill.

Usually we allow statesmen to pass on to their just reward before enshrining them on the map, and since Mr. Pickersgill is still in robust middle life I feel that this haste to embalm him is rather indecent—like giving a man a coffin for Christmas.

Besides, I don't think Pickersgillville will last. It is too long and hard to say. People are bound to start calling it Pickersville instead. Once this process of corruption begins there is no telling where it will end. But in this case we can guess. It will be elided to Piggersville, which is still easier to say, and from that it is but a step to Pigsville or even Pigville. It is bound to happen, and what will the Post Office do then, poor thing? It will be faced with just another ugly name, fully as bad as Famished Gut, and it will have to go through the painful process of changing it to Silverdale or something of the kind.

TOPICS FOR EXPLORATION

1. What examples of "place names with punch" can be found in Newfoundland? Where do these names come from?

2. Why is the Canada Post Office trying to get rid of the old place names? What are some of the proposed replacements for the old names?

3. Harold Horwood uses anecdote to capture the spirit of Newfoundland folklore. What do we learn about Newfoundlanders from the story about Fom and the tale about George Coles?

4. Why is "Pickersgillville" quoted as an example of "a doubtful improvement"? What does this example prove when compared with the old names rejected by the Canada Post Office?

5. What is Horwood's attitude to the process of renaming initiated by the Canada Post Office? Find examples of his sarcasm and satirical humour in the story.

6. Check the meaning of "fumigate" in a dictionary. What effect is created by Horwood's use of this word in the title?

Dionne Brand

Dionne Brand, born in 1953 in the Caribbean, has lived in Canada for over twenty years. She has studied English and philosophy at the University of Toronto, and has also done postgraduate work in the field of education. From 1990 to 1991, she was writer-in-residence at the University of Toronto. She has published six books of poetry, the most recent of which is No Language Is Neutral *(1990). She co-authored* Rivers Have Sources Trees Have Roots—Speaking of Racism, *and edited* No Burden to Carry: Narratives of Black Working Women in Ontario 1920s to 1950s. *Our selection comes from her first collection of short stories,* Sans Souci and Other Stories *(1988).*

St. Mary's Estate

St. Mary's Estate was further on. Past the two rum and grocery shops, past Miss Dot's, past the savannah, past Miss Jeanne's parlour—paradise plums in large bottle jars. Then a piece of bush. Then St. Mary's.

Most of it is still there I notice, as the jeep misses the St. Mary's entrance and drives a little way on to Schoener's Road, the dried-out river bed in which duennes used to play all night, or so the story goes. I tell my sister this is where the spirits of dead unchristened children used to live, duennes, calling children in the evening to come and play. Our friend, driving the jeep, asks if I want to write down the correct spelling of the name of the road. I tell him it does not matter. I have known that road and that dry river bed for thirty-four years with a mixture of fear and curiosity, though I've only ever stood this distance from it. The story might still be true. The trees and the stones have been preserved in my head with their sign of silence, yellowness and eerie emptiness. When we look toward the river bed, the three of us, we look as if we're watching something or someone. Not emigration, not schooling, not brightly lit cities have managed to remove the shapes of duennes in the river bed by Schoener's Road. Not even Schoener, probably a Dutch privateer, with all his greed and wickedness, debauchery and woman-burning, not even he could remove the shapes of duennes in this river bed, by putting his strange name to it. It is still quiet, waiting for dusk for duennes to come out calling to play whoop.

The jeep turns around. The two male passengers of a truck leaving Schoener's Road stare at us as the vehicles negotiate passage. Then the jeep turns right into the gravelled entrance of St. Mary's. There is still a white sign board on a post, now leaning into the ditch at the entrance, now woodlice eaten. The letters are worn, but officious and distant; painted a long time ago, they survive like the post. A vigilant reminder and a current record of ownership and property. At this point you can see the sea straight ahead, in back of the house where I was born. This entrance gives you a sense of coming home, the same sense I've always had upon seeing it. The eyes light on the completeness of the scene it guards. There are two long barracks, one on each side of the gravel road. In front of the right barracks there is a great tamarind tree, now a little shrivelled but still protecting the place underneath, dirt swept clean, where people, mostly men, used to gather and play cards, drink rum and talk. Of the two barracks this one still houses people. All that is left of the other are the nine to twelve thick white pillars which it stood on once and the triangular moving roof under which copra is put to dry. Bush has overgrown the floors and the walls have been removed, perhaps from fire, or perhaps from ancient wear, sunk into the ground. That's where Cousin Johnny used to live. He was deaf and did not speak. He made beautiful soups and mouth-watering coconut bakes and saltfish. The whole compound would smell sweetly of his bakes on a Saturday evening.

The jeep eases along for another fifty yards; my eyes rest on the place, old and familiar like watching the past, feeling comfortable and awestruck at once. Then too, resentful and sad. A boy atop the left barracks stops raking the copra to watch us. No one else is about. The air is very still, yet breathing, a breeze, quiet and fresh, blowing from the sea. The sea here, too, is still. A country beach, a beach for scavenging children, thinking women, fishermen. The sea is not rough or fantastic, nothing more stupendous than an ordinary beauty, ever rolling, ever present. The kind of sea to raise your eyes to from labour. This must have been the look toward the sea that slaves saw as they pulled oxen, cut and shelled coconut, dug provisions from the black soil on the north side of the road. This must have been a look of envy.

There used to be a big well near the tamarind tree. Plait Hair and Tamasine used to live over there, in the third place of the back row of the right barracks. She had seventeen children; he plaited his hair, refusing to cut it. He worked hard, always in silence, his cheeks sucked in. Tamasine was a big red woman, as big as Plait Hair was slight and wiry. The walls separating each quarter of the barracks from the other did not go up to the roof, so everyone could hear what was going on in the other. Each quarter was one room. People used to wonder how Plait Hair and Tamasine had seventeen children, since it was difficult to be private. Maybe they'd wait till everyone was asleep, including their children. Even now, I find myself speculating.

There used to be a lagoon on the left, past the left barracks, off into the bush ...

The gravel road slows the jeep, as it edges toward the small wood house where I was born. Set in the centre to observe the two barracks, its back is toward the sea, its legs standing halfway in sand, halfway in dirt. It's the same house, thirty-four years later. The jeep moves even more slowly because of the silence of the place. As it passes the barracks there is no sign or sound of life except the boy on the copra house gone back to his work.

"It's the same house," I say; and to my sister, "Do you remember it?"

"No," she says, "I wasn't born yet."

Two men come out of the house as the jeep pulls to a stop near the front steps. I recognize one of them as the man who took over after my grandfather was fired as overseer of St. Mary's Estate. An emotion like resentfulness rises in me. It is only a memory of my grandfather, in his sixties; after twenty years, he was to be let go and, from what I could pick up at three or four years old, this new man was the cause. The new man, the overseer, is now an old man. His youth had been thrown in my grandfather's face and his ability to husband cocoa. I'm amused that something learned such a long time ago can still call upon the same emotion and have it come, fresh and sharp like this. I put on a smile and walk up the steps, my hand outstretched, saying, "Hi, I was born in this house. I just want to look around." He cracks a smile in his stern face, as recognition passes over his eyes and confirms, "Oh you is a Jordann," saying my last name as it has always sounded—like the name of a tribe, a set of characteristics ranging from criminal to saint, axe women to shango priestess, obeah woman. My grandfather's life put the sound into my last name. My grandmother's life put the silence after it. Jordann, like a bearing, like a drum.

My grandfather had children and outside women and outside children. He could read and he could write, which made him valuable. He was the overseer for twenty years at St. Mary's. He had an ornate hand and was such a strict parent that all his children wrote exactly like him. He rode two horses, Noble and Buddha. Noble was white and Buddha was black. Noble for show and Buddha for faithfulness. He drank rum at the first shop and the second shop, drinking and gambling out the pittance that he made tending St. Mary's for a white man. He wrote letters and took care of everyone else's business. He gave advice freely, he took only advice which could ruin him. He always walked straight up and stiff, the length of his six feet. Until the last years which he spent here, he lived a life of grace, depending on what was not possible, riches, and escaping payment of the debts he incurred dreaming about it. Grace only lasts forever with God, not with white men, so papa was disposed of when age was tired of holding out on his face and when he was unable to create a vision of acres of rich purple cocoa trees for the estate owner. Then everything caught up with him, mostly his debts and we all went to live in town, except he.

He first went to live in a house up a steep cliff which he could not mount because of his sore foot and then settled into a shack near the road where he sold ground provisions, callaloo bush, okra and pepper. Finally he got a job as an agricultural officer, walking miles into the bush to talk to farmers. The last entries in his diary, the ones before he died, only said, optimistically, "can't go to work, sick today."

The dirt around the house is mixed with sand and broken bits of shells. During deep tide, the sea comes in as far as the front yard, lashing against the pillow tree trunks which the house stands atop. We get the okay from the new man and head toward the beach. My sister and our friend follow me as I tell them,

"There used to be a lagoon over there; once it caught on fire. This is where we used to put garbage. See the shells are better here. This is a place for a kid to hunt shells and stones. This is where I used to play."

They follow me, looking at me a little strangely or perhaps trying to see what I see. My childhood—hunting up and down the beach for shells, stones, bits of bottles, snails, things washed up by the sea, lagan; the blue red transparent shine of 'garlent'; seeing how far you could walk; pointing to Point Galeoto; swearing we could see Venezuela; digging into crab holes.

"This is a place for a kid," I say. "Every Good Friday, a tree would appear in the lagoon. Mama said it was a sign of Christ."

We move away toward the lagoon. It is the dry season. The lagoon is still there despite the years of garbage throwing. Then we walk back toward the house, along the beach, and I point toward a river's mouth rippling into the sea, two hundred yards to the right of the wooden house.

"It was hard to cross there, the tide was too strong sometimes."

And then I see it, and I feel something in me hesitate to walk toward that side. It is a huge green house, hidden from the wood house by trees but visible on the sea side. It used to be yellow, it seems to me; but I could be mistaken. Rust, brought on by the spray of the sea, swells on its sides. It is empty and it is closed. I turn to my sister,

"That fucking house. Do you see that fucking house!"

My sister looks at me, understanding. I cannot bring myself to move toward the house or that part of the beach.

"That goddamned house. It's still there."

I feel such anger and yet, still, my feet do not move toward it. So angry, I feel nauseous. "Fuckers!" I yell, but the wind and the sound of the sea lift the word and balloon it into a feeble scream. The use-lessness of that sound stops me and I explain to our friend who looks perturbed, "That's where they used to live."

In fact, they didn't live there. They came with their children every July. Then we had to be reverential toward them; we could not walk to that side, especially if they were on the beach. They left at the end of August and then, we kids would rush, with my mama who went to clean the house, to see what they had left. Even what they had left we could not touch, thank God, because mama wouldn't allow us. Mostly, we children envied the real doll's head that lay here or there and the shoes discarded. Their children always wore shoes and socks. We ran about like mad things in bare feet and washed-out clothing.

For two months, this wasn't our place. For two months papa bowed and scraped, visibly. And mama warned us grandchildren not to misbehave or embarrass the family.

And still after this long, the imperative of habit and station causes my legs to stand where they are. Do not go near the house. It is the white people's house. It is their place and we are 'niggers'. Reaching back into me, thirty-four years, a command, visceral, fresh as the first day it was given. It still had the power of starvation, whip and ... blood. I turn and we walk back toward the wood house and the stern-faced new man.

This is where I was born. This is the white people's house. This is the overseer's shack. Those are the estate workers' barracks. This is where I was born. That is the white people's house this is the over-seer's shack those are the slave barracks. That is the slave owner's house this is the overseer's shack those are the slave barracks.

This estate has been here for hundreds of years. Papa was the overseer. It is the end of the twentieth century and the slave barracks are still standing; one, with people living in it; the other refusing to drop into the earth, even though it has no walls. Tamasine and Plait Hair used to live in the barracks. Uncle Johnny used to live in the one that's half gone. The walls were thin cardboard and the daily gazette was used as wallpaper.

To sleep beneath the raw stench of copra, night after night, for two hundred years is not easy; to hear tired breathing, breathless fucking, children screaming, for five hundred years is not easy. And the big house was always empty, except for two months of the year. The slave barracks whose layers of gazette paper stretched for hundreds of years, was packed with Black humanity, rolling over and over and over without end, and still. This is where I was born. This is how I know struggle, know it like a landscaper. An artist could not have drawn it better.

"Fuckers. Fuckers. Fuckers." I hear myself muttering, under my breath. "Fu-u-ck, they're still there."

I go up the steps of the wood house, asking the new man,

"Sir, who owns this place?"

"Hackens and them, nah," he replies, leaning his now gray head as if I should know or remember, "They always own it."

"Always?"

"Yes." The new man nods as he speaks, "You know, them is big shot."

I must not have remembered about the house; because now, I can see it from the front of the wood house, too. Twenty of us were born in the two rooms of this wood house, while that one stood empty, locked. I'm looking to where I had instinctively not looked before. The house is still there, green, the windows locked, rust bleeding from its joints.

We climb into the jeep saying good-bye to the new man.

Always.

The jeep hobbles up the gravel road past the quiet barracks. The boy on the roof doesn't stop his work this time to look at us. We get to the sign post. "St. Mary's Estate," it says once again, judiciously. Red-eyed, I have a picture of the green house in my head, ablaze.

TOPICS FOR EXPLORATION

1. What do the "duennes" represent for the narrator? How are they symbolically related to her present situation?

2. What gives the narrator "a sense of coming home"? What part does memory play in enlivening the scenes of her visit? Find concrete sensory images or descriptive details that recapture the past for her. Is there any indication early in the story that her attitude to this place has changed since she was a child?

3. The narrator is a member of the Jordann clan. What is the significance of this identification with family, and how does a sense of belonging affect the narrator?

4. As overseer of St. Mary's Estate for twenty years, the narrator's grandfather lived a "life of grace." What happened to him later?

5. What are the main symbols of colonial exploitation that inflame the narrator's anger? What is the significance of the big house inhabited two months a year and the slave barracks inhabited "for hundreds of years"? What does it mean for "Black humanity"?

6. How is the narrator's rage signalled by different stylistic devices used by Dionne Brand, such as repetitions and parallel structure? Why does she use the pronoun *they* rather than the name of the estate owners?

7. How does this visit to the place where she was born affect the narrator? Has anything changed since her childhood? What is the meaning of the repetition of the word *always* at the end of the story?

SUGGESTIONS FOR
FURTHER STUDY

1. Compare Alootook Ipellie's response to the imposition of white culture with the reactions of Pat Deiter-McArthur (Unit One) and Carol Geddes (Unit Four). How do they differ in tone and method from one another?

2. Compare the importance such authors as Gabrielle Roy and Harold Horwood attribute to the meaning of place in the preservation of cultural heritage. What different writing styles and strategies do they choose to talk about Manitoba and Newfoundland respectively? What can account for the difference in perspective between these two pieces?

3. Compare "homecoming" in any two of Minni, Brand, and Stachniak (Unit Five). How have the different experiences that emigration has provided changed their characters? What feelings are raised by renewed contact with the places of their origin?

4. Compare the role of memory in the pieces written by Boston King (Unit One), Gabrielle Roy, and Dionne Brand. What is the significance of memory for both individual and collective identity?

5. Gabrielle Roy expresses nostalgic feelings about her childhood in Saint-Boniface, Manitoba. Compare this kind of nostalgia with the immigrant nostalgia experienced by the characters in Salwa Mohareb Said's story (Unit Two) and Genni Donati Gunn's story (Unit Three).

DOUBLE BIND: CANADIAN IDENTITY

INTRODUCTION

The "double bind" of Canadian identity consists of several paradoxes. For many Canadians, especially those with recent experience
as immigrants or a strong ethnic identity, belonging to two cultures
can be either enriching or bewildering. While this double bind could
apply to any author in this collection, in this Unit we are
concentrating on some specific problems. First, double-bind identity
can mean feeling at home in both cultures, compartmentalizing life

into two discrete, complementary modes which can easily be reconciled. But the double bind might also mean being more at home in one culture than the other. If their cultural identity is more ethnic than Canadian, people may feel stigmatized and isolated from their community; if it is more Canadian, they might be estranged from their roots, unable to understand their cultural origins, and perhaps regretful of the loss. Finally, the double bind could mean alienation from both cultures. If people cannot identify with either culture (or both cultures) strongly—or are rejected by both as "inadequate"—they may feel lost in the ambiguous "no man's land" between the two cultures.

Tony German examines the double standard of Canada's colonial relationship with the "mother country," Great Britain. He recalls his discovery that English "superiority" is more imaginary than real. German shows how he needed to overcome the ethnocentric British domination in his own life before he could assert his pride of identity as a Canadian.

Ramon Sepulveda, in "The Reception," pictures the anxiety of a new Canadian, shifting among several scenes in his mind, during the formal ceremony of citizenship in the new country. Such anxieties, which confront the present experience with the rigid values of the past, are the crust of all culture shock.

Canadian members of visible minorities often have difficulties with their ancestral culture, if they have become "too Canadian." David Suzuki confronts this problem in his visit to Japan, where he observes how the expectations based on his physical similarity to the population are broken by his Western language, tastes, and attitudes. Although there is a "biological connection," he is a *gaijin* (foreigner), who is unfamiliar with traditional Japanese values. Unlike his immigrant grandparents whose motives are a mystery to him, he is caught between two cultures as a Canadian in Japan and a third-generation Japanese in Canada. Sun-Kyung Yi also experiences the "immigrant's split personality" as a Korean-Canadian. Unable to sustain a difficult double role—at home, at school, and at work—she finds herself drifting away from the very conservative cultural expectations she encounters in a Korean company in Toronto, from which she is demoted for being "not Korean enough." Although a member of both cultures, she feels that she is "accepted fully by neither."

Drew Hayden Taylor has turned this ambiguous situation to comic effect. As a blue-eyed Ojibway, he is called "pretty like a white boy" and is often mistaken for a white by Native people. He savours, in his essay, the paradox of being a minority in his own minority group. Often he has to argue for his Indian status. Caught between two cultures that judge identity by appearance, Taylor feels suspicious of the reaction he provokes in both cultures. In a final gesture of asserting his identity, he humorously secedes from both Ojibway and Caucasian races to become an "Occasion"—a one-of-a-kind.

Finally, Camille Hernandez-Ramdwar, a woman of mixed heritage, records her difficult search for a sense of belonging and identity. The child of an interracial couple (Ukrainian-Canadian and Trinidadian), she feels deprived of any right of cultural inheritance. The experience of racism has profoundly changed her perception of what it means to be Canadian. She discloses the hidden presumption of whiteness in the definition of a Canadian; she also reveals the racist and sexist stereotypes that Black women are bombarded with. In the end, defining herself as Ms Edge Innate, she chooses to situate herself on the periphery of the world that becomes ever more "divided, departmentalized, tribalized."

This "cultural schizophrenia," for some Canadians, persists as long as discrimination and stereotyping force us into definitions we refuse to identify with. On the other hand, feeling at home in both, one, or neither of the cultures seems to be a condition of living in Canada that we cannot—indeed, may not wish to—resolve.

Cultura Canadese

pick and shovel
    in a ditch
    calloused hands
    hard hats
boots planted in sewage
is the clay mud of Ontario fertile?

    la bella vita in America
pasta lancia
primo unico
mamma bravo
CHIN radio*

telejournale
"doferin e san cler"
    where are we now?
    the snow falls
    the wind is cold
where is our history in this land?
do the indian spirits understand italian?
have they heard of da Vinci or Verdi
or even Columbus?

    speak english only
not italian not even french
is this a paese**
or a geographical hypothesis?

—*Joseph Pivato*

*Joseph Pivato was born in Italy. He has a B.A. from York University and an
M.A. and Ph.D from the University of Alberta. Since 1977 he has taught
literature at Athabasca University in Edmonton. His books include*
Contrasts: Comparative Essays on Italian-Canadian Writing *(1985, 1990)*

and Echo: Essays on Other Literatures *(1994)*. *His poems and essays have appeared in many anthologies and literary journals.*

* CHIN radio: the call letters of a Toronto radio station featuring multicultural programming.

** paese: a community of like-minded citizens.

Tony German

Tony German is an established author, a screenwriter, an experienced naval officer, staff officer, and businessman. He writes historical fiction for young adults, including such titles as Tom Penny *(1977),* River Race *(1979),* Tom Penny and the Grand Canal *(1982), and* A Breed Apart *(1985). He is the author of a major history of the Canadian navy,* The Sea Is at Our Gates *(1990). His articles and stories have been published in different Canadian magazines, newspapers, and professional journals; he has also done work for film and radio.*

Bloody Brits

One of those scenes that sticks in the young mind and stays forever happened to me in 1935 when I was eleven years old. My mother, who'd been born English, had taken my sister and me "home" with her for a visit and we were at a Sunday tea-party in a country garden. It was quite lovely I remember, the garden. Bright with sunshine and summer flowers and a table laden with goodies. But I was trapped. Trapped by a tall and stately lady clad in tweeds. She talked at me, looking down from under the brim of her bee's-wing hat, the kind that English ladies wore pulled firmly down with both hands to cover the ears. Her head was tilted somewhat back. Her eyes were hooded and they sighted down her high-bridged nose, lining me up for a broadside.

"Ahhh," she said to me, with that commanding confidence I came to know. "Ahhh," she said, "Tony." Pause. "Tell me. Do you have the whaah-less. Yet. In Canadah."

The Wireless. Yet. In Canada. That's what she said. Actually said. And she'd said it, not asked it. And here we were staying near by with my aunt and uncle in their charming (my mother insisted) cottage in Kent just half an hour by train from Charing Cross, and their whaah-less was run by one of those big glass-jar batteries full of water and electrodes because their charming cottage had no electricity, no heat, and to get to the toilet and the bath you had to go out a side door into the perishing cold. And it wasn't a summer cottage either. They lived there year round. Did we have the bloody wireless. Yet.

I don't really remember what I said back. Perhaps I muttered something about my prized crystal set or listening to Jack Benny en famille on Sunday nights. But I do remember looking up at those flared nostrils and hooded eyes with the eyebrows arched above. And I remember what I felt. Condescension. I was being patronized. I may not have known the actual words but deep down I got the feeling. I was a colonial, jolly good little chap and all, but everything stems from the Mother Country and in due course Canadah would get the wireless and other such wonders as Imperial majesty might bestow. QED.

It was the single jarring event of that whole summer and it cracked the romantic picture of this England I had crossed an ocean to view wide-eyed. It was a fabulous time for wide-eyed viewing. Nineteen thirty-five was the Silver Jubilee of King George V and I saw it all. The gilded coach, the bearded King and bejewelled Queen, the magnificent escort of Household Cavalry, plumes and sabres and helmets and breastplates all agleam. Hooves clattering. Massed bands playing and banners curling and lines of scarlet Guardsmen stretching ad infinitum down the Mall.

Then Spithead, the fabled roadstead where the might of the Royal Navy lay in awesome, ordered ranks. Their guns thundered salutes, sailors raised their caps and hurrahed precisely thrice as the Royal Yacht steamed grandly by. Britannia ruled as she must have done forever. In Portsmouth, to confirm it, mighty *Victory* lay with her hundred guns, soaring masts, and the snowy quarterdeck where Nelson fell to the villainous French in deathless glory. And the gundecks below, painted entirely red—oh, joy—for when the scuppers ran with blood.

The Tower of London had real Beefeaters and the Crown Jewels, and at night a breath-taking floodlit pageant in the moat. It peaked, I remember well, when a splendidly costumed Sir Walter Raleigh laid his head, unflinching, on the block. With an astonishing piece of stagecraft it was lopped clean off. Madame Tussaud's wax warriors and heroes, kings and queens in splendid cavalcade, surely lived, and lived right here. And where else, as attested by her Chamber of Horrors, could murders be so gorgeously bizarre? Everywhere we went it seemed there were castles, courtyards, battlements, hill forts, and standing stones. At a cousin's ancient country house was a gigantic oak, quite hollow—we climbed inside—which had hidden King Charles from the Roundheads just as sure as local legend said.

I was stirred by all these deep-rooted wonders that were England. Truly excited. But I was not at all surprised. Seeing it all merely confirmed that the world and its story and all things wise and wondrous did indeed spring from this sceptred isle. I knew because I'd been reading about it all my life.

I'd Changed the Guard at Buckingham Palace with Christopher Robin, thrilled to Scrooge's ghosts. I'd braved shot and shell as a powder-monkey under Drake's flag. G.A. Henty sent me off too, *With Clive in India, With Wolfe at Quebec.* I'd even been *In the Thick of the Fray at Zeebrugge* in a Royal Navy motor torpedo-boat kindness of a somewhat lesser talent called Percy F. Westerman. And Stevenson of course. I *was* Jim Hawkins.

Now, this summer, I was face to face with it all. Even the strange Englishisms like Red Indians and ice hockey (as though there were some other kinds) didn't faze me. Nor did the fact that kiddies bathed, not swam, off stony beaches while fathers dozed in rented deck-chairs wearing braces, trousers rolled and handkerchiefs on heads, knotted at the corners. Those were excusable foibles and quite familiar in advance because we got the English comic papers at home. There was *The Tiger* for young fry, which I'd devoured, and, for my advanced age, *The Champion.* It cost a dime I think and it was full of stories similar to those in the luscious fat maroon-coloured annual called *Chums* that was under the Christmas tree each year.

The tales were all of British boys, nigh-fatally encumbered with instincts of decency and fair play, prevailing over all. The enemy might be the bully of the Lower Fifth, an avaricious mine-owning Portugee, a boastful American athlete. There were treacherous Spaniards, inscrutable Chinese, whole armies of Arab fanatics riding the Sahara, and even crafty, sneaking half-breeds in ever-frozen Canada. ('Breeds, they called 'em, and they used knives against our hero's fists.)

Oh, yes. Britain had become my world. This subtle and pervasive and surely calculated Imperial campaign to recapture with the written word each succeeding generation that occupied those red bits on the map had me in thrall. It was not just cricket and the law that cemented the Empire. It was books, books, books. And I was part of it. Until my tweedy lady. It was right then, when I think back, that I knew I wasn't English. That there was a difference that went much further than accent. Canada was mine. This England was theirs. And this happy breed looked at us colonials down its snoot. Tweedy lady's condescension, like the Parsee's cake crumbs under the rhinoceros's hide, has been under mine ever since.

British was not just best, mind. It was only. Viz. another tweedy lady some years after. A different one, gentler this time, dowdy and seemingly quite sweet. She was with her husband, who had "Brigadier General, British Army, Retired" stamped on his forehead, and they were on board the same boat in which my wife and I were enjoying a sightseeing cruise of the Amsterdam canals. Among the points of interest was the waterside view of a fine old house-cum-warehouse with curlicued gables. In it was born, as our young tour-conductor told us fluently in four languages, the great Admiral Maarten Tromp. Tromp did bloody battle with Admiral Robert Blake off Dover and Dungeness, he said, and swept the English Channel with the legendary broom at his masthead. Then, in the last few minutes under way, the young man circulated engagingly for his tips.

He paused at the two elderly Brits.

"Ah, yes," said she, speaking loudly as to any foreigner. "We did enjoy the tour. Your English is really excellent and we were so impressed with your knowledge of English history. Oh...." She stopped. On her face astonishment, revelation. The scales of ages fell away and her last look was of betrayal. "Oh," she said softly, and her shoulders sagged, "I suppose it was Dutch history too."

The droves of Brits who came to Canada post-Second World War from demi-paradise, wracked and riven as it was, brought talents and skills and thwarted energy. And the same old blithe conviction of superiority inherited from generations long past. As one who had been devastated by arch-Brit as a tad, I watched with baleful interest, awaiting, I suppose, some ultimate revenge. But as I watched, these newcomers permeated. I think that's the word. For they did not follow form. They did not come to the immigration sheds, awed and grateful, as entering a promised land. Commonwealth was a palatable synonym for British. Their slice of Canada was only proper due. And they utterly ignored a basic thrust of the new Canada by failing to cluster in an ethnic group.

They eschewed the staunch title "New Canadian." Nowhere did they form tight-knit communities with street signs in Olde English. No restaurants boasting English cooking did they start, thank heaven, though other-ethnic entrepreneurs did hire them for their accents to dish up cock-a-leekie and steak-and-kidney pie and bring their quaint hygienic practices to ersatz pubs. No distinctive dress came with them from across the sea. We'd seen kilts before, though Scots were never really Brits, and the bespoke-tailored set with bowler hat and brolly and county tweeds largely stayed behind.

They brought no new high days with them, no special New Year's to get sozzled on. The Irish had long since staked out St. Patrick's Day and the Glorious Twelfth and booze-worship generally. St. George's Day didn't take. Guy Fawkes could have sparked an annual spectacle had the wretched man succeeded in blowing up the House of Commons, but failure doesn't wash. Victoria Day stood as a reminder of past glory. Acting smartly, some properly organized Brits could have clinched it for themselves with, say, a maypole in front of each town and city hall. But the-24th-of-May-is-the-Queen's-Birthday was lost to Canadian compromise, adjusted so everyone could have a long week-end in spring. That made it a fair cop for any ethnic group. A pity, because Multiculturalism today would certainly pick up the tab for the maypoles.

Canadian tax money is available from one source or another to any group claiming cohesion by some exotic cultural glue. But while Ukrainian, Greek, and Caribbean groups flourish, I am told the Canada Council has had not a single application for morris-dancing. Gaelic and Celtic chairs abound at universities. Fair enough. But Gaels and Celts are tribes really and not your basic Brit. There are good things galore in the mystic net of Canadian cultural programs. Why don't Brits group up and climb aboard?

Their trouble is they just cannot come to grips with the simple fact that, once outside their blessed plot, they are in fact an ethnic group. Nowhere in the world—much less in a country where one of the languages approximates their own—can they consider themselves to be dubbed, nay, branded thus. Who? Us? Ethnic? No bloody fear. But you are, you know. You bloody are.

By and large Canadians are a welcoming and tolerant lot. There are some ugly exceptions in our history. Mackenzie King's denial of the Jews and forty years of foot-dragging over the West Coast Japanese come to mind. We are rather too easily put upon, a pushover for invasion by pseudo-refugees on the one hand, and on the other too bureaucratically clogged to welcome the genuine with expedience and compassion. Sure, there are red-neck pockets here, and the odd cry that the taxi business is cornered by Haitians, that Italians are railroading nomination meetings, and that the Hong Kong Chinese will own us all. But where else—wisely or not—are people given money to nurture their own ways, to live in the country but stay in their own cultural stream? Strange it is. But in the main, ethnic groups are not resented by Canadians. With the prime exception, dear friends, of you, you bloody Brits.

Because you are the only group that has ever dominated Canadians, first the French, then the English-speaking, on their own turf. Dominance spawns resentment, and Canadians still rest uneasy with the memory of yours. Earlier waves, don't forget, swept the Plains of Abraham and behaved as though they'd settled things. They fashioned the Château Clique and the Family Compact in their own image and brought world-class experience to diddling the Indians. More Brits came as professional soldiers to stop the unspeakable Yankees, to hang about the garrison mess and make off with the richest girls in town. They came as skilled administrators to establish peace, order and maternal government; as trained servants, too, who knew their place and ruled these less cultivated households cunningly from below stairs.

Courtiers even, direct from London, brought vice-regal splendour to Rideau Hall in boozy backwoods Ottawa. They excluded lumber barons and back-benchers and spittoons from their ken. Generations of social aspirants were withered by their savoir-faire. Then came the stream of idly well-bred remittance men to set social levels through dressing for dinner and to establish cultural leadership with what D.H. Lawrence described as "The Oxford Voice". It was, he said,

> so seductively
> self-effacingly
> deprecatingly
> superior.—
> We wouldn't insist on it for a moment
> but we are
> we are
> you admit we are
> superior.—

Now, post-war, it was not only that specific accent, that Voice, that caste. Brit social strata had sprung some leaks and the juices of the old aristocratic self-assurance had seeped throughout its many layers. Accent of course never could overcome the accident of British birth. But from Oxford to the Old Kent Road, whatever nuance they might possess, these new-wave types would cow you with it, seize control of the home and school or union local or whatever with nothing but articulate aplomb. The very sound could plough the diffident native under with subliminal avocations of deeper, richer reservoirs of wisdom and of power in fact long gone. The old arrogance could be called up in a trice, and, if all else failed, that ultimate weapon, calculated condescension. Tweedy lady had come by it with no effort at all. Domination? Let me try to count the ways.

When my eldest child was eight I took him on his first canoe trip. It was not ambitious. In the Gatineau, quite close to home, a couple of portages and you can leave the world behind. Our first night we settled into our sleeping-bags with that special luxuriousness that stems from a day of pack and paddle. The tent flaps were turned back to the embers of the fire, the silhouetted pine, the glassy stillness of the lake. A beaver splashed. A loon called. I lit the candle and pulled from my pack the book I'd selected with such care. This was a great enchantment to open to my son. Reading. In a tent with the wilderness outside, going on forever. His eyes shone. He was captured along with me as I read the wondrous tale.

Then the loon laughed. And laughed. And the sound of it echoed round and round the lake, mocking. He'd heard me, that loon. No wonder he laughed. I was reading *The Wind in the Willows*. Here. By this gem of a lake in the Canadian Shield I was reading to my own son about an English water-rat rowing an English mole up a peaceful English backwater. What was I doing?

But hold, Loon. What had we on our shelves at home for kids in 1958 other than English books? And a few American. Fine books, wonderful books. But, give or take Ernest Thompson Seton and L.M. Montgomery, scarce a Canadian book in a carload. Even the Grey Owl I'd read so avidly had betrayed my whole generation by turning out to be a Brit. And the books I read to all my kids were the ones I'd read myself, or that had been read to me. Bears in a London street. Rabbits in Mr. McGregor's garden. Cheshire cats in thin air. Moles in row-boats ...

In any loon's language now, that's an ethnic group. And burrowing mole-like, the lot of them. Right into my own offspring's heart. Going on this way, what possible protection would my grandchildren have?

Attack is the best defence. Right at the source. With my confidence puffed by modest success in Canada, I took the first book I'd written for young fry to a London publisher. Right in that panelled sanctum the senior editor, gracious lady, allowed it was good stuff. But, "The setting, you know. The background. The way things are in Canada. So different. Our young readers would just not feel at home. You know."

I knew all right and I snarled at her. I snarled that London publishers had waxed fat for generations selling Billy Bunter to the Sikhs, and they never cared a brass farthing what young Sikhs felt about anything. "Besides." I rose to leave, groping for the most devastating thrust I could muster. "Besides," I said, "we bloody do have the whaah-less. Yet. In Canadah."

She stared, uncomprehending. I stomped down Long Acre to Leicester Square in a fine rage, feeling better every step.

TOPIC FOR EXPLORATION

1. What is significant about the discussion of the wireless (radio) in the cottage in Kent in 1935? What contrast is it designed to reveal? What do "colonial" and "Mother Country" mean to the British woman? Find other ironic examples of British ethnocentrism.

2. What spectacles does Tony German see as a boy at the jubilee in England in 1935? How do "these deep-rooted wonders that were England" affect German's view of himself as a colonial?

3. What picture of British boy heroism does the author discover in books and magazines? How is he affected by literary exploits of British imperial glory? What role does literature, including literature for children, have in imposing the dominant culture and shaping one's sense of identity? How has the lack of Canadian literature, in the past, contributed to German's view of himself?

4. For what reason did British refugees, after World War II, reject the status of immigrant and "cluster in an ethnic group"? Why did they refuse to see themselves as "ethnics"? Is part of German's purpose in his essay to prove that the British *are* "ethnic"?

5. How does the "Oxford voice" attempt to establish itself as a force of superiority over other Canadians? Does it succeed?

6. How long does it take for German to free himself from the British-centred outlook? How does he turn the tables in his encounter with the British publisher's editor? Does he manage to overcome the expected British ethnocentrism?

David Suzuki

David Suzuki, born in Vancouver in 1936, is a writer, educator, journalist, TV and radio host, and a world-renowned geneticist. He appears regularly in the popular CBC television series The Nature of Things. *He has been an active spokesperson on social and environmental issues. This excerpt comes from his book* Metamorphosis: Stages in a Life, *published in 1987.*

Ancestors—The Genetic Source

My genes can be traced in a direct line to Japan. I am a pure-blooded member of the Japanese race. And whenever I go there, I am always astonished to see the power of that biological connection. In subways in Tokyo, I catch familiar glimpses of the eyes, hairline or smile of my Japanese relatives. Yet when those same people open their mouths to communicate, the vast cultural gulf that separates them from me becomes obvious: English is my language, Shakespeare is my literature, British history is what I learned and Beethoven is my music.

For those who believe that in people, just as in animals, genes are the primary determinant of behaviour, a look at second- and third-generation immigrants to Canada gives powerful evidence to the contrary. The overriding influence is environmental. We make a great mistake by associating the inheritance of physical characteristics with far more complex traits of human personality and behaviour.

Each time I visit Japan, I am reminded of how Canadian I am and how little the racial connection matters. I first visited Japan in 1968 to attend the International Congress of Genetics in Tokyo. For the first time in my life, I was surrounded by people who all looked like me. While sitting in a train and looking at the reflections in the window, I found that it was hard to pick out my own image in the crowd. I had grown up in a Caucasian society in which I was a minority member. My whole sense of self had developed with that perspective of looking different. All my life I had wanted large eyes and brown hair so I could be like everyone else. Yet on that train, where I did fit in, I didn't like it.

On this first visit to Japan I had asked my grandparents to contact relatives and let them know I was coming. I was the first in the Suzuki clan in Canada to visit them. The closest relative on my father's side was my grandmother's younger brother, and we arranged to meet in a seaside resort near his home. He came to my hotel room with two of his daughters. None of them spoke any English, while my Japanese was so primitive as to be useless. In typical Japanese fashion, they showered me with gifts, the most important being a package of what looked like wood carved in the shape of bananas! I had no idea what it was. (Later I learned the package contained dried tuna fish from which slivers are shaved off to flavour soup. This is considered a highly prized gift.) We sat in stiff silence and embarrassment, each of us struggling to dredge up a common word or two to break the quiet. It was excruciating! My great uncle later wrote my grandmother to tell her how painful it had been to sit with her grandson and yet be unable to communicate a word.

To people in Japan, all non-Japanese—black, white or yellow—are *gaijin* or foreigners. While *gaijin* is not derogatory, I find that its use is harsh because I sense doors clanging shut on me when I'm called one. The Japanese do have a hell of a time with me because I look like them and can say in perfect Japanese, "I'm a foreigner and I can't speak Japanese." Their reactions are usually complete incomprehension followed by a sputtering, "What do you mean? You're speaking Japanese." And finally a pejorative, "Oh, a *gaijin!*"

Once when my wife, Tara, who is English, and I went to Japan we asked a man at the travel bureau at the airport to book a *ryokan*—a traditional Japanese inn—for us in Tokyo. He found one and booked it for "*Suzuki-san*" and off we went. When we arrived at the inn and I entered the foyer, the owner was confused by my terrible Japanese. When Tara entered, the shock was obvious in his face. Because of my name, they had expected a "real" Japanese. Instead, I was a *gaijin* and the owner told us he wouldn't take us. I was furious and we stomped off to a phone booth where I called the agent at the airport. He was astonished and came all the way into town to plead our case with the innkeeper. But the innkeeper stood firm and denied us a room. Apparently he had accepted *gaijin* in the past with terrible consequences.

As an example of the problem, Japanese always take their shoes off when entering a *ryokan* because the straw mats (*tatami*) are quickly frayed. To a Japanese, clomping into a room with shoes on would be comparable to someone entering our homes and spitting on the floor. Similarly, the *ofuro*, or traditional tub, has hot clean water that all bathers use. So one must first enter the bathroom, wash carefully and rinse off *before* entering the tub. Time in the *ofuro* is for relaxing and soaking. Again, Westerners who lather up in the tub are committing a terrible desecration.

To many Canadians today, the word "Jap" seems like a natural abbreviation for Japanese. Certainly for newspaper headlines it would seem to make sense. So people are often shocked to see me bristle when they have used the word Jap innocently. To Japanese-Canadians, Jap or Nip (from "*Nippon*") were epithets used generously during the pre-war and war years. They conjure up all of the hatred and bigotry of those times. While a person using the term today may be unaware of its past use, every Japanese-Canadian remembers.

The thin thread of Japanese culture that does link me to Japan was spun out of the poverty and desperation of my ancestors. My grandparents came to a Canadian province openly hostile to their strange appearance and different ways. There were severe restrictions on how much and where they could buy property. Their children, who were born and raised in Canada, couldn't vote until 1948 and encountered many barriers to professional training and property ownership. Asians, regardless of birthplace, were third-class citizens. That is the reality of the Japanese-Canadian experience and the historical cultural legacy that came down to the third and fourth generations—to me and my children.

The first Japanese immigrants came to Canada to make their fortunes so they could return to Japan as people of wealth. The vast majority was uneducated and impoverished. But in the century spanning my grandparents' births and the present, Japan has leapt from an agrarian society to a technological and economic giant.

Now, the Japanese I meet in Japan or as recent immigrants to Canada come with far different cultural roots. Present-day Japanese are highly educated, upper-middle class and proud of their heritage. In Canada they encounter respect, envy and curiosity in sharp contrast to the hostility and bigotry met by my grandparents.

Japanese immigrants to North America have names that signify the number of generations in the new land (or just as significantly, that count the generational distance *away* from Japan). My grandparents are *Issei*, meaning the first generation in Canada. Most *Issei* never learned more than a rudimentary knowledge of English. *Nisei*, like my parents, are the second generation here and the first native-born group. While growing up they first spoke Japanese in the home and then learned English from playmates and teachers. Before the Second World War, many *Issei* sent their children to be educated in Japan. When they returned to Canada, they were called *Kika-nisei* (or *Kibei* in the United States). Most have remained bilingual, but many of the younger *Nisei* now speak Japanese with difficulty because English is their native tongue. My sisters and I are *Sansei* (third generation); our children are *Yonsei*. These generations, and especially *Yonsei*, are growing up in homes where English is the only spoken language, so they are far more likely to speak school-taught French as their second language than Japanese.

Most *Sansei*, like me, do not speak Japanese. To us, the *Issei* are mysteries. They came from a cultural tradition that is a hundred years old. Unlike people in present-day Japan, the *Issei* clung tightly to the culture they remembered and froze that culture into a static museum piece like a relic of the past. Not being able to speak each other's language, *Issei* and *Sansei* were cut off from each other. My parents dutifully visited my grandparents and we children would be trotted out to be lectured at or displayed. These visits were excruciating, because we children didn't understand the old culture, and didn't have the slightest interest—we were Canadians.

My father's mother died in 1978 at the age of ninety-one. She was the last of the *Issei* in our family. The final months of her life, after a left-hemisphere stroke, were spent in that terrible twilight— crippled, still aware, but unable to communicate. She lived the terminal months of her life, comprehending but mute, in a ward with Caucasian strangers. For over thirty years I had listened to her psychologically blackmailing my father by warning him of her imminent death. Yet in the end, she hung on long after there was reason to. When she died, I was astonished at my own reaction, a great sense of sadness and regret at the cleavage of my last link with the source of my genes. I had never been able to ask what made her and others of her generation come to Canada, what they felt when they arrived, what their hopes and dreams had been, and whether it was worth it. And I wanted to thank her, to show her that I was grateful that, through them, I was born a Canadian.

TOPICS FOR EXPLORATION

1. Why does David Suzuki question the validity of the "biological connection" in determining individual identity? How does environment override genes?

2. Although Suzuki resembles them physically, he cannot communicate with his relatives in Japan. He is a *gaijin* (a foreigner). How does being a *gaijin* exclude Suzuki? Why is he rejected at a *ryokan* (a traditional Japanese inn)?

3. What are some cultural practices of Japan that Westerners misunderstand? Find examples in this account of mutual incomprehension based on cultural differences.

4. How have the different generations of Japanese-Canadians responded to the experience of the new land? How do people of Suzuki's generation (*Sansei*) view their immigrant ancestors (*Issei*)? Why are the hopes and motives of *Issei* still a "mystery" to Suzuki?

5. Why does Suzuki feel caught between two cultures when, as a Canadian, he visits Japan?

6. Suzuki takes a pragmatic stance on the question of immigrants' adaptation to life in their new country. Do you agree that Suzuki's assimilation—which might be called cutting off the "link with the source of one's genes"—is part of his process of becoming "Canadian"? How typical is the model represented by Suzuki's family?

Ramón Sepúlveda

*Ramón Sepúlveda was born in Santiago, Chile, in 1951. He came
to Canada in 1974. His short fiction has been published in different
Canadian, American, and Latin American literary magazines and anthologies. He is currently preparing his first collection of stories. This selection
first appeared in 1988, in* Canadian Fiction Magazine.

The Reception

That afternoon I first saw him on the ground floor. He was
nervously looking up at the sign, squinting his eyes to read the first
line: "Secretary of State Canada/*Le Secrétariate d'Etat du Canada.*"
He pulled from his pocket a manila envelope identical to the one I
had, and with his other hand, attempted to dry the drops of sweat
on his forehead. He opened the envelope as he searched for his
glasses, and compared, one by one, the words in the letter with those
on the directory. Then, feeling a little more reassured, put the letter
back in his pocket and walked directly to the elevators.

It must have all started at that party a few years earlier when she
casually said why didn't you give her a call sometime, that you
could have a drink together, ...maybe show her how to cook a
South American dish or something; and you, with your minimal
understanding of local courtesies, answered, "OK, OK," but didn't
ask for her telephone number.

His dark three-piece suit was obviously not his, maybe borrowed
from a friend or a fellow-countryman (at least one or two sizes bigger than he was). His black shoes needed some polishing and weren't
very comfortable either, but his main concern then was to get to his
appointment on time. I pressed the button for the elevator and as
soon as the doors opened he quickly, though hesitantly, jumped

inside it before anyone else. He watched the little red lights above the elevator door, "tree... four... fi... seeks... seven... eih... ni, plink! (*nueve*)," he said, and with barely disguised excitement, rushed quickly out of the elevator. He pulled his envelope out again and made his eyes small in an effort to read the sign on the office door.

"Come with me on Friday, I'll show you the canal," she said. "Don't worry, skating is very simple."

Oh sure, you thought, probably as simple as understanding Canadian football, but you only said, "OK, OK."

"I'll call Bob," she said. "He'll lend you a pair of skates. What size do you wear?"

Good grief, you thought, not your ex-boyfriend. She turned around in the bed showing you her perfect, naked back and started dialing Bob's number. You pulled the sheets down and planted a long kiss on the nape of her neck, "*¡Qué preciosa piel!*," you mumbled, admiring the scattered orange freckles that decorated her back.

"What'd you say?" she asked, smiling and closing her eyes. "... Hello, Bob?"

As people entered the room, the small, blonde woman with a black bow-tie passed a book to the man:

"Good News, The New Testament and Psalms," he read out loud and looked grimly at the blonde: "I'm Católic," he said.

The woman's professional smile reassured him. There were no special books for Catholics; you were either Christian or Muslim, or bring your own book if you wish. "This is a present for the ceremony. You can keep it afterwards," said the blonde woman.

It must have been before the snowfall, you're sure now, probably around October, when the green on the trees fades to orange, yellow and red. She had said to you that she wanted to be photographed naked among those beautiful yellow maples. You thought she was joking and started to laugh. Of course there was nobody around, but it sounded crazy, totally insane.

"What... Are you sure?" you asked.

"Oh, yes." she answered firmly, "sure!" and gave you her Pentax ready to shoot. "Now, please watch the focus."

That was mad, yet incredibly daring. Aren't we all crazy? you thought, all crazy, crazy, and there was no time for hesitation now.

She took off her poncho: "I bought it in Mexico, you know? Last Winter," she said. "Paid no more than ten bucks."

Her jeans had slipped off easily and loosely, but she'd purposely taken a long, teasing time in taking off her flimsy black panties. Soon after, wearing only those white wool stockings and the over-sized cream sweater, ran and sat down with her nude buttocks on the top of an old log. You tried to focus on that wild, orange hair and quickly started shooting pictures as she made faces, crossed her legs, lifted one up and then the other. Click, click, "please, Laurie, come back here, put your jeans back on," and there were more uncontrollable laughs, "...please."

"I Swear (or affirm)," the old lady dressed in black begins to say. "*Je jure (ou déclare solennellement)...*"

The man did not repeat the words; instead, he resigned himself to reading without glasses. He opened the book: "Paul Epistle to the Corinthians. Questions about marriage. Now to deal with the matters you wrote about: A man does well not to marry. But because there is so much immorality, every man should have his own wife..."

"Please Laurie, come back here, put your slacks on."

You barely managed to get a shot of her before she took off the cream sweater and threw it to you. You were obviously thrilled by that and very lucky nobody was around.

"... That I will be faithful and bear true allegiance to Her Majesty, Queen Elizabeth the Second."

What a way of laughing. You couldn't believe your eyes. Luckily all of this was going to be recorded on film, including her cat face covered by orange streams of wind and hair.

"*Que je serai fidèle et que je porterai sincère allegéance à Sa Majesté, la Reine Elizabeth Deux.*"

"All right, Bob... yes... Why don't you drop by and bring the skates over. (Oh, please let me talk.)... no... What am I laughing about?... Oh, nothing... (Can't you see I'm on the phone.)... yes... I said size eleven, didn't I?... (Mmmh, stop that!)... right... yes... no ... (Oh, you're impossible.)"

"Now to the unmarried and widows I say that it would be better for you to continue to live alone as I do. But if you cannot restrain your desires, go ahead and marry—it is better to marry than to burn with passion."

"Queen of Canada. Her Heirs and Successors, according to law and that I will faithfully observe the laws of Canada and fulfill my duties as a Canadian citizen... *mes devoirs de citoyen canadien.*"

You must have shot about twenty before she came back to you, still giggling. She didn't notice when you carefully folded and put her delicate black panties, even more carefully, in your pocket. Then she began slowly sliding her jeans back on without a hurry in the world, and suddenly stopped half way through: "Wait... have you seen my panties?"

"Now, ladies and gentlemen, you are Canadian citizens. You mustn't forget that you are members of a large and vigorous family."

"Thanks, Bob... Yes, I'll see you Friday. Bye, bye."

"That you are in possession of the only plastic card that will pay you dividends."
    "That a wife must not leave her husband; but if she does, she must remain single or else be reconciled to her husband."
    "And you are cordially invited to enjoy a cup of coffee and some delicious pastries, all prepared for the reception of new Canadians by the Ukrainian Ladies Society."

Without smiling, the man shook hands with one of the Ukrainian ladies at the door and politely refused to have any coffee or pastries; instead, he went immediately but clumsily to the exit, still searching for his glasses in his pockets. He looked at the elevator doors again, hesitating to press the button.

"Yes, please get into your pants now. I'll help you." Then you hugged her tightly and kissed her nervously on her lips, smiling and still a bit astonished. You felt that strange and fine sensation of her naked skin against your fully clothed body.
    "Where are my panties?"
    "... Come on, Laurie, get dressed and let's go."

I pressed the button still with a taste of Ukrainian cake, and saw the man out of the corner of my eye. He didn't acknowledge my presence, but started to walk slowly towards the fire exit. Surreptitiously, he looked at the black book in his hand for a few seconds and then spotted a trash can in the corner. He looked at his book again, and all of a sudden, plunk! threw the book into the can. He opened the door and disappeared with the sound of his steps on the stairs.

TOPICS FOR EXPLORATION

1. The author shifts time back and forth among several scenes. Identify the different scenes. You will be helped by Sepúlveda's use of shifting pronouns.

2. How do the serious scenes interact with the frivolous ones? Find examples of the ironic effects of juxtaposing different fragments.

3. How does Sepúlveda show the culture shock experienced by his character? What different messages does he receive in his new environment? How do they affect his cultural habits? What features of his upbringing inhibit his new experience in Canada?

4. Does the story show the author's "appreciation of Canadian courtesy"? What do you think of the parallel between the easy sexual conquest and the ceremony of becoming a Canadian citizen? Is it intended as a criticism of Canada or as a compliment?

Sun-Kyung Yi

Sun-Kyung Yi is a journalist and a producer, living in Toronto. Her television documentary, Scenes from a Corner Store, *about a Korean immigrant family, was broadcast on CBC television. The article reprinted below is from* The Globe and Mail.

An Immigrant's Split Personality

I am Korean-Canadian. But the hyphen often snaps in two, obliging me to choose to act as either a Korean or a Canadian, depending on where I am and who I'm with. After 16 years of living in Canada, I discovered that it's very difficult to be both at any given time or place.

When I was younger, toying with the idea of entertaining two separate identities was a real treat, like a secret game for which no one knew the rules but me.

I was known as Angela to the outside world, and as Sun-Kyung at home. I ate bologna sandwiches in the school lunch room and rice and kimchee for dinner. I chatted about teen idols and giggled with my girlfriends during my classes, and ambitiously practiced piano and studied in the evenings, planning to become a doctor when I grew up. I waved hellos and goodbyes to my teachers, but bowed to my parents' friends visiting our home.

I could also look straight in the eyes of my teachers and friends and talk frankly with them instead of staring at my feet with my mouth shut when Koreans talked to me.

Going outside the home meant I was able to relax from the constraints of my cultural conditioning, until I walked back in the door and had to return to being an obedient and submissive daughter.

The game soon ended when I realized that it had become a way of life, that I couldn't change the rules without disappointing my parents and questioning all the cultural implications and consequences that came with being a hyphenated Canadian.

Many have tried to convince me that I am a Canadian, like all other immigrants in the country, but those same people also ask me which country I came from with great curiosity, following with questions about the type of food I ate and the language I spoke. It's difficult to feel a sense of belonging and acceptance when you are regarded as "one of them." "Those Koreans, they work hard.... You must be fantastic at math and science." (No.) "Do your parents own a corner store?" (No.)

Koreans and Canadians just can't seem to merge into "us" and "we."

Some people advised me that I should just take the best of both worlds and disregard the rest. That's ideal, but unrealistic when my old culture demands a complete conformity with very little room to manoeuvre for new and different ideas.

After a lifetime of practice, I thought I could change faces and become Korean on demand with grace and perfection. But working with a small Korean company in Toronto proved me wrong. I quickly became estranged from my own people.

My parents were ecstatic at the thought of their daughter finally finding her roots and having a working opportunity to speak my native tongue and absorb the culture. For me, it was the most painful and frustrating 2 ½ months of my life.

When the president of the company boasted that he "operated little Korea," he meant it literally. A Canadianized Korean was not tolerated. I looked like a Korean, therefore I had to talk, act, and think like one, too. Being accepted meant a total surrender to ancient codes of behaviour rooted in Confucian thought, while leaving the "Canadian" part of me out in the parking lot with my '86 Buick.

In the first few days at work, I was bombarded with inquiries about my marital status. When I told them I was single, they spent the following days trying to match me up with available bachelors in the company and the community.

I was expected to accept my inferior position as a woman and had to behave accordingly. It was not a place to practice my feminist views, or be an individual without being condemned. Little Korea is a place for men (who filled all the senior positions) and women don't dare to speak up or disagree with their male counterparts.

The president (all employees bow to him and call him Mr. President) asked me to act more like a lady and smile. I was openly scorned by a senior employee because I spoke more fluent English than Korean. The cook in the kitchen shook her head in disbelief upon discovering that my cooking skills were limited to boiling a package of instant noodles. "You want a good husband, learn to cook," she advised me.

In less than a week I became an outsider because I refused to conform and blindly nod my head in agreement to what my elders (which happened to be everybody else in the company) said. A month later, I was demoted because "members of the workplace and the Korean community" had complained that I just wasn't "Korean enough," and I had "too much power for a single woman." My father suggested that "when in Rome do as the Romans." But that's exactly what I was doing. I am in Canada so I was freely acting like a Canadian, and it cost me my job.

My father also said, "It doesn't matter how Canadian you think you are, just look in the mirror and it'll tell you who you *really* are." But what he didn't realize is that an immigrant has to embrace the new culture to enjoy and benefit from what it has to offer. Of course, I will always be Korean by virtue of my appearance and early conditioning, but I am also happily Canadian and want to take full advantage of all that such citizenship confers.

But for now I remain slightly distant from both cultures, accepted fully by neither. The hyphenated Canadian personifies the ideal of multiculturalism, but unless the host culture and the immigrant cultures can find ways to merge their distinct identities, sharing the best of both, this cultural schizophrenia will continue.

TOPICS FOR EXPLORATION

1. What does it mean to be a "hyphenated Canadian"? According to the author, what are the ordeals of people straddling two cultures? Can you think of any advantages of the "split personality" that she discusses?

2. Why does the author say that Koreans and Canadians have such difficulty in merging? Why don't some Canadians view Korean-Canadians as Canadians? Why doesn't the president of "little Korea" tolerate Canadianized Koreans?

3. Find a few examples of cultural differences mentioned in this article. When talking about cultural differences, what are some ways to avoid cultural stereotyping?

4. Although she takes part in both Korean and Canadian cultures, why is Sun-Kyung Yi "accepted fully by neither"? How does this double bind result in "cultural schizophrenia"?

5. What is the ideal of multi-ethnic interactions postulated by the author? What kind of attitude change would it require in both the host culture and the immigrant cultures?

Drew Hayden Taylor

Drew Hayden Taylor was born in 1962 on the Curve Lake Reserve in Ontario. He has worked as a journalist, author, and director for such media as television, radio, press, and theatre. His one-act plays Toronto at Dreamer's Rock *and* Education Is Our Right, *as well as the full-length play* The Bootlegger Blues, *were published in 1990. In his writing, he tries to incorporate elements of traditional Native storytelling, including humour.*

Pretty Like a White Boy: The Adventures of a Blue Eyed Ojibway

In this big, huge world, with all its billions and billions of people, it's safe to say that everybody will eventually come across personalities and individuals that will touch them in some peculiar yet poignant way. Individuals that in some way represent and help define who you are. I'm no different, mine was Kermit the Frog. Not just because Natives have a long tradition of savouring Frogs' legs, but because of his music. If you all may remember, Kermit is quite famous for his rendition of 'It's Not Easy Being Green'. I can relate. If I could sing, my song would be 'It's Not Easy Having Blue Eyes in a Brown Eyed Village'.

Yes, I'm afraid it's true. The author happens to be a card-carrying Indian. Once you get past the aforementioned eyes, the fair skin, light brown hair, and noticeable lack of cheekbones, there lies the heart and spirit of an Ojibway storyteller. Honest Injun, or as the more politically correct term may be, honest aboriginal.

You see, I'm the product of a white father I never knew, and an Ojibway woman who evidently couldn't run fast enough. As a kid I knew I looked a bit different. But, then again, all kids are paranoid when it comes to their peers. I had a fairly happy childhood, frolicking through the bullrushes. But there were certain things that, even then,

made me notice my unusual appearance. Whenever we played cow-
boys and Indians, guess who had to be the bad guy, the cowboy.

It wasn't until I left the Reserve for the big bad city, that I
became more aware of the role people expected me to play, and the
fact that physically I didn't fit in. Everybody seemed to have this preconceived idea of how every Indian looked and acted. One guy, on
my first day of college, asked me what kind of horse I preferred. I
didn't have the heart to tell him 'hobby'.

I've often tried to be philosophical about the whole thing. I have
both white and red blood in me, I guess that makes me pink. I am a
'Pink' man. Try to imagine this, I'm walking around on any typical
Reserve in Canada, my head held high, proudly announcing to
everyone 'I am a Pink Man'. It's a good thing I ran track in school.

My pinkness is constantly being pointed out to me over and
over and over again. 'You don't look Indian?' 'You're not Indian, are
you?' 'Really?!?' I got questions like that from both white and Native
people, for a while I debated having my Status card tattooed on my
forehead.

And like most insecure people and specially a blue eyed Native
writer, I went through a particularly severe identity crisis at one
point. In fact, I admit it, one depressing spring evening, I dyed my
hair black. Pitch black.

The reason for such a dramatic act, you may ask? Show
Business. You see, for the last eight years or so, I've worked in various capacities in the performing arts, and as a result I'd always get
calls to be an extra or even try out for an important role in some
Native oriented movie. This anonymous voice would phone, having
been given my number, and ask if I would be interested in trying
out for a movie. Being a naturally ambitious, curious, and greedy
young man, I would always readily agree, stardom flashing in my
eyes and hunger pains from my wallet.

A few days later I would show up for the audition, and that was
always an experience. What kind of experience you may ask? Picture
this, the picture calls for the casting of seventeenth-century Mohawk
warriors living in a traditional longhouse. The casting director calls
the name 'Drew Hayden Taylor' and I enter.

The casting director, the producer, and the film's director look
up from the table and see my face, blue eyes flashing in anticipation.
I once was described as a slightly chubby beachboy. But even beach-
boys have tans. Anyway, there would be a quick flush of confusion, a
recheck of the papers, and a hesitant 'Mr. Taylor?' Then they would
ask if I was at the right audition. It was always the same. By the way,
I never got any of the parts I tried for, except for a few anonymous

crowd shots. Politics tells me it's because of the way I look, reality tells me it's probably because I can't act. I'm not sure which is better.

It's not just film people either. Recently I've become quite involved in Theatre, Native theatre to be exact. And one cold October day I was happily attending the Toronto leg of a province-wide tour of my first play, *Toronto at Dreamer's Rock*. The place was sold out, the audience very receptive and the performance was wonderful. Ironically one of the actors was also half white.

The director later told me he had been talking with the actor's father, an older Non-Native type chap. Evidently he had asked a few questions about me, and how I did my research. This made the director curious and he asked about his interest. He replied 'He's got an amazing grasp of the Native situation for a white person.'

Not all these incidents are work related either. One time a friend and I were coming out of a rather upscale bar (we were out YUPPIE watching) and managed to catch a cab. We thanked the cab driver for being so comfortably close on such a cold night, he shrugged and nonchalantly talked about knowing what bars to drive around. 'If you're not careful, all you'll get is drunk Indians.' I hiccuped.

Another time this cab driver droned on and on about the government. He started out by criticizing Mulroney, and eventually to his handling of the Oka crisis. This perked up my ears, until he said 'If it were me, I'd have tear-gassed the place by the second day. No more problem.' He got a dime tip. A few incidents like this and I'm convinced I'd make a great undercover agent for one of the Native political organizations.

But then again, even Native people have been known to look at me with a fair amount of suspicion. Many years ago when I was a young man, I was working on a documentary on Native culture up in the wilds of Northern Ontario. We were at an isolated cabin filming a trapper woman and her kids. This one particular nine-year-old girl seemed to take a shine to me. She followed me around for two days both annoying me and endearing herself to me. But she absolutely refused to believe that I was Indian. The whole film crew tried to tell her but to no avail. She was certain I was white.

Then one day as I was loading up the car with film equipment, she asked me if I wanted some tea. Being in a hurry I declined the tea. She immediately smiled with victory crying out 'See, you're not Indian, all Indians drink tea!'

Frustrated and a little hurt I whipped out my Status card and thrust it at her. Now there I was, standing in a Northern Ontario winter, showing my Status card to a nine-year-old non-status Indian girl who had no idea what one was. Looking back, this may not have been one of my brighter moves.

But I must admit, it was a Native woman that boiled everything down in one simple sentence. You may know that woman, Marianne Jones from 'The Beachcombers' television series. We were working on a film together out west and we got to gossiping. Eventually we got around to talking about our respective villages. Hers on the Queen Charlotte Islands, or Haida Gwaii as the Haida call them, and mine in central Ontario.

Eventually childhood on the Reserve was being discussed and I made a comment about the way I look. She studied me for a moment, smiled, and said 'Do you know what the old women in my village would call you?' Hesitant but curious, I shook my head. 'They'd say you were pretty like a white boy.' To this day I'm still not sure if I like that.

Now some may argue that I am simply a Métis with a Status card. I disagree, I failed French in grade 11. And the Métis as everyone knows have their own separate and honourable culture, particularly in western Canada. And of course I am well aware that I am not the only person with my physical characteristics.

I remember once looking at a video tape of a drum group, shot on a Reserve up near Manitoulin Island. I noticed one of the drummers seemed quite fairhaired, almost blond. I mentioned this to my girlfriend of the time and she shrugged saying 'Well, that's to be expected. The highway runs right through the Reserve.'

Perhaps I'm being too critical. There's a lot to be said for both cultures. For example, on the left hand, you have the Native respect for Elders. They understand the concept of wisdom and insight coming with age.

On the white hand, there's Italian food. I mean I really love my mother and family but seriously, does anything really beat good Veal Scallopini? Most of my aboriginal friends share my fondness for this particular brand of food. Wasn't there a warrior at Oka named Lasagna? I found it ironic, though curiously logical, that Columbus was Italian. A connection I wonder?

Also Native people have this wonderful respect and love for the land. They believe they are part of it, a mere chain in the cycle of existence. Now, as many of you know, this conflicts with the accepted Judeo-Christian i.e. western view of land management. I even believe somewhere in the first chapters of the Bible it says something about God giving man dominion over Nature. Check it out, Genesis 4:?, 'Thou shalt clear cut.' So I grew up understanding that everything around me is important and alive. My Native heritage gave me that.

And again, on the white hand, there's breast implants. Darn clever them white people. That's something Indians would never have invented, seriously. We're not ambitious enough. We just take what the Creator decides to give us, but no, not the white man. Just imagine it, some serious looking white man, and let's face it people, we know it was a man who invented them, don't we? So just imagine some serious looking white doctor sitting around in his laboratory muttering to himself, 'Big tits, big tits, hmm, how do I make big tits?' If it was an Indian, it would be 'Big tits, big tits, white women sure got big tits' and leave it at that.

So where does that leave me on the big philosophical scoreboard, what exactly are my choices again; Indians—respect for elders, love of the land. White people—food and big tits. In order to live in both cultures I guess I'd have to find an Indian woman with big tits who lives with her grandmother in a cabin out in the woods and can make Fettuccini Alfredo on a wood stove.

Now let me make this clear, I'm not writing this for sympathy, or out of anger, or even some need for self-glorification. I am just setting the facts straight. For as you read this, a new Nation is born. This is a declaration of independence, my declaration of independence.

I've spent too many years explaining who and what I am repeatedly, so as of this moment, I officially secede from both races. I plan to start my own separate nation. Because I am half Ojibway, and half Caucasian, we will be called the Occasions. And I of course, since I'm founding the new nation, will be a Special Occasion.

TOPICS FOR EXPLORATION

1. How does humour help to communicate a serious subject in this essay of self-definition? Do you think that this humour masks Drew Hayden Taylor's true feelings about his ambiguous status?

2. How does Taylor feel about being part of a blue-eyed minority in a larger brown-eyed minority? Why does he feel he does not fit in either group?

3. How does Taylor present himself as a victim of the "preconceived idea of how every Indian looked and acted"? Why is he treated with suspicion by other Native people?

4. Taylor relates a number of incidents involving misunderstandings about his identity. How do some of these incidents reveal

racial tensions between white and Native people? What is the role of "show business" in creating and maintaining Native stereotypes?

5. What irony is implied by Taylor's talking about being "pretty like a white boy"? What does it tell us about racial self-image among aboriginals and whites?

6. What are the advantages of Native culture, according to Taylor? How does he satirize some of the pretensions of white culture?

7. What does Taylor think about the possibility of living in both cultures? What absurdist solution to the problem of belonging does he find in the end? What are the serious implications of his humorous decision to "secede from both races"?

Camille Hernandez-Ramdwar

Camille Hernandez-Ramdwar is a born TrinCan (Trinidadian-Canadian), who seeks the meaning behind identities, particularly the racial ones we all adopt. Her work has appeared in Miscegenation Blues *(1994),* Fireweed, West Coast Line, Possibilities, *and* Sharing Our Experience *(1993). She currently lives in Toronto with her family.*

Ms Edge Innate

Do you know who I am? I'm the one you can't leave alone. The one who puzzles you, intrigues you. I am the original definition of "exotic." Acceptable in many ways, the café au lait of life, more palatable because I am diluted. Not as offensive, not as threatening—you think. Certainly not as obvious. But hard to ignore.

They call me white, they call me black—they've called me everything in between. Honestly, if one person could claim global citizenship, it would be me, because who could dispute it? But then again, looks count for everything, and I *know*, people see what they want to see. If they're looking for a new member, I'm it. If they're looking for a scapegoat, I'm it. If they're looking for a specimen, I'm it. If they're looking for an excuse, I'm It. I'm It I'm It I'm It—a glorious game of tag and everyone wants to participate.

I don't think my parents realized the complexity of what they were getting into. Like most interracial couples, they just closed their eyes and ears and hoped for the best. Of course the children would be beautiful, of course both sides would ooh and aah over the benefits—the dark (but not too dark) complexion, the wavy (not too curly) hair, everybody should have been happy, everyone should have been satisfied. Those large dark eyes, like the eyes of orphan poster children: "Is she adopted? Where did you get her?" Looks of bewilderment as my mother tries to explain her husband is "foreign," "dark." Dark like the night? Like tar? Like a rapist? Oh dear, you didn't marry one of *those?*

I went to my mother's family reunion when I was sixteen. I guess I went out of respect for my mother, because I didn't go for myself. There was no reason for me to be there, as far as I could see. I didn't resemble anyone in the crowd, and there were over three hundred people there. I remember leaving in the middle of the big barn dance, because I couldn't relate to anyone, and was tired of being asked whose (half-breed bastard darkie nigger) offspring I was.

My mother raised me, she loved me, but upon reaching adulthood, I've realized that there was something very important my mother could never give me—a culture which matched my colour. If women are the bestowers and the keepers of culture, the ones who pass on language, nuance, myth, food, spiritual teachings and values to children, then I have been culturally malnourished. It wasn't my mother's fault. In fact, through many years of struggle, I have learned that there is no one to blame. I could have blamed my parents—my mother for wanting an "exotic" experience, my father for coveting a white woman, but they made their choices, and now I am the one who must deal with the consequences of their actions.

Because I was raised in my mother's homeland, and not my father's, I grew up with my mother's culture. And my parents wanted it that way. If there were women who could have taught me things about my "other" culture—my paternal grandmother and aunts—I was removed from them by an entire continent and a sea.

My mother loved me, she raised me, but she could never quite understand me. She did not live in my skin. In fact she seemed oblivious to my colour, as my father had become oblivious to his. These issues to them were irrelevant, or, in retrospect, too painful. They hoped my acculturation would make up for my colour. They hoped I would automatically assimilate—perhaps even marry white, continue the dilution of our blood, whiten the grandchildren. They never spoke of this, but it was inferred in their actions and statements. I, having no choice, subjected to the isolation of an all-white community (save for the few foster children sprinkled amongst the middle class white families), almost made their wishes a reality.

Because I grew up in this country, because I can speak the language, understand the nuances, the not-saids, the thought patterns, because I can decipher the white response, I am considered Canadian. But I hate this indefinable term. "Oh Edge, you're so Canadian!"

You know what Canadian is to me? A Canadian is someone who likes hockey, likes the winter, the whiteness. A Canadian is someone who spends every summer going to "the lake" ("a pool of stagnant water" my father used to call it). A Canadian is someone who thinks this is the greatest country on earth. Someone who wants to perpetuate the status quo. Someone who travels to the Third World and hangs out with other (white) Canadians, Australians, Brits and occasionally Americans. Someone who thinks of Third World women and men as "an exotic experience." Someone who is ignorant of world history, geography, and is profoundly culturally ignorant. All black people are "Jamaicans" or "from Africa." All South Asian people are "Pakis." East Asians are invariably "Chinese." First Nations people are drunks, or militant troublemakers.

My friend's brother said that the Mohawks at Oka had no right to pick up guns. Oh? I've heard this since many times—they have no right to be angry, no right to defend their land, no right to seek retribution. Canadians have become so accustomed in their psyches to the docility of people of colour that it is reprehensible to them that these "non-whites" are no longer behaving like children, accepting what is thrown at them.

But I digress. It is obvious that, to me, a Canadian is not a person of colour, nor an aboriginal person. A Canadian is white—one of the "two founding nations" or one of the following stream of later immigrants—Jewish, Ukrainian, German, Italian, Portuguese, etc. Therefore, upon meeting black Canadians, I am heard to say "Well, you are black first, then a Canadian by fault of birth," to which they reply, no, my people have been here for five generations and you'd better damn well believe I'm Canadian. To which I counter-attack—oh yeah? When was the last time you WEREN'T asked where you are from? How many of "your people" are represented in government—at *any* level? Why are there race riots in Halifax, where black people have been living as long as white people have? Why are black people being shot by police?

Because I could not identify with my mother's culture, and because I could not acquire whiteness, I strongly adopted my father's culture. I wonder how much of this was choice, how much necessity, and how much instinct. I know I gravitated towards things black and Caribbean long before I knew what those two intertwined yet distinct cultures represented. Everything else (literally) paled in comparison.

When I was small, I would go to parties with the other kids, and someone would put on a record, and I would get up and dance—perfect rhythm, hips, feet—and everyone would stare in amazement and ask—where did you learn how to dance? Who taught you? How do you do it? No one taught me, I would respond—and then think, Edge, you're different. I would sit down to play "Peanut Man" on the piano with my Jewish friend, try to teach her the syncopated beat, but no matter how many times she rehearsed it, it just wouldn't come out right. And I'd think, doesn't she hear what I hear? It's so simple! Again—"I'm different."

And boys—white boys—fascinated by some myth of my sexual powers—dark, musky, hypnotic—would taunt me and tease and abuse me. In Grade One I was called "sex maniac" by gangs of six-year-old boys...and in later years, acquired the trappings of that myth—the oversexed mama, the hot tamale, hot Latin blood, ball-busting black woman who could fuck you in half. They bought it, I dished it out—desperate for love and acceptance and to be considered beautiful in the era of Farrah Fawcett and Cheryl Tiegs. Because black women were to fuck, not to love, because I was a nymphomaniac *anyway,* it was alright to sexually abuse me.

And I've paid a price for all this acting, this "assimilation" if that's what it's called. A Trinidadian man told me years ago that people like me were schizophrenic, would always be schizophrenic because we are living in a world that does not allow us to integrate ourselves, our psyches. I don't know about this—there may have been a time in my life when I truly had a hard time feeling whole, but I now know who I am, what I am and where I fit in the scheme of things. Other people may have a problem defining me, but that is their problem. I know where I stand.

(Oh the words of the strong, of the self-knowing—where have I gained such courage? How long have I envied people who simply look into the mirror and state "I Am"? People who can point to one nation on a map, or even continent, and say "This is where I/my people are from." The urge for Wholeness, Completeness in a world that consistently denies it.)

I watch couples on the street very carefully, mixed couples, inter-racial couples, and I always think of the children. If you make children, who will be raising them? Who will be teaching them? Are these white women who mother children of colour really prepared for the struggles that child will endure? Are they willing to accept that they can not and have not walked in that child's shoes? Are they prepared to confront their own ignorance? Can they truly offer support and guidance to that child?

I watch with interest the conflicts over black children placed in white foster homes. The whole movement to end this, to end the assimilation, the "loss of the race," and I can't help but think, yes, but what about those of us who grew up in a mixed race home and *still* did not get culturally nourished? Does it really matter if you are raised by your "blood" parents or not when the issue is culture? That is to assume that your parents' culture is always your own—which isn't necessarily the case. I know I had to fight for my culture; I had to wade and sift through endless genetic memories; I had to tune into ancestral voices and dreams; I had to see myself in eyes that easily reflected my own because they were similar. Eyes that knew richness, pain, history, joy, rhythms of life. I had to seek that, and it was a long journey. I had to leave icicle stares and snow-capped schooling, literally and figuratively, in order to see myself in my natural habitat.

And they call me Ms Edge Innate, precipice girl, riding on the wave of something wholly internal, a calling I can't explain save to say it is in my soul. Innate: i.e., inborn, not acquired. I had to revert back to myself. I had to struggle to claim what was already mine. Something that explains myself to me, something that makes sense.

But I can not expect you to understand—not yet. I watch as people become further divided, departmentalized, tribalized ... and I wonder on the choices I will have to make—again—and that my children will have to make. There is no camp for us to fit easily into, there never has been, and we are always asked to choose, but by reason of our appearance the choice is often made for us.

I am tired of choosing; I long to be whole. The mirror lies, it confuses—appearances are so deceptive and so subjective. My inner voice tells the truth. Ms Edge Innate—here I am, on the periphery of *your* world, but knowing that what is mine is wholly and soully my own.

TOPICS FOR EXPLORATION

1. How does Camille Hernandez-Ramdwar introduce herself at the beginning of her essay? Why does she say that she "could claim global citizenship"?

2. What specific grievances does she have against her parents? Why was she "culturally undernourished"? Why did she feel estranged from her own mother? from her childhood community?

3. How does she define a Canadian? What racist bias does she detect among Canadians? Why does she feel excluded from the definition of a Canadian?

4. How does she justify her identification with her father's culture rather than her mother's culture?

5. How has she been affected by sexist stereotypes about Black women? To what degree did she internalize these stereotypes when she was at school? According to her, what are the reasons why some Black women may feel insecure in their self-esteem?

6. Why is she concerned about the future of children born to mixed couples? In what way is the situation of these children similar to (or different from) the situation of Black children placed in white foster homes?

7. Why is it false "to assume that your parents' culture is always your own"? How does she explain the name "Ms Edge Innate" that she has chosen for herself?

SUGGESTIONS FOR FURTHER STUDY

1. Compare the British self-image of Tony German's memoir with that of Catharine Parr Traill (in Unit One) a hundred years earlier.

2. How does David Suzuki's response to his Japanese-Canadian experience compare with Joy Kogawa's in *Itsuka* (Unit Two)?

3. Both Suzuki and Sun-Kyung Yi have opted for an identity determined by culture rather than the genes. How does this alienate them from their "genetic sources"? Compare the difficulties of this double bind experienced by these two authors.

4. Compare the alienation of Sun-Kyung Yi with that described by Camille Hernandez-Ramdwar. How different are their respective responses to their identity crises?

5. Contrast the identity problems faced by the two authors with Native ancestry, Drew Hayden Taylor and Jenine Dumont (Unit Two). What different ways have they chosen to respond to their dilemmas? What effects have their choices had upon their lives in a predominantly white culture?

6. Compare different strategies of shocking the reader that are used by such writers as Ramón Sepúlveda, Drew Hayden Taylor, and Camille Hernandez-Ramdwar. How effective are these strategies? How does the subject matter in their respective pieces justify the use of shock and surprise?

SELECTED BIBLIOGRAPHY

Begamudré, Ven & Judith Krause. *Out of Place: Stories and Poems.* Regina: Coteau Books, 1991.

Birbalsingh, Frank. *Jahaji Bhai: An Anthology of Indo-Caribbean Literature.* Toronto: TSAR, 1988.

Black, Ayanna. *VOICES: 16 Canadian Writers of African Descent.* Toronto: HarperCollins Publ., 1992.

——. *Fiery Spirits: Canadian Writers of African Descent.* Toronto: HarperCollins Publ., 1994.

Borovilos, John. *Breaking Through: A Canadian Literary Mosaic.* Toronto: Prentice Hall Canada Inc., 1990.

——. *Breaking Free: A Cross-Cultural Anthology.* Toronto: Prentice Hall, 1995.

Brand, Dionne. *No Burden to Carry: Narratives of Black Working Women in Ontario 1920s to 1950s.* Toronto: Women's Press, 1991.

Clarke, George Elliott. *Fire on the Water: An Anthology of Black Nova Scotian Writing.* 2 vols. Porters Lake, NS: Pottersfield Press, 1991.

Dabydeen, Cyril. *Another Way to Dance: Anthology of Asian-Canadians.* Stratford, ON: Williams-Wallace, 1990.

Fanning, Peter & Maggie Goh. *Home and Homeland.* Oakville, ON.: Rubicon Publ. Inc., 1992.

Fife, Connie. *The Colour of Resistance: A Contemporary Collection of Writing by Aboriginal Women.* Toronto: Sister Vision, 1993.

Goh, Maggie & Craig Stephenson. *Between Worlds: A Collection of Writings on the Canadian Immigrant Experience.* Oakville, ON: Rubicon Publ. Inc., 1989.

Grant, Agnes. *Our Bit of Truth: An Anthology of Canadian Native Literature.* Winnipeg: Pemmican Publication AB, 1990.

Harris, Claire and Edna Alford. *Kitchen Talk: Contemporary Women's Prose and Poetry.* Red Deer, Ab: Red Deer College Press, 1992.

Hutcheon, Linda & Marion Richmond. *Other Solitudes: Canadian Multicultural Fictions.* Toronto: Oxford University Press, 1990.

King, Thomas. *All My Relations: An Anthology of Contemporary Canadian Native Fiction.* Toronto: McClelland & Stewart, 1990.

Lee, Bennett & Jim Wong-Chu. *Many-Mouthed Birds: Contemporary Writing by Chinese Canadians.* Vancouver: Douglas & McIntyre, 1991.

Leith, Linda. *Telling Differences: New English Fiction from Quebec.* Montreal: Véhicule Press, 1988.

McGifford, Diane. *The Geography of Voice: Canadian Literature of the South Asian Diaspora.* Toronto: TSAR, 1992.

Minni, C.D. *Ricordi: Things Remembered. An Anthology of Short Stories.* Montreal: Guernica, 1989.

Moses, Daniel David & Terry Goldie. *An Anthology of Canadian Native Literature in English.* Toronto: Oxford UP, 1992.

Mukherjee, Arun. *Sharing Our Experience.* Ottawa: Canadian Advisory Council on the Status of Women, 1993.

Oiwa, Keibo. *Stone Voices: Wartime Writings of Japanese Canadian Issei.* Montreal: Véhicule Press, 1992.

Perreault, Jeanne & Sylvia Vance. *Writing the Circle: Native Women of Western Canada.* Edmonton: NeWest, 1990.

Petrone, Penny. *Northern Voices: Inuit Writing in English.* Toronto: University of Toronto Press, 1988.

Rostom, Kamal A. *Arab-Canadian Writing: Stories, Memoirs and Reminiscences.* Fredericton: York Press, 1989.

Scheier, Libby, Sarah Sheard & Eleanor Wachtel. *Language in Her Eye: Writing and Gender. Views by Canadian Women Writing in English.* Toronto: Coach House Press, 1990.

Silvera, Makeda. *Piece of My Heart: A Lesbian of Colour Anthology.* Toronto: Sister Vision, 1991.

The Telling It Book Collective. *Telling It: Women and Language across Cultures.* Vancouver: Press Gang Publishers, 1990.

Tiessen, Hildi Froese & Peter Hinchcliffe. *Acts of Concealment: Mennonites Writing in Canada.* Waterloo, ON: University of Waterloo Press, 1992.

Waddington, Miriam. *Canadian Jewish Short Stories.* Toronto: Oxford University Press, 1990.

The Women's Book Committee and Chinese Canadian National Council. *Jin Guo: Voices of Chinese Canadian Women.* Toronto: Women's Press, 1992.

COPYRIGHTS AND ACKNOWLEDGEMENTS

We wish to thank the publishers and copyright holders for permission to reprint the selections in this book, which are listed below in order of their appearance.

UNIT ONE

MULTICULTURALISM By Cyril Dabydeen. Reprinted by permission of the author.

SASKATCHEWAN'S INDIAN PEOPLE—FIVE GENERATIONS By Pat Deiter-McArthur (Day Woman). Reprinted from *Writing the Circle: Native Women of Western Canada* (Edmonton: NeWest Press, 1990). Reprinted by permission of the author.

MEMOIRS OF THE LIFE OF BOSTON KING, A BLACK PREACHER, WRITTEN BY HIMSELF DURING HIS RESIDENCE AT KINGSWOOD SCHOOL By Boston King. This article originally appeared in *Methodist Magazine* 21(1798):105–110, 157–61, 209–213, 261–65.

THE EARTHQUAKE By Marie de l'Incarnation from *Word From New France: The Selected Letters of Marie de l'Incarnation*, edited and translated by Joyce Marshall (Toronto: Oxford University Press, 1967). Reprinted with permission.

A HOLOCAUST SURVIVOR'S STORY By Miriam Rosenthal. Transcribed and edited by Allan Gould. Reprinted from *Toronto Life* (November 1981). Reprinted by permission of Miriam Rosenthal.

LEND ME YOUR LIGHT From *Tales from Firozsha Baag* by Rohinton Mistry. Used by permission of the Canadian Publishers, McClelland & Stewart, Toronto.

BREAKING THE BARRIERS: REFUGEE WOMEN IN CANADA By Helga (Kutz-Harder) Mills. This article originally appeared in *Canadian Woman Studies/Les Cahiers de la femme* (Spring 1989). Reprinted by permission of the author.

UNIT TWO

UNIT THREE

(Montreal: Guernica Editions, 1989). Reprinted by permission of the author.

WHY MY MOTHER CAN'T SPEAK ENGLISH By Garry Engkent. From *Many-Mouthed Birds: Contemporary Writing By Chinese Canadians* (Vancouver: Douglas & McIntyre, 1991). Reprinted by permission of the author.

AN IMMIGRANT CHILD REMEMBERS By Lucy Fazio. Reprinted from *The Gazette*, January 23, 1994. Reprinted by permission of the author.

MULTICULTURALISM IN PUBLIC DISCOURSE By Karim H. Karim. Reprinted from *Language and Society*, 1989. Reproduced with permission of the Minister of Supply and Services Canada, 1996.

UNIT FOUR

WHO ARE YOU? © Rita Joe, from *Poems of Rita Joe*, published by Abanaki Press, Halifax, Nova Scotia. Reprinted with permission from Ragweed Press, PO Box 2023, Charlottetown, PEI.

AS IT WAS IN THE BEGINNING By E. Pauline Johnson. From *The Moccasin Maker* (Tucson: University of Arizona Press, 1987).

A MINOR INCIDENT From the collection *A Nice Gazebo* by Robyn Sarah (Montreal: Véhicule Press, 1992). First appeared in Canadian Author and Bookman (Fall 1989).

A CLASS OF NEW CANADIANS From *A North American Education* by Clark Blaise. Copyright © 1973 by Clark Blaise. Reprinted with the permission of the author.

GROWING UP NATIVE By Carol Geddes. Reprinted from *Homemaker's Magazine* vol. 25, no. 7 (1990). Reprinted by permission of the author.

FINDING A NATIONALITY THAT FITS By Isabel Vincent. Reprinted from *The Globe and Mail*, December 3, 1990. Reprinted by permission of *The Globe and Mail*.

UNIT FIVE

TARA'S MOTHER-IN-LAW: From *Trishanku* by Uma Parameswaran (Toronto: TSAR Publications, 1988), pp. 50–51. Reprinted by permission of the publisher.

UNIT SIX

UNIT SEVEN

INDEX OF AUTHORS
AND TITLES

READER REPLY CARD

We are interested in your reaction to *Pens of Many Colours: A Canadian Reader*, Second Edition by Eva C. Karpinski. You can help us to improve this book in future editions by completing this questionnaire.

1. What was your reason for using this book?
   - ❑ university course
   - ❑ professional
   - ❑ college course
   - ❑ personal development
   - ❑ continuing education course
   - ❑ other interest _____

2. If you are a student, please identify your school and the course in which you used this book.

   _____

3. Which chapters or parts of this book did you use? Which did you omit?

   _____

4. What did you like best about this book? What did you like least?

   _____

5. Please identify any topics you think should be added to future editions.

   _____

6. Please add any comments or suggestions.

   _____

7. May we contact you for further information?

   Name: _____

   Address: _____

   _____

   Phone: _____

(fold here and tape shut)

MAIL ⮞ POSTE

Canada Post Corporation / Société canadienne des postes

Postage paid
If mailed in Canada

Port payé
si posté au Canada

Business Reply

Réponse d'affaires

0116870**399**   **01**

0116870399-M8Z4X6-BR01

Heather McWhinney
Director of Product Development
HARCOURT BRACE & COMPANY, CANADA
55 HORNER AVENUE
TORONTO, ONTARIO
M8Z 9Z9